Young Bilingual Learners in Nursery School

BILINGUAL EDUCATION AND BILINGUALISM

Series Editors
Professor Colin Baker, *University of Wales, Bangor, Wales, UK*
Professor Nancy H. Hornberger, *University of Pennsylvania, Philadelphia, USA*

Other Books in the Series
Becoming Bilingual: Language Acquisition in a Bilingual Community
    JEAN LYON
Bilingual Education and Social Change
    REBECCA FREEMAN
Building Bridges: Multilingual Resources for Children
    MULTILINGUAL RESOURCES FOR CHILDREN PROJECT
Child-Rearing in Ethnic Minorities
    J.S. DOSANJH and PAUL A.S. GHUMAN
Curriculum Related Assessment, Cummins and Bilingual Children
    TONY CLINE and NORAH FREDERICKSON (eds)
Foundations of Bilingual Education and Bilingualism
    COLIN BAKER
Japanese Children Abroad: Cultural, Educational and Language Issues
    ASAKO YAMADA-YAMAMOTO and BRIAN RICHARDS (eds)
Language Minority Students in the Mainstream Classroom
    ANGELA L. CARRASQUILLO and VIVIAN RODRIGUEZ
Multicultural Children in the Early Years
    P. WOODS, M. BOYLE and N. HUBBARD
Multicultural Child Care
    P. VEDDER, E. BOUWER and T. PELS
A Parents' and Teachers' Guide to Bilingualism
    COLIN BAKER
Policy and Practice in Bilingual Education
    O. GARCIA and C. BAKER (eds)
Teaching and Learning in Multicultural Schools
    ELIZABETH COELHO
Teaching Science to Language Minority Students
    JUDITH W. ROSENTHAL
Working with Bilingual Children
    M.K. VERMA, K.P. CORRIGAN and S. FIRTH (eds)

Other Books of Interest
Beyond Bilingualism: Multilingualism and Multilingual Education
    JASONE CENOZ and FRED GENESEE (eds)
Encyclopedia of Bilingualism and Bilingual Education
    COLIN BAKER and SYLVIA PRYS JONES

Please contact us for the latest book information:
Multilingual Matters, Frankfurt Lodge, Clevedon Hall,
Victoria Road, Clevedon, BS21 7HH, England
http://www.multilingual-matters.com

BILINGUAL EDUCATION AND BILINGUALISM 18
Series Editors: Colin Baker and Nancy Hornberger

Young Bilingual Children in Nursery School

Linda Thompson

MULTILINGUAL MATTERS LTD
Clevedon • Buffalo • Toronto • Sydney

In memory of my parents, Ned and Máire

Library of Congress Cataloging in Publication Data

Thompson, Linda
Bilingual Education and Bilingualism: 18
Includes bibliographical references and index
1. Education, Bilingual–Great Britain. 2. Language arts (Preschool)–Great Britain.
3. Children of immigrants–Education (Preschool)–Great Britain. 4. Children of
minorities–Education (Preschool)–Great Britain. 5. Nursery schools–Great Britain.
I. Title. II. Series.
LC3723.T47   1999
370.117'0941–dc21   99-36331

British Library Cataloguing in Publication Data

A CIP catalogue record for this book is available from the British Library.

ISBN 1-85359-454-7 (hbk)
ISBN 1-85359-453-9 (pbk)

Multilingual Matters Ltd

UK: Frankfurt Lodge, Clevedon Hall, Victoria Road, Clevedon BS21 7HH.
USA: UTP, 2250 Military Road, Tonawanda, NY 14150, USA.
Canada: UTP, 5201 Dufferin Street, North York, Ontario M3H 5T8, Canada.
Australia: P.O. Box 586, Artarmon, NSW, Australia.

Copyright © 2000 Linda Thompson.

Typeset by Bookcraft Ltd, Stroud.
Printed and bound in Great Britain by the Cromwell Press Ltd.

Contents

Acknowledgements

There are a number of people whom I should like to thank formally. Firstly, my supervisor, colleague and friend, Professor Mike Byram; Anne McNamara who assisted with the data collection, and the first set of maps; Mr Byram Senior (Mike's dad) who so expertly tailored the children's clothing to carry the recording equipment. All the staff in the School of Education Library: Joyce, Mary, Brenda and Susan, whose expertise I still rely upon. I should also like to thank the many colleagues in Durham University School of Education who made me laugh and helped me think. The reviewers, Colin Baker and Nancy Hornberger helped with encouragement and comments. Financial support for the project came from Durham University Research & Initiatives Committee. However, none of this would have been possible without the time and trust of the children, their families and teachers in Box Hill Nursery. I can only apologise for reducing you all to data. Finally, my very special thanks to Dave who took on the onerous process of computerising the maps and who above all has provided seemingly limitless understanding and support.

My sincere thanks to you all.

Linda Thompson
Singapore, 1999

Chapter 1
Who is Bilingual in Britain?

He imagined himself back in his native village … for this was the ideal
that every man looked forward to during all his working life: the return
to the native village, the ultimate peace. Yet even this was denied him:
his native village in the Panjab had been incorporated into Pakistan
and the ancestral strip of land was lost to him and his. The only home
he had now was in the city, if a home in the city could be called a home.
(Ruth Prawer Jhabvala, *The Nature of Passion*, 1986: 177)

Introduction

This book reports on the Box Hill Nursery Project, an ethnolinguistic
study of the social and linguistic behaviour of a group of eight children of
ethnic Pakistani origin, aged between three and four years, during their
first term in an urban nursery school. The children are all third generation
British, born to British-born parents. It has become acceptable to speak of
British Asians as a homogeneous group but, while there may be some
shared elements in their histories and in their experiences as migrants, their
origins, histories and languages are richly diverse. The pupils in the Box
Hill Nursery study are children whose families originated from the Mirpur
region of the Panjab. In order to understand the school experience for these
children it is important to begin with a description of their families, the
history of their heritage, the languages which they speak, and the background to their settlement in Britain.

This chapter sets out the international, national and regional context for
the study. It outlines the political and economic backgrounds to the migration of particular groups to the UK throughout the 1950s, 1960s and early
1970s, which account for the heterogeneous linguistic, religious, ethnic and
cultural composition of present-day British society and the subsequent
educational provision for the children of the groups who eventually settled
more permanently in Britain.

Britain's Linguistic and Cultural Heritage

The social, ethnic and linguistic composition of present-day British society is the legacy of former British social, economic and political policy. The focus of this study is England. The situation in other parts of the UK differs in a number of ways. In particular the policy and language of education in Wales would stand in sharp contrast and will not form part of the study.

The 1987 Language Census found that 172 different languages were spoken by children in Inner London Education Authority schools. Which languages are they and who speaks them? An overview of the main language groups from which the 172 are derived has been summarised by Alladina and Edwards (1991: 13) into geolinguistic areas. These are presented in Figure 1.1.

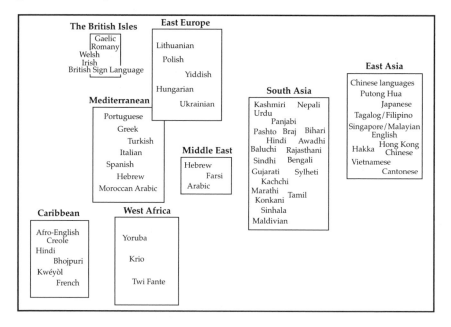

Figure 1.1   Geolinguistic areas identified by Alladina and Edwards (1991: 13). Reprinted by permission of Pearson Education Ltd.

While this comprehensive overview is useful, it also presents difficulties. For example, there are problems with defining minority groups in terms of the language(s) they speak or the region from which they originate. Indeed it is not even possible to provide a satisfactory definition of a linguistic minority in purely linguistic terms. This derives from the difficulty of settling two crucial issues on the basis of linguistic data alone: the definition of (and agreement on) geographical boundaries, and the ethnic composition of the peoples who live within them. The boundaries of particular languages cannot in reality be easily established. The study of variation within language, of linguistic change, and of bilingual repertoires has led sociolinguists to the conclusion that it is not possible in the real world to regard languages as fixed structures or systems. This is particularly true of the region frequently referred to in the literature as the subcontinent of Asia, or by Alladina and Edwards (1991: 13) as South Asia. To understand the linguistic composition of this region it is necessary to examine both geographical boundaries and ethnic composition more closely.

The Geography and History of the Panjab Region

The complexity of the linguistic situation is better understood from the historical perspective. Before partition of the subcontinent in 1947, the whole of the Panjab was part of a single state. The majority of the population spoke one of the local dialects of Panjabi as their first language. Partition in 1947 realised the vision of the two-nation theory outlined by a number of intellectuals, including Rahmet Ali, who died in 1951. Partition institutionalised religious divisions with the creation of two new nation states, India and Pakistan. The former state of the Panjab became divided between these two new nation states. The name of the new nation, Pakistan, is believed to have been coined by Rahmet Ali. The word takes the letters from the different areas that he hoped would make up the state: P for Panjab, A for Afranistan, K for Kashmir, S for Sind, and -tan from Baluchistan. There are two explanations for the I. One is that it makes the word pronounceable. However, *istan* in Sanskrit means 'place', while *pak* in Persian and Urdu means 'pure'. So Pakistan means 'land of the pure'. As described by Rahmet Ali's biographer Khursheed Kamal Aziz, the word and its underlying concept were outlined in a pamphlet entitled *Now or Never*, written by Rahmet Ali and published on 28 January 1933. The sources of this derivation give insight into the linguistic complexity of the place. For the purposes of clarification, further detail is offered.

Urdu, a language based on the speech of educated Muslims of northern India, was declared the official and national language of Pakistan. The written form, based on the Perso-Arabic script, reinforced the link with Islam, the state religion. Urdu itself was not the native language of any

indigenous group that fell within the post-1947 borders of Pakistan. Native speakers of Urdu were mainly migrants and refugees (Khan, 1991). Post 1947 all education and official business in Pakistan was conducted in and through the Urdu language. Urdu also became established as the language of written literature.

Present-day Pakistan is divided into four regions, each of which has its own regional language: Panjabi in the Panjab; Sindi in Sind; Baluchi in Baluchistan and Pashto in Sarhad. Urdu, however, as the official state language remains the language of power and prestige, although it is suggested by Khan (1991) this has not been established without some internal resistance.

From 1947 until 1971 Pakistan was divided into East and West. In 1971 East Pakistan became the new nation state of Bangla Desh. Bangladesh (as it is now known) is an Islamic state. The language situation here is similar to that in other countries in the region. Like Pakistan, Bangladesh has a national official language, Bengali, in addition to regional languages. The official language policy is equally as complex as in present-day Pakistan.

Post-colonial geographic divisions mean that since 1971 the former state of the Panjab has become three separate nations. From west to east these are Pakistan, India and Bangladesh. Taylor and Hegarty (1985: 43) provide a map of these post-1971 geographical boundaries. This is presented in Figure 1.2. The map shows the main areas of emigration from Pakistan, India and Bangladesh to Britain during the 1950s and 1960s, the concentration of ethnic groups within these boundaries and the national languages and religions. The main areas of emigration to Britain are shaded. Mirpur is one of those areas.

The Linguistic Composition of the Panjab

The Linguistic Minorities Project (1985) identified Urdu as one of the 12 languages most commonly spoken in London primary schools. This group includes two sub-groups of Urdu speakers: a small number of people (from both India and Pakistan) who speak Urdu as their first language, and a much larger number of Urdu speakers who originate from the former West Panjab state, now known as Pakistan. The latter group learned Urdu after it became the national language of their home country, Pakistan. The language they speak has been identified by Khan (1991) as Urdu-Panjabi, to distinguish it from the Sikh, Hindi-Panjabi spoken in India. The Linguistic Minorities Project (1985: 23) presents a diagram (Figure 1.3) which

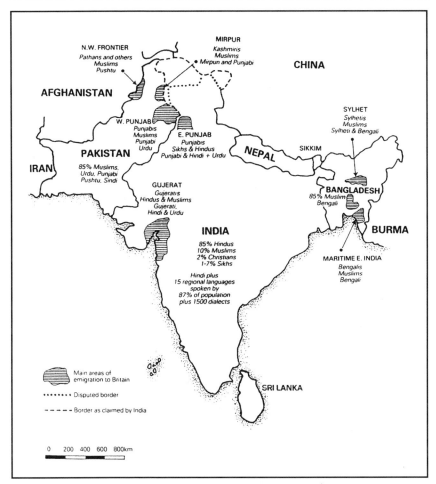

Figure 1.2   Post-1971 geographical boundaries and ethnic, religious and linguistic composition within South Asia (Taylor & Hegarty, 1985: 43). Reproduced by permission of National Foundation for Educational Research.

summarises the complexity of the linguistic, religious and ethnic composition of the former state of the Panjab.

Khan (1991) suggests that the vast majority of Urdu speakers in Britain are Muslims from the Pakistan Panjab who speak Panjabi as the main language of the home. They can be distinguished from Sikh and Hindu speakers of Panjabi by their commitment to Urdu as the symbolic

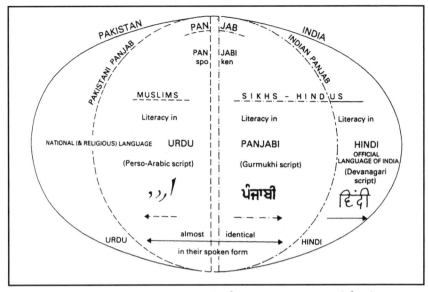

Figure 1.3   Linguistic, religious and ethnic composition of the former state of the Panjab (Linguistic Minorities Project, 1985: 23). Reproduced by permission of Routledge and Kegan Paul.

expression of their religious identity. It should be noted, however, that not all peoples from this region are Muslims.

The Historic Development of Urdu

The Urdu language was originally one of the languages spoken in the Hindi region alongside Brah, Bihari and Kari Boli Hindi. During the sixteenth century large parts of India fell under Muslim rule. These Muslim dynasties were of mainly Turkish and Afghan origin, their language and culture predominantly Persian. While Urdu remained an essentially Indian language in structure, as with all languages in contact situations with others, change began to occur. Although Persian (or Farsi) was the official language, Urdu spread throughout India via army encampments, bazaars and administrative channels. This diffusion is evident in the etymology of the name 'Urdu' which originated from the Farsi *Zaban-e-Urdu-e-mu'alla*, meaning 'language of camp and court'.

Urdu has a strong literary tradition. The written form takes its script from the Perso-Arabic and it draws some of its lexicon from the same source. Although Urdu-Panjabi and Hindi-Panjabi may be mutually intelligible by some in the spoken forms, the written varieties, derived from different alphabets, are not. The samples in Figures 1.4 and 1.5 illustrate this visually.

ਇੰਗਲੈਂਡ ਦੀਆਂ ਦੂਸੀਆਂ ਭਾਸ਼ਾਵਾਂ

Figure 1.4 A sample of Panjabi script

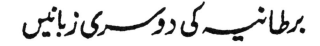

Figure 1.5 A sample of Urdu script

Describing and Defining Urdu

The definition and description of Urdu is contentious. The 1961 census of India and Mobbs (1981) both suggest that Urdu and Hindi be treated as a single linguistic system in the spoken form. However, Grierson (1927) describes the significant difference between the two systems and uses the word order to demonstrate this. Alladina (1985), Mehdi (1974: 207–8) and Pattanayak (1981) all argue for the acknowledgement of Urdu and Hindi as separate describable linguistic systems, and their justification for this goes beyond the mere linguistic to include both the language loyalties and the sense of ethnic and religious identity associated with speakers' language choice. In addition to being the official language of Pakistan, Urdu is one of the 15 official languages of India, spoken as either a first or a second language by an estimated 30 million Muslims (Khan, 1991: 129). In Pakistan Urdu is the first language of around five million people and is used as a second language by an estimated 40 million more (Katzner, 1977). The linguistic and geographical heritage of this region may in part account for the inaccuracies that have arisen in ascribing people to heritage languages and lands. Migrants from the subcontinent are frequently referred to collectively as 'Asians'. However, I should like to suggest that this term is now too general to be meaningful. It fails to capture the diverse complexity of the cultural, linguistic, religious, ethnic and national heritage of the peoples of this region.

Patterns of Migration and Settlement in Britain

The main area of interest for this study is people of ethnic Pakistani origin, so they will be the focus of comment. However, some points remain pertinent to other migrant groups and communities. The family backgrounds of migrants are not easy to contextualise within Britain because of the difficulty in obtaining precise and accurate information about the number of people of Pakistani origin now settled here. This complexity is due in part to the political changes which have taken place in the region since partition, and in part to the subsequent changes in the nomenclature adopted in Britain by officials when defining and classifying origin. These changes have been further compounded by the reformulation of policy and legislation regarding British immigration, which have in turn given rise to further redefinition and reclassification. One example of this can be seen in the classification of those born in the Mirpur region of West Panjab before 1947 as 'Commonwealth', while those born after 1947 would not be included in this category. The term 'New Commonwealth' was introduced to replace the term 'British Commonwealth' which did not include the two new nations, Pakistan, created in 1947, and Bangladesh, created in 1971. Difficulties also arise in providing accurate statistical information on patterns of migration and settlement in Britain throughout the 1950s, 1960s and early 1970s, the most vigorous eras of resettlement.

The most recent and comprehensive survey of patterns of immigrant settlement was undertaken by Taylor and Hegarty (1985: sec. 5), who outline the demographic settlement of Asian groups in Britain. Their sources include Rose *et al.* (1969), the 1971 and 1981 censuses, and two sample surveys: the National Dwelling and Housing Survey, 1977–8 (NDHS), and the Labour Force Survey, 1979 and 1981. All of these provide information on ethnic origin but a number of difficulties are encountered in compiling separate data on Pakistani-born individuals because they are subsumed under two separate groups, namely the 'New Commonwealth born' (NCW) and the 'New Commonwealth and Pakistani born' (NCWP).

An earlier attempt to survey patterns of immigrant settlement was the 1971 census, which collected information on the birthplace of individuals and their parents and classified all individuals born in India, Pakistan and East Africa under the single heading of 'New Commonwealth born'. However, by 1973 West Pakistan had become Pakistan and susequently left the Commonwealth, whereas East Pakistan, renamed Bangladesh, remained a member of the Commonwealth. This development gave rise to the newly created category of 'New Commonwealth and Pakistani born'

(NCWP). Birthplace figures for the NCWP-born population are further confused because they also include expatriates born in Pakistan to parents on some form of overseas service. This group may not necessarily perceive Pakistan as their land of heritage, but only as their place of birth. An important distinction is to be made here. This group was recorded separately in the 1971 census, which did not collect information on ethnic origin of individuals but only on their place of birth. This added a further difficulty to the compilation of separate figures for those born in Pakistan not of Pakistani origin, and those ethnic Pakistanis born in their homeland.

In an attempt to draw a more comprehensive picture of immigrant settlement patterns in Britain, Taylor and Hegarty (1985: 44) augmented the 1971 census figures with information held on the registration of births, deaths and marriages. Using these data they were able to estimate the number of NCW-born of ethnic origin, based on 'persons born in the New Commonwealth who are not of United Kingdom descent plus children born in Great Britain to parents of NCW ethnic origin, including children with only one such parent' (Taylor & Hegarty, 1985: 44).

Ethnic Pakistanis and Bangladeshis are included in this category (Office for Population Census and Surveys (OPCS), 1977) but such inferences can only be drawn with increasing difficulty and uncertain reliability (Taylor & Hegarty, 1985: 44). OPCS figures for 1977 contain only one set of figures for all of those children born in Pakistan within a given period. This global figure includes three categories of Pakistani-born: those born to ethnic Pakistani parents; those born to parents resident in Pakistan but who were not ethnic Pakistanis; and a growing number of individuals of mixed descent and parentage. Thus it is difficult to obtain, from these figures (Commission for Racial Equality, 1979), accurate and precise information on the number of ethnic Pakistanis born to parents resident in their homeland.

Similarly, figures for the NCW-born ethnic groups can only be estimated. These estimates show that between 1961 and 1976 the NCW born numbered 3.3% of the total population of Great Britain, with people of South Asian and Afro-Caribbean origin accounting for an estimated two-thirds of this percentage (Field *et al.*, 1981). The 1981 Labour Force Survey showed 4.1% of Britain's population to be of NCWP origin, with those of Indian, Pakistani and Bangladeshi origins representing a combined total of 1.9%. There are however acknowledged difficulties in compiling such statistics. The difficulties encountered in compiling figures on the Pakistani-born individuals is compounded when attempting to estimate the number of ethnic Pakistanis who subsequently settled in Britain. Since no comprehensive or systematic figures exist of ethnic Pakistani settlement in Britain, all figures presented (here and elsewhere) can only be regarded as mere estimates. Leaving aside the precise number of people involved, it is nevertheless possible to draw the following profile of the permanently settled communities from South Asia who represented 1.9% of the British workforce up to 1981.

The First Migrants

The primary motivation for migration from South Asia was economic, the desire to find work. As a result, the majority of those first immigrants were male. A nationally representative survey carried out in 1974 (Smith, 1976) included 2103 Asians, of whom 16% were Pakistani and Bangladeshi, and revealed that 37% of the Pakistanis came from the Mirpur region. Some 89% of the Pakistanis questioned said that their primary motive in coming to Britain was to earn money; 13% of the Pakistani and Bangladeshi men said that they had come for education. The survey seems to confirm the trend for male migration which began in the late 1950s. Almost a quarter of the ethnic Pakistanis arrived in Britain between 1960 and the middle of 1962, with a further 38% arriving between 1962 and 1968. Of all those who came, 38% were aged between 15 and 24 years. The 1974 Survey revealed differences in the regional distribution of groups from various districts. Table 1.1 presents a profile of newly settled migrant communities in Britain. It is based on Taylor and Hegarty (1985: 52) from Thapar (*The Times*, 1982) and shows patterns of migrant settlement within Britain.

Table 1.1   A profile of migrant communities from South Asia newly settled in the UK (© Times Newspapers Ltd, 1982)

Area of origin	Religion	Language	Main areas settled in UK	Main castes
INDIA				
Panjab	(1) Hindu	Panjabi	Southall, Birmingham (Handsworth)	Brahmin, Khatri, Baniya, Chura
	(2) Sikh	Panjabi	Southall, Birmingham (Handsworth)	Jat, Ramgarhia, Tarkhan, Chura
Gujerat	(1) Hindu	Gujerati Kutchi	Wembley, Leicester	Patel, Lohana, Solanki, Shah
	(2) Muslim	Gujerati Kutchi	Wembley, Leicester	Bhora, Ismaili, Sunni

Table 1.1 (*cont.*)

Area of origin	Religion	Language	Main areas settled in UK	Main castes
PAKISTAN				
North Western Frontier Province (Pathan)	Muslim	Pushto	Bradford (Hanover Square)	According to Pathan tribe system
Mirpur	Muslim	Mirpuri	Bradford	Based on rural patterns of Pakistan's Azad Kashmir
Panjab	Muslim	Panjabi	Manchester, Birmingham (Sparkbrook)	Rajput, Khan, Gujjar, Nai etc.
BANGLADESH				
Sylhet	Muslim	Bengali	Camden and Brick Lane, London; Bradford	Similar to castes of the state of Bengal in India
EAST AFRICA				
Kenya, Uganda,	(1) Hindu	Panjabi Gujerati	Southall, Leicester	Same as Panjabi Hindu or Gujerati Hindu
Tanzania,	(2) Sikh	Panjabi	Southall, Birmingham	Same as Panjabi Sikh
Malawi, Zambia	(3) Muslim	Panjabi Gujerati	Leicester, London	Same as Gujerati or Panjabi Muslim

Source: Taylor and Hegarty, 1985: 52

There are many reasons for this pattern of settlement. Following the passing of the 1962 Commonwealth Immigration Act, the mass migration which started in the late 1950s was regulated by a selective system of employment vouchers designed to meet the needs of the British labour market. There were three categories of voucher: A for those who had specific jobs to come to in Britain; B for those who possessed special skills or qualification; and C for unskilled workers without definite prospects of employment. Applications for category C vouchers were highly organised by a network of travel agents. Taylor and Hegarty (1985: 61) report that between 1962 and 1967 migrants from India and Pakistan were allocated 42,450 of the 72,940 vouchers issued, a figure they describe as of 'disproportionate benefit' to the region.

The majority of migrants from the subcontinent had previously worked on the land. They came to Britain to take up jobs as unskilled labourers in manufacturing industries. Some Pakistanis, with previous experience in textiles, were able to find similar work in the north of England through the sponsorship scheme, whereby immigrant labour was recruited into a gang of Pakistani employees, responsible to an English-speaking foreman, frequently in order to work unsocial (night) shifts.

Taylor and Hegarty (1985: 52) identify Bradford as the main area of settlement for Mirpuri-speaking Muslims from the Mirpur region of Pakistan, of the Azad Kashmir caste. However, the official information on which they base their statement is too insensitive to feature the relatively small number of migrants from the Mirpur district who were recruited directly to Yorkshire and Cleveland factories under the voucher system. Nor do these official figures include those migrants who were self-financing and paid their own passage to Britain. They would not fall within the 'voucher' figures.

The variation in timing and composition of the migration of ethnic Pakistani origin is reflected in the settlement patterns and characteristics of the migrant communities in Britain. Although no systematic records exist on these national settlement patterns (Taylor & Hegarty, 1985), certain factors, including the languages spoken, the region of origin and personal network links, seem to be connected in the establishment of these settlements.

The Mirpuri Community in Pakistan and Cleveland

Until 1994 Cleveland was an administrative region in the north-east of England. In 1989 the county's Research and Intelligence Unit published the results of surveys carried out to establish the composition and demographic concentration of ethnic minority groups in the region. The results are shown in Table 1.2.

This figure of approximately 14,000 from ethnic minority groups comprises a number from the Muslim community of ethnic Pakistani origin. The 1981 census records a total of 2071 people born in Pakistan, but information available does not identify the number from the Mirpur district separately. The local geographical distribution of the group of Pakistani origin has been reported by the Cleveland Research and Intelligence Unit (1989) and is shown in Figure 1.6.

Table 1.2 The composition and demographic concentration of ethnic minority groups in Cleveland

Year	Cleveland's total population	Cleveland's ethnic minority population
1981	565,800	12,150
1989	554,467	14,010

Source: Cleveland Research and Intelligence Unit, 1989

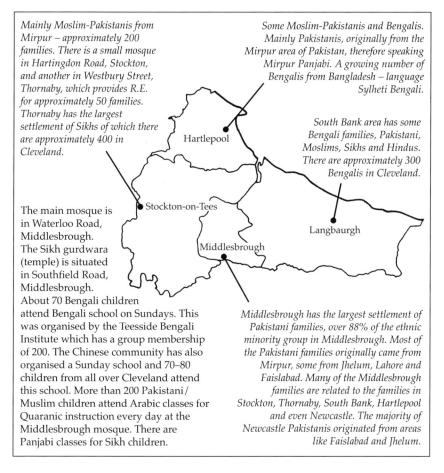

Mainly Moslim-Pakistanis from Mirpur – approximately 200 families. There is a small mosque in Hartingdon Road, Stockton, and another in Westbury Street, Thornaby, which provides R.E. for approximately 50 families. Thornaby has the largest settlement of Sikhs of which there are approximately 400 in Cleveland.

Some Moslim-Pakistanis and Bengalis. Mainly Pakistanis, originally from the Mirpur area of Pakistan, therefore speaking Mirpur Panjabi. A growing number of Bengalis from Bangladesh – language Sylheti Bengali.

South Bank area has some Bengali families, Pakistani, Moslims, Sikhs and Hindus. There are approximately 300 Bengalis in Cleveland.

The main mosque is in Waterloo Road, Middlesbrough. The Sikh gurdwara (temple) is situated in Southfield Road, Middlesbrough. About 70 Bengali children attend Bengali school on Sundays. This was organised by the Teesside Bengali Institute which has a group membership of 200. The Chinese community has also organised a Sunday school and 70–80 children from all over Cleveland attend this school. More than 200 Pakistani/ Muslim children attend Arabic classes for Quaranic instruction every day at the Middlesbrough mosque. There are Panjabi classes for Sikh children.

Middlesbrough has the largest settlement of Pakistani families, over 88% of the ethnic minority group in Middlesbrough. Most of the Pakistani families originally came from Mirpur, some from Jhelum, Lahore and Faislabad. Many of the Middlesbrough families are related to the families in Stockton, Thornaby, South Bank, Hartlepool and even Newcastle. The majority of Newcastle Pakistanis originated from areas like Faislabad and Jhelum.

Figure 1.6 Map of the geographical distribution of ethnic minority groups within the Cleveland area (compiled by Perveen Ahmed; statistics taken from Cleveland Research and Intelligence Unit, 1989)

Mirpuris differ from other settled Asian migrant communities in Cleveland in a number of ways. It is therefore worth outlining their history and traditions, although there is a dearth of published information to draw from. There are no known detailed accounts of the Mirpuri community in Cleveland. However, the Mirpuri community in Bradford has been written about. These accounts can be found in 'The Pakistanis: Mirpuri villagers at home and in Bradford' (Saifullah Khan, 1977: 57–89) and in 'The Urdu speech community' (Khan, 1991: 128–140). From these sources the following profile of the Mirpuri community in Pakistan has been drawn.

The Mirpuri community in Pakistan

The origins of the Mirpuris lie in the Mirpur district of that part of Kashmir held by Pakistan. It is known as Azad (free) Kashmir. Its geographical position as a border area has contributed to its history and experience. Mirpuris are subjects of the old state of Jammu and Kashmir and are citizens of Pakistan. A cease-fire line demarcates Azad Kashmir from the Indian-held Kashmir. The Mirpur district lies in the foothills and is bounded by mountains. Saifullah Khan (1979a) describes the Mirpuris as essentially Panjabi in culture, speaking a vernacular, dialect form of Panjabi. The Mirpur district is situated to the north of the Panjab, where the rain-fed land is divided into smaller holdings than in the more fertile, irrigated land of the Southern Panjab. The land is more hilly than in other parts of the Panjab. There are no through communication routes and in the past there have been harsh regimes which are held responsible for preventing the development of the agricultural, social and educational initiatives evident in other parts of South Asia. As a border state, Mirpur experienced the consequences of partition as well as an influx of people from Indian-occupied Kashmir. The topography has determined, to some extent, the slow progress of internal communication networks by road, rail and air.

Villages within the region vary in size from a few hundred to several thousand. Some settlements are dominated by large landowners, while others are characterised by individuals farming their own land. Those who do not own land include tenant farmers, hereditary craftsmen and village artisans. Mirpur also has its share of new settlers. Those who arrived during or after partition are known as *mahajars* (refugees). Within the villages the primary social unit is the household, frequently a three-generation unit comprising grandparent(s), married son(s) and their wives and children, along with unmarried sons and daughters, and less often, unmarried, divorced or widowed uncle or aunt. Daughters move to their husband's family on marriage. Property is held in common and resources, whether derived from land-work or wage labour, are pooled. Decisions are made communally, with final authority resting with the head of the household, the eldest male. Each position within the family comprises a complex set of rights, duties, attitudes, expectations and sentiments, which are balanced to create the effective functioning of the unit. Roles are precisely and clearly defined into a pattern of mutual interdependence with individual subordination to the group. Houses consist of two or three rooms leading into a walled courtyard or compound which contains animal shelters and an open-air kitchen. The courtyard is usually connected to a village lane via a high door. Much of the daily life of the household and its individual members is conducted in the public arena of the courtyard. In the summer months people sleep outside in the courtyard or on the flat rooftops.

There is an established tradition of migration from Mirpur. Some Mirpuris have moved to more fertile agricultural land in the south of the region, while others, facilitated by improved transport links, have joined the trend to urban migration within Pakistan. During the Second World War many Mirpuri men joined the British army and navy (Tinker, 1974, 1977). Since then they have remained a major source of recruitment for the Pakistani army. There is therefore an established tradition of migration for economic purposes. As a result, Mirpur has probably been more exposed to external influences than many other districts in the region. At any rate, the extent of contact with external agencies may not always be fully realised by those from outside the Mirpuri community.

This trend towards external contact has continued. In the 1950s a joint international venture between Britain, Canada, Australia, New Zealand, Germany and the USA began the construction of the Mangla Dam, the world's largest earth dam. This resulted in the displacement of large numbers of people. Between 1963 and 1967 100,000 people, estimated at 18,000 families, were relocated from 20 villages and one small town. Some moved to farmland in Southern Panjab, some were resettled into newly built villages or absorbed into old villages like Chak Sawari and the new Mirpur City. Displaced persons were compensated with cash which some used to migrate to Britain.

Saifullah Khan (1979b) suggests that the rural communities of the region are neither isolated nor static, and she attributes their gradual adaptation over the decades to the strength of traditional institutions rather than to the absence of external influence. She also notes, though, that recent developments, including the extension of communications, transportation, electricity, the introduction of consumer items and a cash economy, have all served to undermine the traditional power structure of the Mirpuri community. Dependent tenant farmers have become independent land-owners with access to an income and capital; traditional landowners have sold land, and some have sent sons abroad to ensure continued access to new sources of wealth. The flow of money, the sale of land and more contact between East and West have all increased. Many of the original migrants to Britain (and elsewhere) were men joining relatives or close family friends with whom they already had established contacts. This meant an absence of men in the villages, which inevitably altered tradi-tional practices. However, the tradition of what Saifullah Khan (1979b) terms the 'joint family system and community life' has provided support for those remaining and minimised disruption. The migration to Britain was probably the less disruptive for the Pakistani-based Mirpuri commu-nity because it adhered to a pattern, established over decades. A journey to Britain was only one of several options available to villagers threatened with the political instability and limited economic opportunities of Azad Kashmir.

Saifullah Khan (1979a) suggests that the conditions and opportunities in Mirpur influence the degree of economic and emotional identity and involvement with both England the adoptive land, and Pakistan the home-land. The nature of traditional relationships within the villages of Mirpur is a crucial factor in understanding the Mirpuri communities in Cleveland and Pakistan. In village society, the individual is at the centre of a complex network of rights, obligations and duties. An individual's rights and duties are dictated by a number of factors including age, gender, order of birth and other people within the community. Individualism and independ-ence, valued by some cultures, are perceived within the Mirpuri community as secondary. Interpersonal relations are determined by respect for a strict hierarchy, characterised by the authority of elders, the public authority of men and the difference of women. Family and kin take priority over individuals. Close friendships are characterised by the use of the terms 'sister' or 'brother', as appropriate, and gradually acquire the loyalty and interdependency of siblings. Interactions between the sexes are usually subject to close public scrutiny and severe restrictions. The pre-ordained rigid rules of social and personal behaviour can provide a certain stability and security for individuals. Those who deviate from the norm, whether by chance or choice (Saifullah Khan, 1979b, cites widows and the disabled as two examples), are subject to severe reprimand or control. Those perceived as vulnerable, for example the young and unmarried, are controlled, and those who do not fulfil expectations lose esteem and influence.

Beyond the household is the kinship group or *biradari*. This word, meaning brotherhood or clan, describes an endogamous group whose members claim descent through paternal ancestors to a common male ancestor. It is also used to refer to individuals or groups with whom there is a brotherly (loyal) relationship. *Biradari* elders are respected and hold the powerful position of maintaining *izzat* (prestige or pride) within the group. Deviants who threaten the *izzat* are reprimanded. *Biradari* members are bound by highly defined rights and duties, sentiments and general conduct. The *biradari* fosters a strong sense of identity and psychological security. Through it, advice, welfare and banking services are conferred. It is supported financially through a system of gifts and in return extends financial support to *biradari* families at times of considerable expenditure, for example rites of passage and family events such as the birth or marriage of a child. It offers a crucial support system for a relatively poor population, living in a country with no formal welfare system and limited medical facilities.

The *biradari* defines social and interpersonal behaviours both inside and outside the group. Group members are discouraged from forming special alliances within it and from extravagant gifts or donations which could not be matched by the less fortunate members of the network. The *biradari* defines and reinforces strict codes of personal and public behaviour. It also encourages preferential cousin marriage. This is one way of avoiding anguish over the status of the partner in the match and of ensuring that land and property remain within the kinship group. For the bride, it provides a way to remain in contact with her natal family and to avoid the hazards of an unknown household after marriage. The *biradari* extends beyond the village; those who live long distances away remain in close contact and return to attend important family occasions.

Mirpuri villagers are mostly Muslims of the *Sunni* sect. Islam remains a strong influence on daily life in village society, with no distinction made between the religious and the secular. Central to the Islamic faith is belief in *Allah* (God) and submission to the will of Allah (the meaning of *Islam*), which is manifest in the *Qur'an* (holy book). The tenets of the Islamic faith pervade the daily routines of village life, with prayers five times a day and the annual calendar built around periods of fasting, mourning and Islamic festivals.

If the Mirpuri attitude towards geographical mobility is pragmatic, the attitude towards *vilayat* (Britain, derived from Blighty Englander) is perhaps idealised. *Vilayat* is perceived as a land of wealth and security where fortunes are amassed. However, personal symbols of success and fortune, even if accrued for the collective good, are achieved at a cost. There is no respect for the morality of *vilayat*, where the women behave immodestly, travel alone, talk freely with unrelated men and do not cover their bodies. Nor is there envy of the Western family, which appears small and without love, where children in their teens leave their parents and old people live alone.

The Mirpuri community in Cleveland

A general profile of the ethnic minority communities in Cleveland County (including the Mirpuris) has been summarised by the Research and Intelligence Unit (September 1989: 6–7) as:

> a young population, with a relatively high number of births, growing since 1981. The growth is likely to continue whilst ... [the] total population is declining. Hence the ethnic minority population will represent an increasing proportion of [the] population.

This rapid increase in the number of young children within the community will make education a growing community concern. For the children who are the focus of this study, born to parents whose families originate from the Mirpur district of Pakistan, religion is a central part of life in their community. Social customs are justified in terms of religious belief and religion remains one of the bonds important in the maintenance of the community's social solidarity and cultural cohesion. Since Arabic is the language of Islam, religion also has implications for language learning and teaching within the community. Most communities now have the mosque as their focal point. The mosque is more than just a meeting place for life cycle and religious celebration. It serves an educational function, teaching the *Qur'an*, Urdu and Arabic to children at the weekend and in the evenings. It is also the meeting place for five times daily prayers. The Friday sermon from the Imam reminds the community of their duties, reinforcing the sense of group solidarity derived from the *biradari*.

In addition to the local mosques which reinforce the Muslim religion there are other religious centres. These include the Islamic foundation, the UK Islamic Mission, the Muslim Welfare Association, the Muslim Youth Organisation, the Pakistan Welfare Organisation, the Pakistan Social and Cultural Circle and Urdu Markaz (the Urdu Centre). They all contribute to strengthening community identity through the Islamic tradition, via a range of social and cultural as well as religious functions and activities. These include the celebration of the major Islamic festivals of *Id-ul-fitr*, the end of *Ramadan*, the month of fasting; *Id-ul-Azha*, associated with Abraham's intended sacrifice of his son; and *bara-wafaat*, the prophet Mohammed's birthday.

The earlier description of the *biradari* presents it as a very important concept in describing Urdu-Panjabi communities in Britain. *Biradari* members maintain close relationships even in Britain. They frequently pool resources to buy a house or start a business. Contact is frequent, with regular visits for family celebrations, including births, weddings, religious festivals and cultural ceremonies. As a powerful social network the *biradari* also serves to maintain and reinforce boundaries and cultural practices, in particular the practice of *purdah* which restricts the movements of women, although today *purdah* rarely means their total seclusion within a household, as was traditionally the practice.

Another distinctive feature of the Mirpuri community in Britain is the regular links maintained with 'the homeland'. It is usual practice for families to send children to Pakistan on a regular basis for visits which can last for several months. This serves as an enculturation process for the generations of children born in Britain, an opportunity to experience at first hand life in the rural Muslim community of their ascendants, an experience which the community does not believe it is possible to provide in Britain, even within the Mirpuri community. Reciprocal visits from Pakistan are equally usual.

Cultural and social activities reinforce both the *biradari* and links with the homeland, Pakistan. Videos of Urdu, Panjabi and Hindi films and their music are popular entertainment. So are events like *Mushairas* and *Qawwalis*. *Mushairas* are public gatherings where poets recite lyrics known as *gazal*, the most popular of the classical forms of Urdu poetry. *Qawwali* music is the devotional music of the *Sufis*, the mystics of Islam. It dates back to the tenth century and the lyrics are usually in Urdu, Panjabi or Farsi. Both *Mushairas* and *Qawwalis* are organised by the local community and may take place three or four times a year.

Education Provision within the Biradari

Cleveland's Mirpuri community have established a number of organisations and associations to provide for a variety of social, cultural and educational needs. These include the education needs of different sectors of the community. The 1989 Research and Intelligence Survey identified the following organisations (presented in alphabetical order) affiliated to Cleveland Community Relations Council:

- Asian Girls' Class

- Cleveland Asian Women's Association

- Islamic Society

- Middlesbrough Mosque Committee

- Pakistani Students' Association

- Stockton Mosque

- Teesside Pakistani Association

- Thornaby Muslim Association

These represent the largest, most well-founded and officially recognised groups. Doubtless other, less official groups also exist.

Attitudes to Language Learning within the Mirpuri Community

The migrant groups from Pakistan, India, the Panjab and Bangladesh bring with them to Britain, their adopted homeland, more than just their cultural and linguistic heritage. They also carry personal and collective expectations of linguistic pluralism. Within the communities there is the expectation that official and regional languages will differ from the vernacular of the home and interpersonal contacts. The Mirpuri community in Britain holds to the expectation of both personal and societal multilingualism as the norm. They carry this expectation with them from their homeland where language learning is not linked directly with formal education or regarded as synonymous with other aspects of educational success. Learning languages is regarded as a necessity of everyday life. New languages are learned because they are needed for routine communications. Different types of exchange with different interlocutors require different languages.

The expectation within the Mirpuri community is that individuals will learn and use different languages and language varieties for different purposes in different situations or domains. This reinforces the description of bilingualism and language choice as 'domain determined' (Fishman *et al.*, 1971). The Mirpuri orthodoxy of language learning is different from the prevalent attitude in Britain, particularly from that within the formal education system. Within the Mirpuri community language learning is not necessarily a formal school-based activity. Many young children learn the varieties of language used within the family and kinship groups, before they enter formal education. The *biradari* has a tradition of community support which although present in the homeland has assumed new roles and functions in the adopted country. These expectations of personal, community-based multilingual proficiency contrast sharply with the personal aspirations of the indigenous British community and the education provision for language-learning experiences within Britain. This attitude to multilingualism is explained by the Commission for Racial Equality (1982) in a discussion document:

> Throughout Asian history groups of people have expressed a desire to learn another language which they see as functionally more relevant than theirs. Asian children who speak Panjabi at home may well want to learn Urdu instead of Panjabi because this was the traditional language of learning for their parents. Those from East Panjab may well choose to study Hindi for religious reasons.

This positive attitude to linguistic diversity, not prevalent among the monolingual English-speaking community, was probably not anticipated by educationalists and language planners. It is a feature of the Mirpuri community's educational needs which deserves attention.

Summary

This chapter has set the historical context for understanding the heterogeneous composition of present-day Britain. One of the newly settled migrant communities from the Mirpur region has been identified for detailed discussion, and the geographic, linguistic, cultural, social and religious features of this group have been described. This has set the context for the children who are the focus of the Box Hill Nursery Project, children who represent the second or third generation to be born into the families of these early migrants. They were all born in the UK to UK parents (and frequently grandparents, too). All of these children expect to be educated in the UK and will hence be on the receiving end of government education policy. Chapter 2 will outline the development of statutory education provision within Britain for bilingual children, including the children and grandchildren of these early Mirpuri migrants.

Chapter 2

The Development of Education for Bilingual Children in Britain

They behave this way not because I'm Black but because they are white. (Alice Walker, *Possessing the Secret of Joy*, 1992: 38)

Introduction

Chapter 1 presented a view of Britain as a multilingual, multi-ethnic society; a society comprising many languages, religions, many customs, cultures and characters who have made Britain their permanent place of residence. This heterogeneity has not always been welcomed or even acknowledged. In schools, an absence of recognition has resulted in a lack of clearly stated policy for the education of these children, many of whom have the potential to become bi- and even multilingual. The aim of this chapter is to provide a critical overview of the development of education provision for such children that has taken place in Britain since the 1960s. These comments do not apply to Wales, where the situation differs.

The newly settled communities of ethnic Pakistani origin are not the only groups to contribute to the cultural, linguistic, ethnic and religious diversity of British schools. Since the mid nineteenth century there has been a variety of such groups, Polish, Ukrainian, Chinese, Yiddish, French and many others, speaking languages other than English (Bourne, 1990). However, no major educational discussion of their needs began until the mid 1960s when, with the arrival of migrants from the New Commonwealth, multilingualism began to be perceived as an issue both for society and for educational policy makers. From the outset, therefore, the presence of bilinguals from Pakistan (and its neighbouring region) provoked a response from society at large and education authorities in particular that was different from their response to other bilingual migrant groups.

The Assimilationist Approach

Throughout the 1960s the education provided for bilingual children was characterised by its emphasis on assimilation into the dominant British

22

culture through the English language. Its focus on teaching English as a second language (ESL) was frequently at the expense of the wider curriculum and always at the expense of the pupils' home language(s). The teaching methodology was 'borrowed' from the British secondary school tradition of foreign language teaching, despite the inappropriateness of this approach for primary-age pupils, some of whom were as young as five years.

By 1966 the need for the intensive teaching of English as a second language (TESL) was recognised under Section XI of the Local Government Act 1966. This enabled LEAs to claim a grant, at the rate of 75% of the salary paid to each teacher employed for this purpose. One outcome of this separate funding was the establishment of TESL provision outside mainstream education. LEAs established peripatetic teams of ESL teachers to serve in primary schools and language centres (where older children were placed on arrival in Britain). TESL was seen as the key to assimilation and to the newcomers' rapid adaptation to the British way of life. Pupils' existing language skills were disregarded. This led the Swann Report to comment: 'It seems to have been assumed that the children's own languages would simply die out and be replaced by English' (DES, 1985: 388).

With the benefit of hindsight, current thinking sees this policy as discriminatory in effect, if not in intent. In summary, it can be said that Section XI funding led to separate English language teaching for children whose home language was not English. ESL teaching was made available to children whose community language was accorded language status. Children of Caribbean origin whose first language was Creole were not included in ESL provision.

The emphasis on assimilation did not, however, extend to religious practice in what was fast becoming a secularised Britain. The central importance of places of worship (in the case of the Mirpuri community this meant the mosque) played an increasingly important role in the everyday lives of these communities. This influence soon spread beyond the initial religious focus to include cultural transmission and the reinforcement of ethnic group identity. For example, the teaching of home or community languages frequently took place in religious centres. This wider role, encompassing ethnic, cultural and linguistic as well as religious aspects of life, meant that places of worship assumed an increasingly significant role in the maintenance and reinforcement of ethnic identity within some of the settled communities.

The 1970s witnessed significant developments in the official recognition of the language needs of bilingual children outside Britain. In the United States the 1974 case of *Lau* v. *Nichols* established the rights of a non-English-speaking child to a meaningful education which acknowledged the child's home language (in this case, Chinese). A year later, in Britain, the move from the assimilationist approach to the education of bilingual children towards integrationist thinking was precipitated from an unexpected source. The 1975 Bullock Report presented the findings of a committee of enquiry into the teaching of reading in primary schools. The committee felt unable to isolate the teaching and learning of reading from other aspects of language learning, for example oracy and writing. The Bullock Report *A Language For Life* (DES, 1975) addressed in its recommendations the language needs of those children still perceived at that time as 'of immigrant origin', and was critical of language teaching which required a child to 'cast off the language of his [*sic*] home as he [*sic*] passes the school threshold' (DES, 1975: Chapter 5: 20). The report suggested that 'the school should adopt positive attitudes to its pupils' bilingualism and wherever possible should help maintain and deepen the[ir] knowledge of the[ir] mother tongues' (DES, 1975: chap. 5: 20). It also described bilingualism as 'an asset ... something to be nurtured' (DES, 1975: 293) and suggested the school as one of the agencies which should nurture it (DES, 1975: 294). This statement, together with a further recommendation for schools to formulate a language policy which included ESL provision, constituted a recommendation to schools to broaden their perception of ethnic minority educational needs, and to offer a wider curriculum that included broader cultural elements.

Although the report raised awareness of the existing linguistic skills of ethnic minority pupils there was little sign of the education system, or society at large, valuing these abilities as relevant to the pupil's educational achievement and progress. However, another factor combined with the Bullock Report to give impetus to the move away from educational policy dominated by assimilationist philosophy. This was the change in status of black ethnic groups from an immigrant workforce to a settled community of British citizens (Mullard, 1984). The shift in status changed both society's and the groups' perception of their educational and social needs. This change was reflected in the British education system, when assimilationist education gave way to the development of multicultural education and the subsequent change in educational provision for bilingual children.

This national trend within Britain was supported by the international developments of the late 1970s. In 1976 a draft EC directive on the language education of migrant workers was issued to interested parties throughout the European Community. It proposed that member states should offer free tuition in the national languages of migrant workers as part of the curriculum for full-time education. However in 1977, only one year after the draft was first published, a significant modification was made that required member states merely to *promote* mother tongue teaching (European Community, 1977). (An expanded discussion on Britain's specific response to the modified directive will be presented in the next section.)

The Pluralist Approach of Multicultural Education

The development of the concept of multicultural education broadened educational provision beyond English language teaching (ELT) to include cultural and religious teaching. Multi-faith celebrations and world religions joined the school curriculum. More significantly, the new approach expanded language teaching to include mother-tongue teaching (as it was then called) and bilingual support in ESL provision. Multicultural education placed increasing emphasis on developing the child's full linguistic competence. ESL teaching became sensitive to the existing linguistic competence of pupils for whom English was a second language. Their community languages were seen as a linguistic resource for ESL and other teaching.

However, this wider view of the role of language in the educational experience of ethnic minority pupils impinged only marginally on ESL provision, much of which, in terms of its underlying aims and assumptions, remained unchanged from the earlier days of assimilationist thinking. English remained the medium of instruction in all primary classrooms, as well as the medium used for testing educational achievement, particularly in the field of language development, reading, writing and oracy, and for assessing verbal reasoning or intelligence testing. Thus bilingual children were compared and assessed in their educational achievements with their monolingual, English-speaking peers. Bilingual pupils' seeming lack of achievement (as measured in English) was perceived as problematic. Bilingualism remained an unacknowledged resource which still did not feature as significant in educational assessment profiles or pupil records. The development of the home language, in those schools where community languages were taught, was seen only as a means of accelerating children's learning of English, their second or subsequent language, rather than as a learning activity of intrinsic worth and value.

In retrospect it is possible to see how multicultural education failed to meet the needs of ethnic minority pupils in a number of ways. It was in some respects simply another form of compensatory education, essentially no different in form from the assimilationist programmes which preceded it. It also failed to address the institutional practices and procedures identified in the Swann Report (DES, 1985) as the real causes of educational underachievement among some bilingual children.

An alternative perspective on the educational underachievement of certain groups of pupils from ethnic minority backgrounds was argued by Troyna (1991), who suggested that bilingual pupils are underrated rather than underachieving. However, current institutional practices identified by the Swann Report as disadvantageous to bilingual pupils remain in place even today. These include the testing and assessment procedures (SATs) which are now carried out annually as part of the 1988 Education Reform Act. Bilingual children are currently assessed through tests in English and their performance compared with mean scores that had been standardised on monolingual English-speaking pupils.

With hindsight it seems that the multicultural education movement, with its focus on a marginal curriculum for black, ethnic minority children which taught aspects of their everyday lives (characterised as the tokenism of 'samosas, saris and steel bands'), was no less marginalising than its predecessor, the assimilationist approach. Through this misfocus, the multicultural education movement failed to improve bilingual children's performance in mainstream curriculum activities. A society's values can be seen encapsulated within its education provision. Britain was still not acknowledging the multilingual nature of its population and this attitude was reflected in the education system.

In 1977, only two years after the publication of the Bullock Report, the European Economic Community issued a directive on 'The Education of the Children of Migrant Workers' (July 77/4861). Article 3 stated that it required member states 'in accordance with their national circumstances and legal systems and in co-operation with the state of origin, to promote the teaching of the mother tongue and culture in accordance with normal education' (European Community, 1977: 2). EC member states were required to comply with the directive from 25 July 1981, and the Commission issued a report on its implementation on 10 February 1984. In Britain, Circular No. 5/81, issued on 31 July of the same year, outlined the DES guidelines on compliance with Article 2. It stated:

For the local education authorities in this country, [the directive] implies that they should explore the ways in which mother-tongue teaching might be provided, whether during or outside school hours, but not that they are required to give such tuition to all individuals as of right. (DES, 1981: 2)

Thus it could be inferred that the British education system was not making adequate provision for the educational needs of bilingual pupils. A follow-up EC report in 1984 on the implementation of the 1977 directive showed that Britain was at that time lagging behind other member states in complying with it, with only 2.2% of the primary school-age children from homes where languages other than English were spoken receiving home language teaching at school, compared with, for example, 80% of children of the same age in the Netherlands. Furthermore, Article 3 met with a mixed response from within minority communities. It was regarded (from both inside and outside these groups) as separating ethnic minority groups and differentiating their right to educational provision. Linguistic minorities from EC states who were not living in the EC state of their birth (those for whom the EC directive was originally intended) were entitled to home language teaching when resident in their host community, whereas linguistic minority groups who were British citizens and living in the EC state of their birth (Britain) enjoyed no such entitlement.

Thus the settled migrant communities in Britain felt disenchantment on two fronts: firstly with their exclusion from the EC directive, and secondly with the multicultural education initiative, which they perceived as conceptually unsound in both its theoretical foundation and its practical implications. This dual disenchantment coincided with a developing political awareness within black ethnic minority groups whose newly found confidence accompanied their change in status from that of 'immigrant' to that of British citizen. The dissatisfaction felt amongst educationalists representing ethnic minority educational rights stemmed from the disregard of education planners for the theoretical and practised models of bilingual education that existed both elsewhere throughout the EC and internationally.

The multicultural education movement has been criticised from a number of sources. Churchill's (1986) overview of the principles used by policy makers in OECD countries in their attempts to meet the educational needs of linguistic and cultural minority groups has identified a number of ways in which the various attempts (including those in Britain) failed to meet the needs of the groups that they were established to serve, namely the ethnic minorities. His view is that:

the policy making process that emerges from the analysis is one where policy is rooted in societal assumptions about the role of linguistic and cultural minorities, based in turn upon historical factors, in which the strongest is the development of public education ... mainly in a context of linguistic uniformity ... These assumptions result in definable types of problem definitions that are in large measure a function of the characteristics of minority populations concerned and of the level of educational provision available for them at a given point in time. Minority aspirations depend in turn on the level of educational provision made at a given time, and the response to their need is a function of their level of aspiration, a sort of circular relationship. (Churchill, 1986: 155)

Churchill (1986: 3) also suggests that 'the often abysmal results obtained by educational policies are traced in large measure to the limits placed by public opinion and by accepted problem definitions on the range of policy options that can be considered and adopted by authorities'.

His are not the only criticisms. Bourne (1990) has identified specific ways in which the recommendations of the Swann Report (DES, 1985) have not been achieved, a decade after its publication. These will be discussed later in this chapter. Thus it was that disenchantment with the multicultural education initiative gave rise to the anti-racist education movement.

The Anti-racist Education Movement

Mullard (1984) presents the case for anti-racist education as a development within the black consciousness movement of the mid 1960s. He worked with the National Association for Multicultural Education (NAME) and was instrumental in changing the name and focus of that group. In 1985 it became the National Anti-racist Movement in Education, retaining the acronym NAME.

For Mullard (1984: 29) the move from multicultural to anti-racist education is not a mere question of alternatives. He perceives the shift in emphasis as linked closely with the change in status of black ethnic minority groups from that of immigrant to that of black British citizen. He suggests (1984: 9) that the anti-racist approach to education reflects the socio-political values of the black ethnic groups 'in their ... struggles and resistances against colonialism, imperialism and metropolitan racism. Mullard (1984) and Sivanandan (1982) both view the growth of anti-racist education as a parallel to the life experiences of black people in a white society, Mullard presenting the argument for anti-racist education as 'the re-articulation of black ethnicity through the structural–cultural experiences of Black people in British society' (1984: 24).

The study presented here, the Box Hill Nursery Project, is about the experiences of young bilingual pupils in formal education. Mullard (1984: 50-1) identifies the pre-school nursery as the most important and yet most difficult educational institution in which to address the needs of black ethnic minority children, in terms of acknowledging and nurturing their ethnic identity. This he attributes to the informal organisation and structure of the nursery school curriculum and its classroom procedures. His view is that despite the seeming informality of the pre-school context, nursery education is 'one of the most rigid situations of all' and that it overemphasises the caring role at the expense of the educating function.

The Swann Report – Education for All?

In 1985 (the same year that the acronym NAME changed its meaning) a report of major significance for the education of bilingual children was published. The report, *Education for All*, contained the recommendations of the Swann Committee, established in 1979, whose terms of reference included 'recognising the contribution of schools in preparing all pupils for life in society which is both multiracial and culturally diverse' (DES, 1985: vii). Although the primary focus of the committee was the children of Afro-Caribbean origin and their educational underachievement in relation to their peers, the report included a broader discussion of the educational needs of other children of former migrant communities. Swann's response to educational provision for bilingual pupils was that:

> essential to equality of opportunity, to academic success and broadly, to participation on equal terms as a full member of society is a good command of English … first priority in language learning … must therefore be given to the learning of English. (DES, 1985: 426)

Although committed to English as the language of education, the report stated suggested changes in provision: it favoured a move away from separate ESL teaching, and recommended that the needs of bilingual learners be met within mainstream school as part of a comprehensive programme of language education for all children (DES 1985: par. 5.2).

The Swann Report acknowledged the importance of fostering positive ethnic identity. The committee recommended a broader base for doing this through cultural and religious teaching as well as through language use. They did attempt to incorporate a broader definition of bilingualism. However, on the subject of bilingual education the report did little to advance thinking amongst educationalists, stating unequivocally, 'We cannot support the arguments put forward for the introduction of programmes of bilingual education in maintained schools' (DES, 1985: par. 2.15).

The report was equally unequivocal in its response to the provision for languages other than English. While recommending that community languages and home languages should be valued in the mainstream curriculum, enriching the linguistic awareness of monolingual pupils, the committee remained firmly opposed to any separate provision for language maintenance classes or bilingual forms of education. They pronounced that mainstream schools should not seek to assume the role of community providers for maintaining ethnic minority community languages (DES, 1985: par. 2.18).

The committee did however, make two important exceptions. Their first recommendation was for the provision of bilingual support to help pupils make the transition between their home languages and English, the medium of instruction in the early years. This was really the starting point for the study presented here. It was felt that the use of language in the classroom at the stage of transition from home to school, in the nursery school, would provide an opportunity for observing the transition and the role played by language in the process.

The second recommendation was for community languages to be included in the foreign language curriculum of secondary schools wherever there is likely to be sufficient demand. This recommendation will also have implications for the future education of the children included in this study, when they reach secondary school. The statement says that all pupils in those schools where community languages are in demand should be encouraged to consider studying them (DES, 1985: pars 3, 19 and 2.20). While this support was welcome, it failed to go far enough in its support of community languages within mainstream secondary foreign language provision. It confines the community languages, including Urdu, Arabic, Hindi, Bengali and Panjabi, to name but a few, to those schools where there is a concentration of pupils interested in learning these languages. This contrasts sharply with the provision and resourcing of the other languages included in the foreign language curriculum and automatically affects the status of these community languages in comparison with those already established within the foreign language curriculum. It also reinforces the place of foreign language teaching within the secondary school curriculum.

If the Swann Committee's recommendations had been implemented after 1985, Bourne outlines six developments that one would expect to find five years after the Committee made its recommendations. These are:

(1) A movement away from the provision of English language support provision in separate centres and withdrawal classes, and increasing efforts to provide structures of support within the mainstream classroom.

(2) An increase in in-service training and support for mainstream teachers to enable them to meet the needs of learners with a range of linguistic backgrounds.

(3) A change of emphasis from specially funded 'Section XI' English language support posts towards seeing language support as a mainstream responsibility, perhaps with fewer, but more experienced and specialised 'ESL' teachers.

(4) An emphasis on the recruitment of community language teachers, both in mainstream subject areas, and for 'bilingual support' (primary) and community languages teaching (secondary).

(5) An increase in the provision for 'bilingual support' (primary) and community languages classes (secondary).

(6) Increasing support for voluntary community group organised language classes in after-school hours. (Bourne, 1990: 5)

However, the findings of a national survey conducted by NFER between 1985 and 1988 into Local Education Authority (LEA) provision for language support for the curriculum learning of bilingual pupils, and for the teaching of the languages of local linguistic minority groups in the schools of England and Wales, identified seven constraints on the further development of provision for bilingual pupils:

(1) The absence of clear structures for consultation with minority linguistic groups at national and local levels on appropriate provision.

(2) The absence of forceful policy and funding targeted at teacher training institutions to increase the admission and training of bilingual teachers as language specialists and on mainstream subject courses.

(3) The absence of explicitly targeted national in-service priority funding for helping schools to respond to bilingualism effectively.

(4) The absence of any central curriculum and materials development body for bilingualism and community languages.

(5) The expectation among LEAs that any provision for bilingual pupils should be supported by extra, special funding.

(6) The lack of clarity in Home Office 'Section XI' regulations for funding, and the absence of any more appropriate source of funding for educational provision specifically to meet the needs of minority linguistic groups in England.

(7) The paucity of widely available documented models of good practice in adopting mainstream provision for multilingual classrooms, and of models of practice for community languages teaching in mixed first and second language classrooms. (Bourne, 1990: 12)

Such findings illustrate that there is a visible shortfall in the recommendations made by the Swann Committee (DES, 1985) and the subsequent implementation of those recommendations with regard to the education of bilingual children. If the purpose of the committee was to identify ways in which all pupils could benefit from the compulsory education provision, and if their recommendations were designed to provide a structured move towards equality of access to education for pupils, and greater participation in educational decision making for ethnic minority groups, the question raised by Bourne's (1990) findings is, have these recommendations been implemented, and if the answer, as Bourne's findings suggest, be no, then the cornerstone of Swann's Report, *Education for All*, is questionable.

The omission from the Swann Committee's recommendations pertaining to home language teaching and bilingual support was a disregard of the existing evidence which indicates the central role of languages (both first and subsequent) in the learning process. A separate professional report carried out by HMI for the DES into *Mother Tongue Teaching in School and Community* (DES, 1984) took a slightly different view on the education issues raised by the topic. Their report stated that progress in community language teaching would depend on 'establishing a firmer base of accurate knowledge of pupils' existing language skills in their mother tongues' (DES, 1984: 24). The report perceived a gap in existing knowledge of the language use of bilingual children and suggested that a linguistic description of bilingual children's language repertoire was needed before more concrete recommendations could be made (Linguistic Minorities Project, 1985). In their survey report of four LEAs (Ealing, ILEA, Manchester and Walsall) the HMI took a slightly different view from Swann in the question of first language provision within mainstream education. The DES (1984: 7) 'strongly endorsed' the six principles identified by one of the authorities in its documented policy statement. One principle endorsed by the DES is particularly significant. They state that 'it is educationally desirable that bilingual children in primary schools should be given the chance to read and write their mother tongues and to extend their oral skills in these languages' (DES, 1984: 7).

Current Policy in Britain

Since 1988 there has been provision for a national curriculum in Britain. The Cox Report was the discussion document which preceded the introduction of the National Curriculum for English. The terms of reference of the Cox Committee (DES, 1989) stipulated that the committee concern itself with the English curriculum for all pupils, whatever their first language. The supplementary guidance to the working group stressed that 'the framework [for English] should ensure, at the minimum, that all school-leavers are competent in the use of English – written and spoken, whether or not it is their first language' (DES, June 1989: Par. 10.1). The working group was informed that it 'should also take account of the ethnic diversity of the school population and society at large, bearing in mind the cardinal point that English should be the first language and medium of instruction for all pupils in England' (DES, June 1989: par. 10.1).

In their recommendations the Cox Committee reaffirmed the Swann Committee's belief that 'the key to equality of opportunity, to participation on equal terms as a full member of society, is a good command of English' (DES, 1985: chap. 7, par. 2.16). Their report included a chapter on 'Bilingual Children' (DES, June 1989: chap. 10). In this chapter, the committee reiterated the 'cardinal point that English should be the first language of and medium of instruction for all pupils in England' (DES, June 1989: 10.1).

However, it should be noted that pupils in Welsh medium schools in Wales were to be excluded from the supplementary guidance from the Secretary of State for Education. This exclusion clause once again differentiated between groups of bilingual British and EC citizens. Dissatisfaction with this differential treatment is now evident from an unexpected source. Parents in Wales are to appeal to the House of Lords after a five-year campaign against Dyfed (a Welsh LEA) County Council's bilingual education policy, under which English-speaking children in predominantly Welsh speaking areas are required to attend Welsh language schools. The appeal (reported in the *Independent*, 11 July 1994) is based on the right of the child to be educated in the home language. If successful, the implications will spread beyond Wales. This is but one example of the anomalies of statutory provision to exist within the 1988 Education Reform Act. This exclusion clause once again differentiates between groups of bilingual British citizens.

English in the National Curriculum

English is now decisively defined as the language of compulsory education provision in Britain for the majority of pupils aged between five and 16 years (except in Wales, as we saw above, where the situation is more complex and will not be included in this discussion). The programmes of study for English (and other core subjects of the National Curriculum) are linked closely to attainment targets and pupil assessment. This inevitably means that if all children are to be taught and assessed in the English language, community language bilingual children are still to be compared with their monolingual English-speaking peers, and the full range of their linguistic repertoire will continue to be unrecognised in their learning and formal school assessments. Irrespective of the Cox Committee's disclaimer of inconsistency and unreasonable discrimination, it is likely that the assessment profiles of ethnic minority pupils (a statutory requirement of the 1988 legislation) will record a lower level of performance because the assessment will be carried out in English and will exclude from the assessment those languages in which such pupils may be competent. It will not therefore be a comprehensive record of their linguistic repertoire and may even result in an inaccurate record of their linguistic competence. This is one way in which the Cox Report and the subsequent legislation can be interpreted as 'discriminatory'. There is another, namely, the proviso under Section 19 of the 1988 Education Reform Act which allows disapplication of the provision of the National Curriculum and enables headteachers to exempt some pupils from the assessment requirements for English, if it is considered that those pupils have language difficulties so severe as to render the assessment unworkable. In practice this could lead to some bilingual children being separated from their monolingual peers for assessment purposes. Since assessment procedures are to be linked to attainment targets, which in turn are linked to programmes of study, this could lead to the same pupils being separated for teaching purposes also. Section 19 of the 1988 Education Reform Act is a conundrum. It allows for the possibility of preclusion from the National Curriculum by the very act which is said to ensure entitlement to this curriculum for all pupils aged between five and 16 years in compulsory education.

Assessment takes place at the age of seven years, in Year 2. Even if bilingual pupils are not excluded from the assessments (SATs), it seems reasonable to speculate that some children may achieve a comparatively low level of performance. This achievement will be marked on education records, with the result that precisely those institutional practices and procedures identified by Swann as being discriminatory to ethnic minority pupils have been perpetuated and enshrined in the 1988 legislation. To reiterate Troyna's (1991) point, bilingual pupils will remain underachievers simply because their abilities are underrated.

Despite the fact that the Cox Committee continue to refute accusations of inconsistency or discrimination against community language bilinguals, the position of community language-speaking pupils does seem anomalous when they are compared with the committee's recommendations for their Welsh-speaking bilingual peers. If education policy decision at national level chooses not to address the educational needs of significant numbers of the population, the stated aim of the 1988 Education Reform Act regarding each pupil's entitlement to education is questionable.

Future Policy for Bilingual Pupils in Britain

In January 1995 the National Curriculum (post-Dearing) documents were issued with the promise that there would be no major changes in the curriculum content for the next five years. How the educational needs of bilingual children in British schools is to be met remains unstated. Yet the 1988 Education Reform Act gives each child an entitlement to education. One of its stated aims is to prepare pupils for adult life. This has frequently been represented to mean preparation for the workplace. However, there is a broader meaning to preparation for adult life which encompasses active citizenship. The real success of the 1988 Education Reform Act is still to be assessed. Success can be judged in many ways, and the ability to create an appropriately trained workforce is one measure. Another might be the value-added element, such as how compulsory schooling develops individuals beyond the official curriculum. In order to achieve this, British schools will need to meet the challenges of both the 1976 Race Discrimination Act and the 1988 legislation. Thus the challenge identified by Swann (DES, 1985: 90) of 'evolving an education system which ensures that all pupils achieve their full potential' should once again be under active consideration by the teaching profession, educational policy makers and politicians. While community groups have the ability to be polyglots, official recognition should come from within the education system if these abilities are to become meaningful within the workplace.

Progress in education provision from assimilation through multicultural education and anti-racist education reflects the change in status of certain ethnic minority groups from that of immigrant to that of British

citizen. However Britain, despite its heterogeneous, multilingual population, and unlike (for example) Canada, Wales, Singapore and Australia,
does not have an official national language policy. In the description and
analysis presented above of the education provision for bilingual children
in British schools since the 1960s, up to and including the introduction of
the National Curriculum in 1988, the inherent value system of education
policy makers is clear. English is now firmly established as the only official
language of mainstream education in Britain. Foreign languages are taught
in secondary schools, but these are almost exclusively defined in terms of
modern European languages. French and German are widely taught, while
Urdu and Panjabi are not.

Despite the lack of a national language policy Ingram (1990) suggests
that it is still possible to infer policy in Britain:

> Language-in-education planning is the process involved in demon-
> strating how the ideals, goals and content of a language policy can be
> realised in practice. In case a country does not possess a clearly formu-
> lated and stated language policy ... it is possible to infer a policy from
> the State's social, demographic, and economic structure, its interna-
> tional relationships, and general developments in policy nationally.
> (Ingram, 1990: 1)

Policy statements are important because, as Kroon and Vallen (1994) re-
mind us, language and education policy are not just abstract; they
influence individuals and sometimes can determine how they go about
their daily lives.

The current situation in Britain is that the full linguistic repertoire of
some pupils is not being reflected in classroom teaching and assessment.
Bilingualism is ignored as an individual, societal and national resource.
Both the 1944 and the later 1988 Education Acts omit specific education
provision for bilingual pupils. This neglect fails to acknowledge bilingualism as a positive intellectual, social and educational advantage for
individual pupils, as well as an economic, social and cultural national
resource. Current education provision in England is therefore undervaluing, undermining and underselling significant groups within British
society. At present there has emerged a practice of unofficial English
language immersion programmes. This has come about almost by default.
What is needed for the future is *planned* education provision that accords
the teaching and learning of language(s) and culture(s) a more central role
within compulsory education, beginning at the point of transition into
school in reception classes and continuing throughout the primary school.

Without an official policy statement it is not possible to monitor the impact and changes that are taking place. It is also difficult to ensure that all children are receiving the education best suited to their needs.

Bilingual Children in Pre-school

At present, nursery education within Britain is not compulsory. It falls outside statutory provision and hence official education policy. However, there is support from a variety of sources (DES, 1975; Fishman, 1989; Mullard, 1984) for the view that the point of transition to formal schooling is an important one in the life of bilingual children. There is also support for the view that this period of transition is difficult for young children to make (Tizard & Hughes, 1984; Willes, 1983). There is a paucity of research into the effects of the transition on young bilingual children. However, research into the experiences of monolingual pupils suggests that nursery education may have a formative influence on later academic achievement and success (Tizard *et al.*, 1988) and that, despite the fact that it falls outside statutory provision, it is an important component in the process of education as a whole.

Since 1988 and the introduction of the Education Reform Act the education system has experienced unprecedented change and legislation. Alongside this, there has been increased public scrutiny as well as calls for greater transparency of education process and accountability of the teaching profession. These changes have impacted on early years education in the nursery and reception classes. Initiatives have included the introduction and subsequent abolition of the Nursery Voucher Scheme, the instigation of Ofsted inspections of nursery schools and a policy statement on curriculum, *Desirable Outcomes* (1996). All of these have been very expensive to implement. Despite all of these opportunities to introduce changes that specifically address the educational needs of young bilingual pupils, little has happened to enhance their prospects of achieving bilingualism through mainstream education. From September 1998 all children will be assessed on entry into mainstream schooling. These assessments are known as Baseline Assessments (BLAs), and are required by law. There are currently some 90 BLAs available to schools, and since many are observational the individual child's language proficiency is central to the assessment. Yet despite this, few BLAs are available in languages other than English. An exception is the Performance Indicators in Primary School (PIPs) BLA (Tymms *et al.*, 1997) which can be carried out in the child's home language, and includes British Sign Language. Many of the other BLAs rely on knowledge and proficiency in English. By comparison around 10 BLAs are available in Welsh for pupils attending schools in Wales. This leaves an anomaly in the education provision for different groups of UK citizens.

Summary

This chapter has outlined the development of educational provision for bilingual children in Britain since the 1960s up to and including the introduction of the National Curriculum in 1988. From the analysis of the documentation presented it is suggested that explicit statements of support for bilingual pupils in British schools (DES, 1975, 1985) have been resisted. Due to the lack of a clearly stated national policy for the education of bilingual pupils there has emerged a practice of unofficial immersion programmes for teaching English. To date, no systematic national programme exists to meet the language needs of bilingual children. Criticism of the current state can be found in Pattanayak's (1991) statement in the Foreword to Alladina and Edwards (1991: vii) when he suggests that:

> the multicultural debate in the UK, unfortunately, has … got bogged down in the spurious controversy between multicultural and anti-racist education. Instead of discussing cultural variation and the cultural interaction between shared values and culture-specific values, this debate has been lost in the metalanguage of models and the muddles they have created.

A further criticism of the education provision for bilingual pupils is that it has been conceived by British educationalists in the early stages, without reference to or liaison with the community groups for whom they were planning and providing a compulsory education system. It is therefore hardly surprising that current education provision has failed, at least in part, to meet the personal and educational aspirations of the bilingual groups it was designed to serve.

Finally, it is suggested that nursery education is important for monolingual children because it has been identified by Tizard *et al.* (1988) as influencing later academic achievement and success at school. If this is the case for monolingual children, it is suggested that nursery education may be equally influential in the lives of young bilingual pupils. Transition from the home to formal schooling has been identified as a critical stage in the development of the bilingual child (DES, 1975; Mullard, 1984; Fishman, 1989) and a worthy but neglected focus of research interest.

Chapter 3
Theoretical Frameworks:
Influences and Inspirations

> Murderers, or great criminals, should ideally be dons: plenty of time to
> plan the coup and no curious questions or inquisitive glances once it is
> done. (Anita Brookner, *A Start in Life*, 1991: 9)

Introduction

This chapter will outline the theoretical paradigms that have provided
the foundations for the Box Hill Nursery Project. It is difficult to trace
precisely all that has influenced one's ideas, but the chapter outlines the
key influences on my developing ideas about language learning in young
children. It brings together ideas from psychology, systemic linguistics,
anthropology and sociolinguistics that are not usually considered simultaneously. The aim is to attempt an integrated approach to the study of
young bilingual learners.

Three equally established theoretical frameworks form the conceptual
framework for this study. The first is Vygotsky's (1962; 1966, 1978) view of
the child as a social being, as one involved in the social order of things from
the very early stages of life. The second is systemic linguistics (in the tradition of Firth, 1968; Halliday, 1973, 1975, 1978, and others) which describes
language as social behaviour. The third is Le Page and Tabouret-Keller's
(1985) description of bilingualism as an 'act of identity'. In order to understand these underpinning conceptual frameworks, a more detailed
examination of each is necessary.

Lev Vygotsky – the Social Psychologist

Central to Vygotsky's view is the idea of the child as a social being. His
view is that language is inextricably tied to cognitive and behavioural
systems, that it interacts with them and serves their continuous development. Vygotsky (1962, 1966, 1978) regards human activity as a tool and
suggests that people use tools as a means of achieving, changing and transforming themselves. He developed this view to cover the use of sign

systems, including spoken language, written language and number systems, all of which are created by each society to serve their own unique and differing needs. He suggests that these systems are amenable to change. This is compatible with the description of language as dynamic, evolving and constantly changing.

Vygotsky parallels the child's development in spoken and written language with cultural changes in the use of sign systems. His theory rests on the fundamental premise that development occurs on a social level within a cultural context. He suggests that the child learns by internalising processes witnessed in social activity. The young child moves from a social to an individual plane, or in the terms of Vygotsky's theory, from *inter*-psychological functioning to *intra*-psychological functioning. His view of child learning can be summarised as determined by social functioning. In his view the structure of an individual child's mental processes mirrors the social milieu from which they are derived. Language development is embedded within societal and cultural contexts.

Central to Vygotsky's theory is the view of intellectual growth contingent on learning language (the social means of thought). This view has been developed and expanded by Luria (1978). The Vygotskyan perspective has a number of key concepts that help to explain how this ontogenesis takes place. Speech, which begins as a shared social activity on the part of the child, becomes a principal means of the mental regulation and refinement of individual behaviour. Vygotsky describes three types of regulation in communication activities. These are:

(1) *Object-regulation*: where a person is object-regulated when directly controlled by their environment. Within the education context a number of examples of object-regulation can be found. For example, the organisation of the school and the learners within it; the choice of teaching materials, textbooks and teaching styles; the organisation of the curriculum, syllabus and the methods of assessment, all assume intrinsic power because they are symbolic within the society, and they exert some influence on learners because of the ways in which they are used by teachers as controlling mechanisms. A National Curriculum can be regarded as a reflection of a society's values.

(2) *Other-regulation*: when one person is regulated by another person who can influence and regulate through their position of authority, status, choice and use of language or other behaviour. The teacher in the classroom, for example, can be described in this way. Other-regulation can exert influence in a number of ways, which may be either positive or

negative, and can be used by a teacher (or any adult) as a means of influencing the child or children in their care. It may be achieved directly through interpersonal contact and interactions or, less directly, through structuring the environment in which interactions and contacts take place.

(3) *Self-regulation*: where speech or spoken language is used to control oneself through self-directed utterances. Vygotsky (1962) suggests that this denotes mature linguistic ability. This feature of language use will be discussed in greater detail in Chapter 10 when describing individual children's language behaviour.

A central concept in Vygotsky's descriptions of language learning in young children is that of 'inner' or 'private speech'. This is sometimes referred to as 'speech-for-oneself'. He suggests that children find it helpful to speak (sometimes aloud, but not loudly) when they are engaged in activities. This talk can take the form of either dialogue or monologue. The latter is described as abbreviated structures that may not be meaningful to a listener who is unlikely to be able to share the speaker's thoughts. Private speech is a feature of child language also noted by other psychologists, including Piaget. However, there is a significant difference between Vygotsky and Piaget on the function and importance of inner speech. Vygotsky suggests that it plays a central role in both the language and cognitive development of the individual, whereas Piaget proposes that it merely 'withers away' as the child grows older. Vygotsky attaches greater significance to the child's private speech. He suggests that speech-for-oneself becomes internalised as verbal thinking. Thus speech-for-oneself assumes a much greater significance in the development of the child's language, thoughts and cognitive functioning.

Vygotsky's zone of proximal development

Vygotsky makes a distinction between 'learning' and 'development'. He suggests that learning is related to formal educational situations and contexts, while development happens in a less contrived way. This distinction leads him to describe a central notion of his theory, the 'zone of proximal development', which he uses to explain the distinction between a child's *actual* development, as measured by, for example, IQ tests, and their *potential* development. Vygotsky suggests that in order to assess the potential development level it is necessary to present the child with a problem, the solution to which is just beyond their present mental capacities, and then to allow them to interact with another (more experienced) person while working out the solution. He suggests that these processes by which the child arrives at the solution provide a more accurate assessment of the intellectual capacity than traditional IQ tests.

Vygotsky's theoretical construct of a zone of proximal development concurs with the social nature of learning. He suggests (1962: 104) that 'what a child can do in collaboration today, he can do alone tomorrow'. This is a view of learning reinforcing the social nature of the activity. It stands in contrast to the Piagetian view of the child as the lone scientist trying to work out a view of the world independently and alone, a view that has been criticised by Donaldson (1978) because it underestimates the capabilities of young learners.

Vygotsky's theory of a zone of proximal development is not a stage confined to childhood. He suggests that it is evident at every stage of human development, whenever a person is moving from 'not knowing' through a learning phase, aided by external agencies, people or other learning supports. This idea has been developed and extended by Bruner (1986), who describes the critical function of the support given to the learner through the zone of proximal development as 'scaffolding', meaning 'appropriate social interactional frameworks'. This element reinforces the social dimension of learning language(s) and other things. In early learning the role of support through the zone of proximal development can be played by adults, competent peers and experienced others. Each can perform a crucial supporting role in helping the learner towards the time when they have a degree of control over a new function or conceptual system. When the child has arrived at the stage of independence, learning can be said to have taken place; the child is then in a position to achieve a degree of control over what has been learned. At this point the new learning can be used as a tool and the external agent or scaffolding is no longer required.

Language plays a central role in Vygotsky's theories of child learning, both as the channel of communication between the learner and those providing support or scaffolding through the zone of proximal development, and as the private, inner speech central to learning success. It is therefore compatible with a socially orientated description of language. This leads us to the second influence under-pinning this investigation, the systemic linguistic description of language as socio-semiotic.

Language as Socio-semiotic

This section will outline the development of linguistic theory from Malinowski and Firth to Halliday. It will chart linguists' recognition of contextual factors and the subsequent influence that these factors exert when people use language. It will be argued that people use language for realising social situations and that context therefore, is an essential aspect of a linguistic description. Specifically, this section will chart the predominantly socially orientated linguistic descriptions provided by the development of systemic linguistics, with its sources in the works of Malinowski, Firth, and later, Halliday.

Systemic linguistics developed out of Saussurian and Bloomfieldian linguistics which, in the pursuit of establishing linguistics as a science, directed linguists towards the study of text in the abstract. Saussure (1916/74: 80) considered text as a unit of social interaction too individual, too momentary, too context-bound to be of general use. Bloomfield (1930/70: 230; 1933/43: 139–57) acknowledged that contextual factors may influence how people use language for realising social activities, but he did not consider it the task of linguistics to account for such matters because he believed that it could not be achieved in a scientific manner.

In contrast to the Saussurian and Bloomfieldian approach, Malinowski and Firth viewed language as realising social acts in the context of situations and cultures. Malinowski's view (1923/66: 310) is that in society, language performs certain functions in the lives of that society's members. He explains that language functions in a number of ways:

(1) It realises action (for example, the handing over of a utensil or instructing a person in its use).

(2) It expresses social and emotional functions (for example, narratives express the social togetherness of a society).

(3) It realises phatic communion (for example, members of a society create 'ties of union' by small talk or by exchanging greetings).

Malinowski's distinctions can be regarded as the first classifications of social activities grouped, according to their function, as either (a) service encounters, or (b) social/emotional genres, or (c) casual conversations. For him, 'a statement spoken in real life is never detached from the situation in which it has been uttered … the utterance has no meaning except in the context of situation' (1923/66: 307). His description (1923/66: 310–11) of how a fishing activity unfolds contextually as a social process is now established as a corner-stone of sociolinguistics. Through this description Malinowski reveals the patterning of the generic structure of the fishing text. This he does in two ways: firstly, by the generic structure of fishing as a social activity, and secondly, by outlining how register (language) choices are made in each structural element of the social activity (or genre).

Malinowski's description of genre patterning can be used as a framework for describing other social contexts. It can be used to show how a social activity unfolds as a generic structure in a text. This it does in a number of ways: by showing the participants' orientations to the relevant institutions and objects ('field') in that text; by revealing the relations between participants ('tenor') and by demonstrating how communications channels ('mode' – that is, the language or register choices of the participants) are selected in each structural element of the genre. At each stage in the unfolding of the social activity there are changes which are recognised as having 'linguistic consequences': 'linguistic material is … dependent upon the course of activity' (Malinowski, 1923/66: 311). The activities which unfold in specific contexts thereby organise the linguistic materials in the text and determine the register choices or modes possible in each stage in the unfolding of the genre. 'Register' or language choice therefore plays an integral role in the construct of social situations. Although Malinowski's original description was of monolingual speakers, it is possible to extend his description to include individuals with linguistic repertoires which include more than one language. Bilinguals may select their mode, register or language choice from any of the languages which they speak and understand.

Malinowski's concept of context of situation has been developed and elaborated by Firth. Central to the Firthian view is the 'actual language text' (Firth, 1968: 173), which has two central tenets. The first is that text should be considered as a constituent part of the context of its situation, and the second is that a text 'should be related to an observable and justifiable grouped set of events in the run of experience' (Firth, 1968: 175). In an expanded description of the first tenet, Firth describes meaning as being created at two complementary levels, the contextual and the linguistic. Therefore, the initial step in the study of a text is to establish situational relations. Firth describes how a text is a constituent feature of the context in which it occurs. His description comprises categories that function in the context of a given situation. For example he establishes the situational relations of:

- who the participants are;
- what the relevant objects and events are; and
- what effect verbal interaction has.

Once these contextual questions have been addressed, then the analysis of a specific text can begin. Firth (1968: 27) suggests that step-by-step analyses are essential because the meanings of texts, utterances and words 'cannot be achieved at one fell swoop by one analysis at one level.'

It is important to note that the study of the relations between contextual categories and language is regarded by Firth (1968: 27) as the study of semantics. Firthian levels have been interpreted in a number of ways. However, there is consensus regarding at least one aspect, namely that the order of the analyses matters less than the agreement that all levels will be included in the analysis. Firth (1968: 174) likens the meanings gleaned from the various levels of analysis to the 'light of mixed wavelengths in the spectrum', and only multiple analyses of texts capture this dispersion. To continue with Firth's metaphor, each level of analysis is seen as shedding light on the meaning of the text. Hence the Box Hill Nursery study presented here will include a number of different levels of descriptive analysis.

Firth's (1968: 200) linguistic analysis recognises two general theoretical relations, the *syntagmatic* and the *paradigmatic*. Syntagmatic relations specify how meanings in texts are composed by language forms or structures and how they are realised at various levels of linguistic description (for example, the phonological, the syntactic, the lexical). Paradigmatic relations are established between features of the systems that specify the values of the elements within the structures.

Firth's second central tenet is the concept of renewal. His view is that when individuals are involved in a social event they are realising a social process linguistically. They are behaving as members of their speech community. They are able to relate the ongoing text in which they are participants to previous texts that they have already experienced, either as observers or as active participants. The current text under negotiation renews these connections with the linguistic events of similar situational contexts, within a given speech community. (This notion has been developed by De Beaugrande and Dressler, 1981, as 'intertextuality'.) This concept of 'typeness' is important for children when they are being socialised into their first or subsequent culture. Social encounters are therefore viewed as social processes that unfold as generic structures, step-by-step, each element contributing to the nature and function of the social process which it is creating. The similarity of contexts for texts can be used by individuals as a method of recognising and classifying the current and other text types. Once a text renews connection with other texts, it can be linguistically stated as a text of a similar or dissimilar type. In this way individuals can learn appropriate linguistic behaviour in a range of contexts. The ways in which individuals anticipate social events (or indeed other people and their behaviour) in terms of previous experiences of similar contexts, events and situations has been described by Bartlett (1932) as 'schemata' and by Tannen (1979) as 'structures of expectation'.

The Hallidayan description of language as 'socio-semiotic'

The Malinowskian-Firthian tradition establishes the study of language as social interaction and communication within heterogeneous speech communities. Continuing in this tradition Halliday (1973, 1975) proposed that discourse is semantic choice in social contexts. His view of language extends beyond an individual's language production to a description of language as social fact. In 1978 Halliday proposed the formulation of language as socio-semiotic. Rooted in the linguistics of Malinowski and Firth, language as socio-semiotic presents language as functioning as an expression of and metaphor for the social processes which it creates and the social contexts in which it occurs. Inherent in the socio-semiotic approach to language description is the notion of language as a dynamic process. Hence, a whole range of modes of meaning are possible (from the concrete to the creative), because language not only facilitates everyday social encounters and supports social action, but it actually creates those contexts.

A socio-semiotic description accounts for the fact that people talk to each other, and that language is not sentences but discourse, that is, naturally occurring interactive connected exchanges which allow for an exchange of meaning in interpersonal contexts and contacts. The contexts where meanings are exchanged cannot therefore be devoid of social or personal values. Contexts cannot be value-free. Language cannot be context-free. Therefore, language cannot be value-free. The context of speech becomes a semiotic structure, taking its form from the culture (or sub-culture) in which it occurs, embracing its mores and values. This form enables the participants to predict prevailing features of the register. Each society and its sub-groups has its own underlying rules which govern acts of communication within its speech community. These rules for appropriate linguistic behaviour are learned. Learning a new language is learning how to behave linguistically in a new culture. Learning a first (or subsequent) language requires understanding how everyday social encounters are organised linguistically in that speech community. Thus individuals who have successfully learned the rules are able to present themselves as members of that (speech) community.

The linguistic tradition as established by Malinowski and Firth and developed by Halliday later became known as British Contextualism and Systemic Linguistics. The basic theoretical principles and development of this tradition are well documented. The most comprehensive accounts can be found in Hasan (1985), Kachru (1980), Kress (1976), Mitchell (1975), Monaghan (1979) and Robins (1971).

This section has outlined some of the main tenets of Firthian and neo-Firthian linguistics with regard to meaning as a socially constructed activity. The accounts support the view that a descriptive account of context is integral to linguistic descriptions, and that language as social semiotic describes discourse as semantic choice made by speakers (or discourse participants) to create social contexts.

Language as socio-semiotic: The implications

Central to the Hallidayan linguistic description of language as socio-semiotic is the notion of language as a dynamic process which not only facilitates social encounters and supports social action but which actually creates those social contexts. Semiotically speaking all social contexts consist of a construct of potential meanings. A socio-semiotic description of a social context needs to account for the social fact that people speak to each other, not in sentences but in naturally occurring, interactive, connected exchanges (discourse). Discourse allows for an exchange of meanings in interpersonal contacts in social contexts. Discourse creates the social context and thus creates the potential for individuals to exchange meanings and create personal encounters. The socio-semiotic description of language use therefore allows for language to create social contexts and personal encounters.

Language as socio-semiotic accounts for the social context of language use. However, there is a further dimension to language use in social contexts which accounts for an individual's behaviour. This behaviour, termed in Hymes' (1972b) taxonomy 'communicative competence', accounts for individuals knowing when to speak, when not to, what to talk about and with whom, when, where and in what manner to interact. To accept both Halliday's description of language as socio-semiotic and Hymes' notion of communicative competence allows for the possibility that each individual can play an instrumental role in constructing a social context, construing meaning from that (and every other) social context, and contributing actively to the language choice or register and the behaviour of other participants in the encounter. Thus individual discourse participants are potentially empowered in social contexts, with discourse rights.

Discourse rights can be realised as social rights. This potential is an important dimension to a social situation where one or more of the discourse participants are, for example, children and hence not accorded social status, or when they represent a linguistic minority in a given context.

Critics of Systemic Linguistics

Sampson (1980: chap. 9) presents a balanced overview of systemic description of language. He identifies specific aspects of the approach that are problematic, for example Firth's claim that phonological choices have direct semantic correlates, and Halliday's notion of 'rank' and 'delicacy' in syntactic structures (Sampson, 1980: 232). However, he admits that 'Halliday's version is at present by far the best known ... in my view, the most attractive version of the theory.' However, he further suggests that:

> the major difficulty in systemic grammar, for one who cares about the methodological issues ... concerns the essential role that intuition appears to play in systemic analysis ... The question whether or not certain constructions express different cases of a single semantic category and therefore belong together in one system ... may be unavoidably an intuitive decision, in which case systemic grammar cannot hope to rank as a science. But then, neither can sociology. (Sampson, 1980: 234)

Despite these stated reservations the Hallidayan and systemic descriptions of language are now well respected by a range of different research communities, including modern linguists (for example Sinclair & Coulthard, 1975), educationalists (Stubbs, 1986) and social psychologists (Wells & Montgomery, 1981). It should be noted that many revisions and refinements to the descriptive frameworks have taken place – and are still under active review – since the early descriptions.

Other Descriptions of Child Language Development

In addition to the Hallidayan description, there are other established descriptions of child language development. The systemic approach can be contrasted with that of Chomsky. The focus of Chomsky's (1968) work is the generic syntactic structures of different languages. The explicitly stated goal of his theory of universal grammar is to define the logic of language acquisition. He defines this linguistic competence as the deep-seated mental state that exists below the level of conscious language use by which even young children are allowed to generate a large set of utterances in their talk. He describes the emergence of grammatical structures as innately determined by the biological function of a 'language acquisition device' (LAD) which is intuitive and unique to human beings. Chomsky (1968) demonstrates mathematically that there exist well-defined classes of morpheme sequences that cannot be generated by any constituency grammar, no matter how complex. It should, however, be borne in mind that Chomsky originally used language to demonstrate an individual's knowledge of systems and rules, the parameters and principles, the configurations of the mind for which the structure of language – grammar – simply serves as evidence. Too frequently this has been misunderstood or misrepresented as meaning that knowledge of the grammar system is a prerequisite for language learning. Nevertheless, Chomsky's description does focus on the grammatical structures of the language as a means of demonstrating the ways in which young children learn one aspect of the 'rules of language'.

Chomsky's seminal description of child language is highly significant. However, it is not without its critics. Romaine (1984) presents an account of child language acquisition that stands in contrast to Chomsky's. By focusing on the sociolinguistic skills that young children must learn, Romaine (1984) describes the acquisition of communicative competence in child language development. Her approach emphasises the sociological aspects of language use, whereas Chomsky's focuses on psychological aspects. Romaine criticises Chomsky because:

he idealises the actual processes of language acquisition. He assumes that it takes place instantaneously. This allows him to ignore the intermediate states attained between the initial and steady state, the role of these intermediate states in determining what constitutes linguistic experience and other kinds of interactions that may be essential for the growth of language in the mind. (Romaine, 1984: 258)

Romaine (1984: chap. 9) further criticises Chomsky's LAD because this views child language acquisition in terms of a progression through a series of more or less discrete stages, becoming ever closer to adult grammar until mature (adult) language use is achieved. This conceptualisation of child language acquisition has reinforced the Piagetian view of the child as a 'lone scientist' or 'mini-grammarian'. From the Chomskyan viewpoint, children's utterances are regarded as merely lesser, underdeveloped and simple versions of adult grammars. However, perhaps the most cogent support for an alternative to the existing Chomskyan descriptions can be found in Romaine (1989: chap. 8) where she suggests that what is required is a comprehensive theory of language use. Ideally, this approach would integrate the social, communicative competence aspects of language use with the Chomskyan dimension.

When it came to choosing a descriptive framework for this study, the choice was not between a right or a wrong one; it was more a question of an appropriate one. Frameworks have to be matched to specific aspects of the intended description. Chomsky's framework is appropriate for some psychological aspects of language behaviour, while the systemic linguists offer an approach more compatible with social aspects of language use. Margaret Berry (1975) in her introduction to systemic theory makes a pertinent point with which I feel empathy. She writes (1975:23), 'While Chomskyan linguistics appeals to the psychologist, systemic linguistics is more relevant for the sociologist.'

Hence for the purposes of this study it was decided that a description of language that emphasised the social functions would provide a better complement to Vygotsky's theories of young children learning, and a description of bilingualism that would emphasise the social aspects of language behaviour for individuals who can speak more than one language. The latter framework is outlined in the next section.

A Social Construct of Bilingualism

Le Page and Tabouret-Keller begin their description of bilingualism by outlining some objections to Barth's (1969) traditional proposition that 'a race equals a culture equals a language', on the grounds that it is misleading (Le Page & Tabouret-Keller, 1985: 234–249). Their account of bilingualism includes the social context of language use in significant ways. They prefer to view individual linguistic behaviour as an 'act of identity'. This approach contrasts with other variationist studies such as Weinreich's (1953), where the languages spoken have been the object of theoretical and descriptive studies, and with psychological approaches to individual bilingualism of, for example, Cummins (1983). The description of bilingualism as the speaker's 'act of identity' emphasises the important relationship between language use, social network structure and ethnic identity. This description has its origins in the hypothesis (and its four caveats) that Le Page (1968: 192) formulated to describe the Creoles of the Caribbean:

> The individual creates his system of verbal behaviour so as to resemble those common to the group or groups with which he wishes from time to time to be identified, to the extent that:
>
> (a)   he is able to identify these groups

(b)   his motives are sufficiently clear cut and powerful

(c)   his opportunities for learning are adequate

(d)   his ability to learn – that is, to change his habits where necessary – is unimpaired.

In order to understand this fully, it is essential to consider it in connection with the metaphor of projection, focusing and diffusion, which Le Page (1978: 80) uses to describe verbal activity. The terminology is borrowed from the cinema, not from psychology. It is the metaphor on which his and Tabouret-Keller's description (1985: 116) of bilingualism as an act of identity is based.

> As an individual speaks s/he is always seen as using language with reference to the inner models of the universe s/he has constructed for her/himself, s/he projects in words, images of the universe ... on the social screen ... as s/he speaks s/he is inviting others to share ... views of the universe (even if that means agreeing to keep out of it!), the feedback s/he gets may lead ... to focus on his/her own image more sharply, and may also lead him/her to bring his/her own universes more into focus with those projected by others. A fresh contact, a fresh point of view, may on the other hand for a time at least make the projection more diffuse.

Le Page and Tabouret-Keller (1985) use 'focusing' to mean greater regularity in the linguistic code with less variability, and 'diffusion' to mean the opposite. This view presents language as a repertoire of socially constructed, socially bound and socially marked systems. Each time the individual speaks they present to the world their view of it. This reinforces closeness to or distance from the interlocutor's view of the world. In this way speakers, through discourse and social interactions, make value statements about their self-perceived identity.

Le Page and Tabouret-Keller (1985) developed their multidimensional description of bilingualism as the result of 30 years' work on the use of English in contact situations in the post-colonial British empire. The term 'multidimensional' is used to include what they call (1985: 1) 'the psychological and social aspects of pluri-lingualism'. Their description seems particularly appropriate to the study presented here because it shares a central concern of:

> the problems of helping children growing up in multilingual communities to profit best from the educational opportunities available to

them – and of helping to improve those opportunities and the understanding of teachers. (Le Page & Tabouret-Keller, 1985: 1)

Central to their description of bilingualism is the belief that bilingual behaviour is normal rather than idiosyncratic behaviour. They share the Hallidayan view that language is dynamic, and that it comes into being, together with those who speak it, through interpersonal behaviour or acts of identity which individuals make within themselves and with each other. They view the individual as the locus of language use, and describe bilingualism as an act of identity. However, they also acknowledge that individual speakers are influenced by other speakers during interactions and that they in turn may influence others:

> a group is any perceived cluster of two or more individuals. Language, however, in use by individuals, is the instrument through which, by means of individual adjustments in response to feedback, both *languages* and *groups* may become more highly focused in the sense that the behaviour of members of a group may become more alike. (Le Page & Tabouret-Keller, 1985: 116)

Le Page and Tabouret-Keller (1985: 2) use the term 'identify' as having two meanings. In the one sense, identify means 'to pick out as a particular person, category or example' by some idiosyncratic feature; in the other, it means 'to recognise some entity as a part of some larger group'. This symbiotic relationship permits an individual's idiosyncratic behaviour to reflect attitudes towards groups, while being constrained by certain boundary markers. Language can be a boundary marker, reinforcing the identity of 'self' against 'others', but this is not necessarily a prerequisite for group membership (Byram, 1990: 85). Other features have been identified by Le Page and Tabouret-Keller (1985: 209). These include physical features of ethnic identity, like jewellery, hairstyle and dress.

Ethnic identity markers need not always be so obvious. Byram (1990: 85) identifies 'return to the homeland' as an aspiration or psychological marker of some immigrant groups. The concept of identity embedded in Le Page and Tabouret-Keller's use of the word reinforces the view that an individual's language use or act of identity is idiosyncratic behaviour that reflects their attitudes towards groups, causes and traditions. The identity of a particular group exists only within the projections individuals make about the group. Language, communities, groups have no independent existence. They depend upon individuals. This view of ethnic groups stands very much in contrast to the definition offered by Giles (1979: 253) as consisting of 'those individuals who perceive themselves to belong to the same ethnic category', and that it is 'usually only in formal, institutional-ised settings that members of different ethnic groups encounter one another' (Giles, 1979: 255–6). The multilingual state of present-day Britain means that people meet in a variety of contact situations, some formal and institutionalised – for example, schools – and others not – for example, inter-ethnic households.

Le Page and Tabouret-Keller (1985: 5) stress that in descriptions of bilin-gualism, groups, communities and their linguistic attributes have no independent existence other than in the minds of individuals; they inhere only in the way individuals behave towards each other. This is compatible with the Hallidayan description of language as socio-semiotic, or (as it is sometimes referred to) social behaviour and social organisation.

Accepting Le Page and Tabouret-Keller's description of bilingualism together with Halliday's description of language use poses certain prob-lems for the researcher. The former (1985: 4) assert that:

> it is extremely hard to carry out sociolinguistic work in a rigorously hy-pothesis-testing manner when one comes to a society as an outsider and tries … to make no prior assumptions about the social divisions within that society … the class assumptions which underlie the work of … Labov in New York or Trudgill in Norwich do not apply.

Their descriptions of language use focus on the social processes by which individuals locate themselves within multidimensional space or the social universe as each perceives it, and the focusing or diffusion of the role-system by which they define their positions in relation to each other, and through which they provide the conceptual foundation for 'language', 'group' and 'community'. Le Page and Tabouret-Keller's description is based on the notion of groups which individual speakers perceive to exist. They hypothesise that individuals create systems from language so that they may resemble those of the group with which from time to time they may wish to identify. This description of language use is compatible with and reinforces the Hallidayan view that language does not exist in the ab-stract but is created in the context of social interaction between speakers, and that different varieties, dialects and languages often do not have clear-cut boundaries at all.

Language use is therefore an explicit statement of an individual's self-perceived identity. Identity can operate on a number of levels, and can relate to affiliation with a number of non-linguistic variables, including age, gender, geographical region, or membership of an ethnic, social, or religious group. An individual's particular language choice in a given social situation will be open to such extraneous factors. These will not necessarily remain constant. However, the ability to perform a linguistic act of identity will always be dependent upon the language varieties (ideolect, accents, dialects and languages) available to an individual in the personal linguistic repertoire. Neither the external factors, nor the individual's linguistic repertoire, both of which can influence language choice, will remain constant. Depending upon the constraining and enabling factors previously discussed, an individual may elect to perform acts of identity which make statements about their age, gender, religion, social status, cultural or ethnic identity. The force of the statement will depend in part upon the individual's communicative competence and in part upon the competence of their audience to comprehend their act(s).

By combining the works of Vygotsky, Halliday and Le Page and Tabouret-Keller it is possible to build a view of thinking and language use as social processes and to view language as simultaneously forming and reflecting experiences from the earliest stages of childhood. The child first learns how to communicate using one or more languages and then develops that communicative competence to participate in the special discourses that society has created. In the case of a child who is learning to be bilingual s/he is simultaneously learning parallel ways of behaving and communicating effectively in the discourses of two (or more) different communities.

All three theoretical frameworks presented here are about social constructs. That is, they have no existence beyond the environment which they create and through which they are constructed. Language and social groups, or networks, are created by people. Individuals' language creates social behaviour. Interaction between individuals creates groups or networks. The individual is the locus of these social constructs. Together these three descriptions of language use provide a description of language as social behaviour, as an evolving, dynamic state, one created by those who perceive it as necessary and which has no independent existence beyond its speakers and the social contexts and functions that they create through language use.

It is, of course, never possible to isolate all that has influenced one's thinking. In the following chapters other influences that have contributed to the design of the research project and the subsequent data analysis will be identified and discussed.

Chapter 4
The Box Hill Nursery Project

At least we can claim that our way of looking at things derives from
close contact with the data. It may be, of course, that we have developed a squint. (R.B. Le Page & Andrée Tabouret-Keller, *Acts of Identity*,
1985: x)

Introduction

Designing a research project always involves elements of risk and
uncertainty. It is essentially a process of making decisions and reasonably
informed choices – some of which will turn out all right and some of which
will not! There is unfortunately no easy route for researchers to take. There
is no single right way and there can be no formulaic approach. Research is a
high-risk activity! This chapter outlines the design of the Box Hill Nursery
Project and discusses some of the methodological considerations involved
and the choices to be made when investigating young children's social and
language behaviour during their first term in the school. The study was
designed to use both qualitative and quantitative methods and to combine
established approaches, such as the observation schedules employed in
similar projects (Sylva *et al.*, 1980; Tough, 1977), with novel amendments. In
keeping with the established conventions, pseudonyms are used to protect
the identity of the informants and the nursery where this project was based.
The Box Hill Nursery is of course a pseudonym. It was located in a real
place, Cleveland, once an autonomous LEA in England, but which no
longer exists.

Rationale for the Study

The aim of the project is to describe the language and social behaviour of
a group of children during their first term in formal schooling in the contact
situation of the nursery school where they constitute a linguistic minority.
It is founded within the established theoretical paradigms previously
outlined in Chapter 3. The rationale for the study is to respond to Mullard's
(1984) call for data to illuminate the debate on the ethnolinguistic behaviour of bilingual children during the initial phase of their secondary

55

sociolinguistic enculturation. The project was devised in the belief that small-scale ethnolinguistic studies can supplement the findings of larger-scale surveys, and are important if we are to understand local patterns of language use for individuals within bilingual communities. It is hoped that the findings will be of interest to nursery school teachers, education policy planners and others interested in the early education of young bilingual children. Although the study is based in the UK the research design and findings may be relevant for other contexts where children are entering an education system where the language differs from the home language(s) they know and use. The scale of the study has been influenced by Le Page and Tabouret-Keller's (1985) view that the individual remains the locus of bilingualism within the community. The primary interest is in individual speakers' choice of language(s) as a means of gaining insights into their enculturation into the nursery school.

Support for the nursery school as an appropriate locus for the study can be found from a number of sources. Fishman (1989: 419) states the view that ethnicity is a major component of mainstream education, particularly at the early levels because it acts as an agent of the socialisation process. Mullard (1984: 50–51) identifies the pre-school nursery as the most important and yet most difficult institution in which to address the needs of black and other ethnic minority children, in terms of nurturing their ethnic identity. He emphasises that, to date, no research findings exist to illuminate the debate on the impact of school on the formation and development of ethnic identity among black children in British schools. Heller (1988) addresses the role of language in the formation of ethnic group boundaries and acknowledges that 'there has in fact been very little work done in this area'. She cites work done in Africa (Scotton, 1976) and her own work in Ontario and Quebec (Heller, 1984), but in England there have so far been few studies of children of the age included in this sample. There are some studies of children in nursery school: these include Moffatt's (1989) observational study of children becoming bilingual in the nursery school, and Spann's (1988) study of codeswitching in nursery-age children. Both of these studies however, differ from the Box Hill Nursery Project in research design, methodology and focus. Further support for the linguistic focus of this particular project can be found in Muysken (1990: 27–28), who observes that Panjabi-English is a language pair not extensively investigated to date.

A summary of previous studies of bilingual learners in various classroom settings is presented in Table 4.1. This overview is not exhaustive. It has been decided to exclude those studies that focus specifically on teacher-talk because those interactions adhere to a highly stylised discourse pattern

(Sinclair & Coulthard, 1975). The table includes research from the USA, Canada and Britain. A significant difference between these groups is the type of educational setting which they explore. In the USA and Canada, for example, a range of different types of education programme is available to bilingual pupils, whereas in Britain, English, the dominant societal language, is the sole language of compulsory education. Although the studies presented in Table 4.1 are not all concerned directly with very young bilingual children at the point of transition into mainstream schooling, they have been included in the overview because they are similar in methodological approach to that adopted for the Box Hill Nursery Project. They also share a focus on children's language use and linguistic repertoire.

Table 4.1 Summary of previous research

Author	Year	Age of subjects	Setting	Languages	Focus
Wong-Fillmore	1976	Kindergarteners	Kindergarten, USA	Spanish–English	Cognitive and social strategies in second language acquisition
Strong	1983	Kindergarteners	Bilingual classroom, England	Spanish–English	Individual's social styles
Shultz	1975	1st- & 2nd-graders 12 children	Bilingual classroom, USA	Spanish–English	Codeswitching in natural speech in classrooms
Zentella	1982	7- & 8-year-olds 3 children: Ana (8), Nora (10) & Juan (7)	3rd grade, Bronx, New York, USA	Puerto Rican Spanish–English	Codeswitching
Cohen, Bruck & Rodríguez-Brown	1977	2 girls: Maria & Rosa	USA		Language use in bilingual classrooms
Moll & Diaz	1985	3 girls: Sylvia, Delfina & Carla	Comparative study of two 4th-grade class-rooms, English–Spanish maintenance programmes, S. California, USA	Spanish–English	Reading for meaning

Table 4.1 *(cont.)*

Author	Year	Age of subjects	Setting	Languages	Focus
Heller	1982	Grades 7 & 8	French-Language School, Toronto, Canada	French–English	Language use
Willes	1983	5-year-olds	Reception class, England	English	Socialisation
Spann	1988	Nursery	Nursery, England	Panjabi–English	Codeswitching
Agnihotri	1979	10- & 11-year-olds	Primary School, Leeds, England	Sikh Panjabi–English	Assimilation process
Moffatt	1989	Nursery	Nursery, England	Panjabi–English	Codeswitching
Bruck, Shultz & Rodríguez-Brown	1972	Maria & Rosa	1st-graders, bilingually schooled, Illinois, USA	Spanish–English	Ethnographic study of language use

Moll and Diaz's (1985) micro-ethnographic study focuses on the reading performances of three girls, Sylvia, Delfina and Carla, in different educational contexts, including language maintenance programmes. Cohen *et al.* (1977) present an ethnographic study of two first graders, Maria and Rosa, and their language use in bilingual classrooms. Two further studies, also from the USA, focus specifically on children's codeswitching. These include Zentella's (1982) study of the codeswitching of three seven- and eight-year-old Puerto-Rican children: Ana (aged eight), Nora (10 years) and Juan (seven years). Shultz's (1975) study on codeswitching focuses on the natural speech of 12 target children in a bilingual classroom of 40 pupils. In some ways this is similar to the Box Hill Nursery context. However, the children in Shultz's study are a little older. While these studies do not exactly parallel the Box Hill Nursery Project, they may be of interest to the reader (and future researcher) because they are related investigations of young bilingual children.

Previous research on children of the same age includes Moffatt (1989), Strong (1983), Spann (1988) and Wong-Fillmore (1976). Although these studies focus on children of the same age (in the nursery and kindergarten) they do not focus specifically on the processes of secondary socialisation.

Agnih
mainst
childre
study f(
mainstr
gual. In(
a numbe
that ther
bilingual
educatio

The Imp

The nu
number o
new social
required t(
how to be
demands o
different kii
These he te
more specia
is associated
that concurs
'embedded l

When the child is moving from a home where the lan
cation is different from that of the school they a
bilingual. At the transition from home to schoo
range of learning experiences and new socia
also be required to learn a new language. I
extra learning challenges. Becoming b
member of a new culture. It entails
values and a different view of on
or who do not share it. In lear
stream schooling, a child w
maybe their first experi
group. This is an ext
experienced by bi
child. This exp
vidual's de
certainly
one is
pu

...ggests that the
...classrooms require a greater degree of
metalinguistic awareness from young children. She maintains that it is
those children who have a more highly developed metalinguistic awareness who achieve most in formal school learning. Tizard *et al.* (1988), in
their study of young children in inner-city schools, found that children
who possess a high degree of metalinguistic awareness in the nursery and
early years of school were those who were good readers at the end of infant
schooling (Key Stage 1 in the UK). These research findings suggest that
classrooms place linguistic demands on young learners and that nursery
education can lay the foundation for their future academic achievement.

In the nursery, children are learning to become sociable, to interact with
a wider range of individuals, both adults and children, some of whom may
be familiar and some hitherto unknown. Even those who are familiar to the
young child may present a challenge of a different kind. Familiar individuals ascribed different roles in new settings will behave in different ways,
using different language codes or registers. All of these factors may
confound rather than confirm previous experience and learning.

guage of communi-
e also learning to be
i, in addition to the new
encounters, the child may
earning to be bilingual imposes
lingual requires learning to be a
earning new ways of behaving, new
self, one's world and the people who do
ing to be bilingual and bicultural in main-
ll encounter many new experiences, including
nce of being a member of a linguistic minority
a dimension to the secondary socialisation process
ngual children. It could have an isolating impact on the
rience may have subsequent repercussions upon the indi-
eloping sense of ethnic identity and self-esteem. It will
mean that the isolated child who finds themselves as a minority of
bereft of appropriate role models able to provide suitable patterns of
il behaviour. For the bilingual child, the transition from home to school
requires secondary socialisation into a new sociolinguistic context, which
may confound rather than reinforce or confirm their existing sense of
ethnolinguistic identity. The child will learn to interact with a wider
network of adults and peers from linguistic speech communities both the
same as and different from their own. The effect of the transition on individual children, bilingual or monolingual, remains underresearched. Due
to the paucity of research in this area, it has been necessary to give particular consideration to the research methods used. The following section
outlines the particular challenges posed by researching very young
children.

A Discussion of Research Methods

Pre-school classrooms have rarely been understood in anthropological
terms. Research in primary school classrooms (Bennett, 1976; Sylva *et al.*,
1980; Tizard *et al.*, 1988) has focused on the 'learning' and 'teaching' activities which take place there. Emphasis has been on knowledge or content of
lessons and the teacher's knowledge-base for teaching has been presumed
to be an index of the quality of the learning (Alexander *et al.*, 1992; Kingman
Report, DES, 1988). However, Mehan (1978) has suggested that the social
organisation of the learning environment may be more influential than an
individual's learning ability in the development of language, cognition
and social competence. Despite this, little research interest has been paid to
how children develop in different social contexts. Ethnography may offer a

descriptive perspective on the understanding of early educational settings and the experiences of children within those settings.

Case study as a research method

Case study as a research method exerts acknowledged limitations, but is considered suitable for this project. There is precedent for the choice, namely Heller's (1984) study 'Language and ethnic identity in a Toronto French-language school'. Using case-study methodology requires consideration of reliability. External reliability of the research is concerned with whether or not the same constructs would be generated by different researchers in this or similar settings. Ethnographic studies are conducted in natural social settings, thus rendering replication highly unlikely. Much is determined by unique circumstances and by the individual and collective personalities involved in a specific context at a given time. The diminished likelihood of replication is an established concern for all ethnographers. It is not unique to this study, nor should it render ethnography less significant as a research approach.

The essential defining characteristic of ethnographic fieldwork procedures are that they are designed to overcome the researcher's bias and that they are grounded in the investigation of communication and other phenomena in natural contexts which they aim to describe. The criterion for 'descriptive adequacy' (Saville-Troike, 1982: 119) is that sufficient data should be collected to provide a description which would enable someone from outside the particular speech community under observation, and who was not present during the periods of observation and data collection, to understand fully both the event described and the participants' behaviour. It is also considered important that the ethnographic account be accepted as *bona fide* by members of the observed community, particularly the participants themselves.

An ethnographic study is one alternative to a research approach which relies on contriving a highly controlled situation. Bruner and Haste (1987: 2) outline one alternative approach to the study of young children learning to cope with new or unfamiliar material with little or no previous experience. Based on Donaldson's (1978) criticisms of Piaget's experiments, that contrived situations can have a negative impact on the child and cause them to underperform rather than demonstrate their true capabilities, Bruner suggests a more naturalistic approach that is in contrast with the Piagetian view of the child as a little scientist, independently interpreting the world as an individual. The more recent emphasis on the child as a social being places that child in a normally complex situation and then observes their efforts to cope with that situation and interpret it. Contextual data on the situation in which the child is being observed constitute an important dimension to this approach. Geertz (1975) terms this contextual data 'thick' data. Since the contextual data form a central contribution to the project and the subsequent interpretation of the behaviours observed, it is perhaps pertinent to outline Geertz's view of culture and the complementary perspective his approach offers to the Hallidayan view of language as social semiotic.

Geertz's thick, contextual data

The anthropologist Geertz presents a view of cultures that he describes as 'an assemblage of texts' (Geertz, 1975: 452). In common with systemic linguists, he views texts as 'an extension of the notion of a text beyond written materials' and states that 'cultural forms can be treated as texts, as imaginative works built out of social materials' (1975: 449). He adopts this approach in his analysis of the cultural form of a Balinese cockfight:

> To treat the cockfight as a text is to bring out the cultural form ... the central feature of it ... that treating it as a rite or a pastime, the two most obvious alternatives, would tend to obscure: its use of emotion for cognitive ends. (Geertz, 1975: 449)

His view of culture is presented in the following statement:

> The concept of culture I espouse ... is essentially a semiotic one ... believing that man is an animal suspended in webs of significance he has spun himself, I take culture to be those webs, and the analysis of it to be therefore not an experimental science in search of law but an interpretative one, in search of meaning. (Geertz, 1975: 5)

In his essay *The Interpretation of Cultures* (1975) Geertz says that thick description is what ethnographers do. Dissatisfied with merely describing the objective, physical behaviour of human beings (the thin description), ethnographers place greater emphasis on context and detail in order to grasp and set down the meanings of human acts. Geertz suggests that the ethnographer is trying to describe 'structures of significance'. For him, culture consists of 'webs of significance' (1975: 5), a 'stratified hierarchy of meaningful structures' (1975: 7); an 'interworked system of constructable signs or symbols' (1975: 14). In order to interpret observed behaviours the ethnographer must write it down. This 'inscription' is the thick description. One method for obtaining thick, contextual data is through participant observation.

Participant observation

Participant observation is an established approach within ethnographic research. It enables the researcher to observe patterned cultural behaviour while immersed in the context in which it occurs. Milroy (1980) suggests that successful participant observation requires 'passing oneself off' as a member of the observed community. In order to do this the researcher needs to leave behind previous cultural experience and acquire the norms and values of the observed community. However desirable this may be it is not so easy for the researcher to achieve. Cultural values are not always consciously held. Individuals are rarely aware of their permeating existence and insidious influence of their own value system. The unconscious nature of cultural experiences and their inherent values makes it very difficult for a person to 'leave them behind' as Milroy (1980) recommends. However, the participant observer can make a conscious effort to suppress previous personal experiences.

There are other views that contrast with Milroy's. Becker (1963) suggests that there are advantages to the researcher in not being a member of the community under investigation; that it is possible for an outsider to act naively and ask questions or for classifications that an insider would be expected to know; that it is possible for an outsider to elicit more knowledge from the informants in a more naturalistic manner, simply because as an outsider they would not be expected to know or understand certain things.

Despite her advocacy of the infiltration approach, Milroy (1980) acknowledges the dilemma faced by ethnographers who are trying to infiltrate a community. She admits that the fieldworker may always remain an outsider to some contexts. This is particularly true if the ethnographer is attempting to describe the cultural and linguistic behaviours of a community as an outsider with no prior knowledge of that community. Adult ethnographers will always face problems when trying to infiltrate children's groups.

Saville-Troike (1982: 121–2) cautions the ethnographer on the academic and professional responsibilities associated with fieldwork: 'The ethnographer should not be "taking" data without returning something of immediate usefulness to the community.'

Potential problems for participant observers include how to introduce oneself to the host community, what information to reveal about oneself and one's purposes and what role to assume in the community during the period of observation. In the case of the Box Hill Nursery Project, the role of teacher was a feasible one for the researcher to assume. However, adults are precluded from child activities for a variety of reasons. In this study it would not have been feasible for the researcher to act convincingly as a member of the observed community, partly on the grounds of language but, more significantly, age, which precluded acceptance as a member of any children's group. This constraint is, of course, not unique to this study. Researchers are adults and will therefore always face this dilemma when attempting candid observations of children's behaviour and activities. Other factors preventing successful assimilation into the observed group can include the physical markers of ethnic identity described by Le Page and Tabouret-Keller (1985: 209), such as modes of dress. These will be referred to in detail in the discussion and analysis of data in Chapter 7.

The researcher is left then with this dilemma. How can an adult, outgroup member gain the right of access to child informants? One way is in the role of professional. A white researcher can play an authentic role as a teacher in a child community and this was the role adopted by the researcher for the purpose of data collection. It is also a role familiar to the researcher and one which it was felt could be played authentically. Saville-Troike endorses the need for the researcher to be on partly familiar territory, stating (1982: 122) that 'ethnographers must first of all understand their own culture, and the effects it has on their own behaviour, if they are to succeed in participant-observation in another.'

The idea central to participant observation is that the researcher is able to enter into various speech events relatively unobtrusively as a participant with whom other participants can feel comfortable. Saville-Troike (1982: 122) recommends a high level of linguistic and cultural competence as a *sine qua non*, and that there should be a shared linguistic and cultural competence between the fieldworker and the observed community. As a complement, I should like to suggest that a professional competence may replace these as genuine grounds for a researcher being present; for example, given a researcher who is a qualified teacher and shares a common concern with the other professionals in the setting. Such a researcher may be able to offer professional assistance and operate in the research setting in a professional capacity alongside other professionals. This does not of course compensate for any lack of linguistic competence, but it can help to justify a presence.

There is also precedent established for the observer not being linguistically proficient in the language of the observed community (Kibrik, 1977), as was the case in the present study. There are, however, a number of ways in which a researcher may compensate for a lack of linguistic competence.

These require the adoption of different techniques, liaison and consultation with more proficient speakers of the language, and the involvement of native speakers in describing and analysing the language. This can actually be a distinct advantage to the researcher because it allows for a wider group of people to become involved in the interpretation of the data. It also helps to overcome bias in the analyses and possible over-interpretation of the data.

Finally, Whiting and Whiting (1975: 312) advise ethnographers 'not to embark on systematic observation which is laborious and time consuming, unless they are convinced that informants cannot report their own behaviour or the behaviour of others reliably.' This comment is pertinent to the children in the Box Hill Nursery Project who were considered too young to undertake this task meaningfully. As a safeguard, older members of the children's families and the Mirpuri community were consulted and involved in the data analysis and interpretation stages of the project.

There are therefore a number of perceived advantages to participant observation as a research method for the collection of linguistic data. Milroy (1987: 78) considers the major advantage to be the high quality of the naturally occurring language which it yields. She also maintains that it is capable of providing insights into the social and communicative norms of the community under observation. This view is supported by Labov (1981:25), who suggests that it is through 'deeper studies of groups and social networks that we gain the possibility of explaining linguistic behaviour.'

The data collected provide complementary aspects of the nursery setting and the informants. They combine to provide a description of the ways in which the informants were learning to be *communicatively competent* in their new social context.

The observer's paradox and the sociolinguist's dilemma

The advantages associated with participant observation have to be considered alongside critical comment. Sociolinguistic research has often been criticised because of the methodological framework in which it is set. Claims that the data are unreliable and the analyses invalid have stemmed in part from the observation that the researcher can exert an undue (and hence distorting) influence on the informants who provide the data, and hence on the data which is gathered and on the subsequent analyses. The claim that the researcher can impact on the phenomenon under investigation is a fundamental philosophical problem in the social sciences. It is referred to as 'the observer's paradox'.

It was Labov (1972: 113) who formulated the observer's paradox with special reference to the sociolinguist. Labov's (1972) claim is that the most consistent and natural data for sociolinguistic analysis are to be found in the vernacular, or casual speech. This naturally occurring language is not easily elicited in interview situations where its use would be inappropriate and hence unnatural. Since Labov's claim much of sociolinguistic theory has put great emphasis on obtaining samples of vernacular speech. In order to achieve this, researchers need to inhabit the social world of the informants: 'To obtain the data most important for linguistic theory, we have to observe how people speak when they are not being observed' (Labov, 1972: 113). This is the observer's paradox.

Labov (1972) and his colleagues adopted several important and interrelated procedures to overcome this paradox. They made radical departures from the established face-to-face interview techniques for collecting linguistic data. The aim was to move away from the social roles of interviewer and interviewee and hence the asymmetrical power relationships and values with which these roles are implicitly encoded. Labov *et al.* focused on interacting groups rather than individuals. This had the effect of the informants outnumbering the interviewer and went some way towards redressing the power imbalance within the situation. Researchers joined informants on social occasions, for example for meals or drinks, and used these opportunities to collect data. The focus on group rather than individual provided an opportunity to observe group dynamics and access more authentic use of the vernacular or casual speech.

The observer's paradox is of paramount concern to researchers eliciting data from very young informants. There are other facets to this paradox which I shall term 'the sociolinguist's dilemma'. Milroy (1980) warns of the possibility that the researcher can be an outsider to some social contexts under investigation. This can be particularly true of the classroom situation, where an adult is marked as an outsider in a number of ways. An adult is marked by age as an outsider to child groups and as a result may exert undue influence, particularly because of the asymmetrical power relations which exist between children and adults, a phenomenon which is compounded when the adult also enjoys the status of teacher. The power imbalance is further accentuated when the adult and child belong to different ethnic groups.

The presence of a white adult (whether researcher or teacher) in the black child culture of the classroom is one more facet to the observer's paradox. While this is a factor, it should not deny the value of the white adult view of the black child-world of the classroom and the description of the child's experiences within that context. Individuals will construct differently even those experiences which they share. Researchers should, however, remain sensitive to the effects which their presence may impose on their informants and hence on the data they collect, and that this influence may impact on the subsequent interpretation(s) of the data.

In this study attempts have been made to minimise this influence and to render misinterpretation less likely. This has been achieved by involving the informants (children, family members and teachers), together with members of the Mirpuri community, in the data analysis and interpretative descriptions. The audio-recorded data was made available to the informants who were present during the periods of observation. They were invited to comment upon the audio-recordings, transcriptions and codings. It was also made clear that sensitive information on the recordings could be erased from the tape and could be omitted from the transcripts if requested. However, no such requests were received.

Issues relating to the collection of discourse data

The research methods used acknowledge the arguments made by linguistic researchers (reported in Stubbs, 1983) for the need to combine different methods as a means of providing cross-validation and of overcoming the difficulties of matching a single research method to the measurement of 'a single pure parameter' of human language behaviour. The selected methods also meet Stubbs' call for a principled approach based on pure analytical rigour. The research methodologies are explicitly stated and attempts are made to make all of the data accessible for scrutiny by others, at all stages of analysis. There are, however, acknowledged constraints in making unedited, audio-taped recordings (the raw discourse data) freely available as a resource to all, for reasons relating to the sensitivity of content (for example inter-group conflicts of a racist nature and other individual antisocial behaviour), and identification of the individual speakers.

Researchers will always face personal and professional ethical dilemmas. In sociolinguistic research (in common with other areas of social science) there is also the general issue of reconciling an academic interest with an ethical commitment to the observed group. This is particularly pertinent when the researcher is not a member of the group under observation. Smith (1985) presents a full (and very personal account) of some of the broad ethical issues which he feels are raised by white academic researchers studying poor non-white minority communities in Britain. The issues explored there are all compounded when the informants are very young children.

The ethics of candid recordings

Collecting naturally occurring discourse data is considered important because it provides the researcher with access to the speaker's vernacular, described by Labov (1972: 208) as the variety of speech adopted by a speaker when they are monitoring their speech style least closely. However, it is acknowledged that gaining access to the vernacular is neither easy nor free from controversy. Candid recordings do provide access, but they also feed the controversy. Linguists are divided in their use and acceptance of such recording. Labov has rejected the practice on ethical grounds (a full discussion of which can be found in Milroy, 1987: 88–93). He remarks (1981: 32) that 'a hidden tape-recorder and a hidden microphone produce data which is as dubious as the method itself.'

Other linguists, including Crystal and Davy (1969) and Milroy (1980), rely on candid recordings and surreptitious observations with some qualification and an accompanying discussion on ethics. Milroy endorses the method as necessary for theoretical advancement of sociolinguistic description. She states:

> The study of the vernacular speech of the individual in its everyday social context is an important task for sociolinguistics. Since most current models of communicative competence and language structure rest on a rather narrow base derived from relatively formal styles or relatively educated varieties, it is particularly important to obtain more information about the facts of specifically non-standard speech in a range of everyday contexts. Not to have such information is undesirable for practical as well as for theoretical reasons. (Milroy, 1980: 173)

Finally, Labov's general principle offers pragmatic guidance. He advises the researcher to 'avoid any act that would be difficult to explain if it became a public issue' (1981: 33). Collecting data in the classroom, a public domain, generally helps the researcher to respect this proviso. Individuals are being observed in a public setting which to some extent prohibits, or at least restricts, displays of very private behaviour. Usually more prosaic concerns dominate, like the difficulties inherent in collecting high-quality audio-recordings in noisy public arenas like classrooms.

The shortcomings of an ethnographic study are acknowledged. It remains a research method chosen by a number of researchers, who consider its merits balance its shortcomings. However, the collection of naturally occurring discourse data remains a challenge for sociolinguist researchers.

A Quantitative Paradigm for the Study of Communicative Competence

The focus of this study is the developing communicative competence of young bilingual children in a new social context. Sankoff (1980) outlines a quantitative paradigm for the study of communicative competence in which she suggests that it is the responsibility of the researcher to do the following:

(1) To define the sampling universe, at least roughly determine the boundaries of the group or community, in which one is interested.

(2) To assess the relevant dimension of variation within the community – this involves constructing stratification for the sample. Thus we must ask whether ethnic group, sex or social class of speaker might affect the kind of language used. Most studies so far have shown that to a very large extent they do.

(3) To set the sample size.

The Box Hill Nursery Project is not designed as a quantitative research project. It attempts to combine quantitative with qualitative data in its descriptions. However, in the planning, attempts have been made to meet Sankoff's three principles for the collection of socially sensitive data. The sampling universe is clearly defined. The community under investigation is defined as a homogeneous group of Urdu-Panjabi/English bilinguals. They are British-born, ethnic Mirpuris, comprising both boys and girls, of similar age, observed in a consistent social context, the nursery school setting. The sample size was fixed from the outset of the study and was reduced (by natural factors) but not increased.

A Suggested Framework for Ethnolinguistic Descriptive Analysis

Bearing in mind the discussion of the previous sections, a suggested framework for ethnolinguistic descriptive analysis will be outlined. The framework addresses issues such as the role of the researcher in analysing ethnographic data and suggestions that the researcher may have a distorting influence on the data. A model that addresses three levels of descriptive analysis ranging from the macro-level of the contextual setting to the micro-level of individual informants' language behaviour will be proposed.

The role of the ethnographer

The primary task facing the ethnographer is to gather information, to capture the data. Ethnographers are primarily concerned with naturally occurring human behaviour. The focus is often aspects of human behaviour that are fleeting, momentary, sometimes too rapid even to be noticed. It is behaviour of which informants are themselves frequently unconscious. Yet if insights are to be gained, the data must be captured and be available for scrutiny and retrospective analysis. Human behaviour occurs in 'real time'. The primary role of the ethnographer is to devise ways by which human behaviour can be captured and recorded for retrospective reflection. This of course poses difficulties and challenges.

There is a point at which actual human behaviour, occurring in real time, is recorded and made available to others who were not present at the events which have been recorded. This is the point of transformation from naturalistic human behaviour to research data. It is the ethnographer who stages and manages this transformation. As manager the ethnographer holds responsibility to two audiences. On the one hand there is an ultimate responsibility for maintaining the authenticity of the human behaviour that has been observed so that it remains recognisable to the original performers; on the other, there is also a responsibility to provide rigorous data sets in a format which makes them both accessible and acceptable to a wider audience. The ethnographer has ethical loyalties to these two separate groups: the individuals observed, the informants, and the wider research community. Since ethnographers are engaged in describing acts of human behaviour it is quite likely that their investigations will also appeal to a much wider group, the general public.

The role of the ethnographer can therefore be described as comprising the following components:

- capturing naturalistic human behaviour;

- transforming human behaviour into data sets;

- analysing the data in terms of the perceptions and cultural values of the informants; and

- presenting insights that are acceptable and comprehensible both within and outside the observed community.

In order to achieve this, it is inevitable that the observed human behaviour will undergo some change and transformation. The data collected for the Box Hill Nursery Project, in the form of audio-taped recordings, thick contextual data and fieldnotes, all underwent these inevitable transformations in the process of becoming data sets. To meet Stubbs' (1983) call for analytical rigour in the studies of human language behaviour, the process of transformation from natural behaviour to data sets will be presented as a series of stages.

Criticisms of ethnography as a research method have included the claim that data undergoes distortion during the process of transformation. The following sections will suggest a series of stages in the process of data analysis. It is hoped that more transparent stages will reduce the potential for this claim of distortion in the transformation process.

The following is a suggested framework for ethnolinguistic descriptive analysis:

Stage 1: collect raw data: audio-taped recordings, observations, contextual data.

Stage 2: prepare the verbatim transcripts.

Stage 3: code the transcripts.

Stage 4: make systematic notation of the transcripts.

Stage 5: establish a computer corpus of the data to facilitate storage and analysis.

Stage 6: analyse the data.

Stage 7: interpret the data.

Stage 8: identify patterns of behaviour.

Stage 9: describe these insights, together with their implications and any applications.

Stage 1: Collection of the raw data

The first stage in the transformation process is the collection of 'raw data'. This is the term used for the naturally occurring human behaviour that is observed in naturalistic settings. These data are recorded as candidly and as unobtrusively as permissible, given ethical constraints. Raw data come in the form of audio-taped recordings; thick contextual data recorded in the observation schedules and the researcher's fieldnotes. In other ethnographic studies they may take different forms and may include, for example, video-taped recordings.

Stage 2: Verbatim transcripts

The second stage in the transformation process is the production of verbatim transcripts from the audio-taped recordings. These were compiled using the standard orthographic alphabet. There are a number of ways available for doing this. A full discussion of the approach adopted for this study will be presented in Chapter 9.

Stage 3: Coded transcripts

At this stage features essential to the analysis and interpretation of the data are added to the verbatim transcripts. For this project, the transcripts have been coded with a number of features. These too will be described in full in Chapter 9.

Analysis of the data

Chapters 5, 6, 7, 8 and 9 present different levels of analysis which aim to describe the linguistic and social behaviour of these children during their first term in the nursery school. These descriptions range from the macro-level of the context to the micro-level of the ways in which individual informants use language. The levels are:

Level 1: a quantitative analysis of how the children spend their time on selected tasks, in the form of a *time-on-task* analysis.

Level 2: a description of the children's use of space within the nursery classroom and grounds.

Level 3: a social network analysis that demonstrates the social dimension to the two previous levels of analyses, showing whom the children spend their time within the nursery.

Levels 4 & 5: the individual informant's choice of language for interactions within and beyond the social networks, including codeswitching.

The Box Hill Nursery Project

The title of the project is derived from the name of the nursery school, the research site where the study was carried out. It has been named retrospectively. At the outset it was known as the Cleveland Project, named after a geographical region in the north-east of England. The Box Hill Nursery Project was designed in three phases:

Phase 1: the preparatory phase

Phase 2: the data collection

Phase 3: the data analysis

This is summarised diagrammatically in Figure 4.1.

PHASE 1	PREPARATION
STAGE 1	IDENTIFYING THE SETTING
STAGE 2	NEGOTIATING WITH PROFESSIONALS
STAGE 3	HOME VISITS, PARENT INTERVIEWS, SELECTING PARTICIPANTS

PHASE 2	DATA COLLECTION
	Collecting discourse data
	Making contextual observations
	Continue interviews with families and professionals

PHASE 3	DATA ANALYSIS
STAGE 1	RAW DATA Audio-taped recordings, observations, fieldnotes
STAGE 2	VERBATIM TRANSCRIPTS
STAGE 3	CODING TRANSCRIPTS Identifying participants, attributing turns
STAGE 4	MAPS OF LINGUISTIC BIOGRAPHIES
STAGE 5	SOCIAL NETWORKS Coterie of significant others
STAGE 6	LANGUAGE USE within the social networks

Figure 4.1 An overview of the Box Hill Nursery research design

Phase 1, Stage 1: Identifying the research site

The project began in January 1987. Following Milroy's advice (1987: 28), the first step was to select 'a community where speakers of the appropriate types might be found'. In this case, the first task was to identify a nursery school that had within its catchment area a significant number of bilingual children who were eligible for nursery education, and who were representative of one of the major community language groups in the UK. Other considerations were also considered important. A research site was sought which met a number of criteria:

- There should be a small (between six and 10) group of children representing one of the main settled ethnic minority communities in the UK.

- There should be both girls and boys in the group.

- The group should be a minority within the nursery.

- There should be both bilingual and monolingual adults working in the nursery on a routine basis.

- Community–school liaison links should be firmly established.

Through consultation with LEA officers, 10 potential nursery sites were identified and contact was made with all of the schools that met the stated criteria. Visits were made to all of these places and discussions held with staff about the feasibility of their involvement in the project. Active involvement of nursery staff was considered important for the retrospective illumination of the data. It was acknowledged that this would make demands on teachers' time and other material resources. Nursery staff were given two weeks in which to consider the full implications of involvement with the project and to respond to the invitation to participate.

The research site eventually selected for the project was Box Hill Nursery School, a 39-place purpose-built nursery school attached to a (then) Group 4 primary school, catering for children aged between three and 11 years. There were a number of nursery schools which were considered to be equally suitable. However, Box Hill was chosen because in addition to meeting all of the stated criteria, the nursery staff were regular attenders at in-service training courses and so the nursery was considered to be reasonably representative of its kind. The nursery, the children and staff were all previously unknown to the researcher. Milroy (1987: 35) stresses the importance of identifying a pre-existing social group with which the researcher has no pre-existing personal ties. All of these factors combined to make Box Hill Nursery a suitable site.

Stage 2: Negotiating with the professionals

For the sake of simplicity, the headteacher, the teachers, the qualified nursery nurses, the bilingual and monolingual classroom assistants, indeed all adults working in the nursery will be referred to collectively as 'teachers'. This is not done with the intention of undervaluing individual contributions.

In the data transcripts, they will be coded as individuals. However, all of the adults working in the nursery were regarded by the pupils and their parents as teachers. This was the case irrespective of the formal qualifications they held or the period of training they had undertaken. Staffing allocation to the nursery was one full-time Main Professional Grade (MPG) teacher who was the head of the nursery; one full-time qualified nursery nurse holding a National Nursery Examination Board (NNEB) qualification; a nursery assistant and the equivalent to one full-time bilingual classroom assistant. In practice this meant that two assistants worked on a weekly rota basis, dividing their time between the adjoining primary school and the nursery unit. Throughout the project the researcher was working in the nursery in the role of teacher. Professional credibility with colleagues with whom she was to be working was important. The researcher was a qualified infant teacher with 15 years' professional experience. It was agreed that she would work in the nursery on an occasional basis, for one term before the data collection began. This enabled her to become established as a member of the community in a number of ways:

- she was enculturated into the nursery routines;

- she established professional working relations with nursery staff;

- she became known by families and within the local community;

- she was able to trial and refine data collection techniques with the help of colleagues.

It is extremely useful for the researcher to be present as a participant-observer in the nursery on a routine basis in this way. It not only facilitates the subsequent interpretation of the data but also, perhaps more importantly, allows the researcher to gain valuable insights into the shared values and understandings that exist between the established nursery team members, the parents and the children.

Stage 3: Home visits and family interviews

There are ethical constraints upon researchers gathering data from young informants. Children are not in a position to make informed decisions about participating in research, and their rights need to be safeguarded.

It was the established practice in the nursery unit to make home visits to potential pupils and their families before the child entered school. This familiarisation procedure provided the ideal opportunity for Stage 3 of the first phase of the project. Between April and June, the researcher visited the homes of each of the bilingual children eligible to begin nursery school in September. During these visits the aims and procedures of the project were explained to families with the help of the bilingual classroom assistant acting as interpreter. To those who expressed an interest, a follow-up visit was made. During the second visit written permission for their child's participation in the project was sought. All information was presented orally in English and in Panjabi (by a native speaker who was known as a member of the Mirpuri community). Written details of the project and permission forms were presented in both Urdu and English. They were returned to the researcher by post or via the school, as preferred. It was hoped that this would reduce (perceived) pressure to participate in the project. The parents and care-givers present, usually female members of the family, grandmother, sisters, sister(s)-in-law, were interviewed and data gathered on the participating child. These data were gathered through semi-formal interviews. The data collected included:

(1) The family's perception of their child's linguistic repertoire. Families were asked to comment on their child's relative competence in Mirpuri-Panjabi, their home language, and in English.

(2) The number of siblings in the family and their ages.

(3) The perceived linguistic repertoire of these siblings.

(4) The family network of children attending the same school.

(5) The composition of the family (siblings, grandparents, etc.).

(6) Whether or not the child had ever made a visit to Pakistan.

The data collected from these semi-formal home interviews formed the basis of a diary record where comments and explanations from a number of sources, including the professionals' and researchers' observations were added throughout the duration of the project. These observations provided, in part, some of the 'thick' contextual data (Geertz, 1975) that were integrated into the analysis of the discourse data. They will not be presented separately here. Their function is to supplement the fieldnotes accumulated to help with the retrospective illumination of the data collected.

The setting: Box Hill Nursery

The research site, Box Hill Nursery School, draws its pupil intake from a multilingual community. It is a 39-place nursery with children attending either a morning or an afternoon session, for five days per week, Monday to Friday. The intake includes a homogeneous group of Urdu-Panjabi speakers, one of the major UK community languages. The observed group comprised both boys and girls. This group constituted a significant, but not dominant group of the nursery intake (12 of the 39 pupils).

Chapter 3 outlined the importance of context as an integral element of linguistic description; the organisation or structure of the nursery setting is therefore significant. The physical organisation and layout of the setting has been determined and influenced by Bruner (1986) and the other post-Piagetian social psychologists. The large open-plan room is divided into 28 learning domains, each containing structured learning activities and materials which have been designed to address specific aspects of social, cognitive, physical, moral or aesthetic development of the child. Each learning domain is delineated by the positioning of furniture and 1.2-metre-high screens, thus allowing supervising adults an overview of the room while simultaneously providing maximum seclusion to the children inside the individual domains. This carefully planned learning environment remained unchanged throughout the four-month observation period, with one exception. During the last four weeks of term, that is after 24 November, Domains 22 and 23 merged to house the Christmas tree which the children had helped to decorate. The educational rationale underpinning the layout and design of the nursery was to encourage maximum learner autonomy. It was a good, but not showcase example of the LEA policy. Children were expected to select their learning activity and to be responsible for the collection and storage of all learning materials required for the chosen activities. Materials were available with each domain, stored in labelled units. Figure 4.2 presents a plan of the nursery setting.

The informants

There are a number of questions relating to the size of the sample chosen for investigation which the researcher must consider. Milroy (1987: 22) reports that many (unspecified) surveys have fewer than four speakers in each cell; that Labov's New York City project included a sample of 88 speakers, but that the data-handling problems characteristic of sociolinguistic analysis mean that frequently only a fraction of the data are selected for analysis. Sankoff (1980: 2) suggests that large samples bring increased data-handling problems, with diminishing analytical returns, and that the selection of the sample may be more crucial than its size.

Originally a group of 12 informants were selected for the Box Hill Nursery Project. They were all born in the UK, as the first-born child to ethnic Pakistani, Urdu-Panjabi-speaking parents, whose origins were in

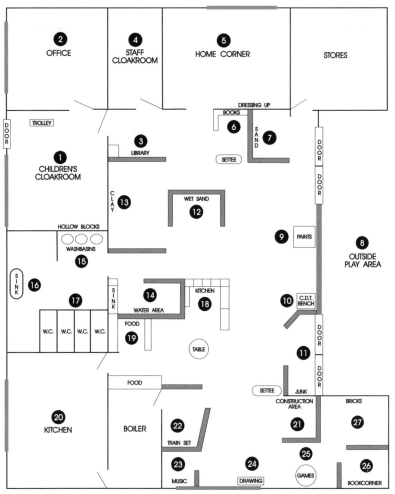

Domain 1	Children's Cloakroom	Domain 11	Junk Table	Domain 21	Construction Area
Domain 2	Office	Domain 12	Wet Sand	Domain 22	Train Set[+]
Domain 3	Library	Domain 13	Clay	Domain 23	Music[+]
Domain 4	Staff Cloakroom	Domain 14	Water Area	Domain 24	Drawing Table
Domain 5	Home Corner	Domain 15	Washbasins	Domain 25	Games
Domain 6	Books	Domain 16	Sink	Domain 26	Book Corner
Domain 7	Dry Sand	Domain 17	WCs	Domain 27	Building Bricks
Domain 8	Outside Play Area	Domain 18	Kitchen	Domain 28	Corridor Areas
Domain 9	Paints	Domain 19	Food		
Domain 10	CDT* Bench	Domain 20	Staff Kitchen		

* Craft, Design & Technology
[+] After 24 November Domains 22 and 23 merge – Christmas tree

Figure 4.2   A plan of Box Hill Nursery

the Mirpur region. All had lived in the UK since their birth and none had attended school before. In family interviews the children were described by their relations as monolingual Panjabi speakers. Their knowledge of spoken English was judged as limited to comprehending a few words only, or as non-existent. These judgements turned out to be underestimations of the children's linguistic competence on the part of the families, who may either genuinely not have witnessed the children's use of English, or else did not want to overestimate competence in English and thereby jeopardise the child's school achievement record, whether through exclusion from specialist ESL support or for other unstated reasons. It is also possible that the informants would not need to use English within their households with family members. The original group of informants included seven girls and five boys, aged between three years and five months (3.5) and four years eight months (4.8) at the beginning of the project. They represented a homogeneous linguistic group of one of the major community languages currently spoken in UK schools, Mirpuri, a vernacular form of Urdu-Panjabi. However, for a variety of reasons that included illness, transfer to other schools and moving house, the final data sets were collected from only eight informants, four boys and four girls.

Table 4.2   The informants

Name	Gender	Age
Sabia	Girl	4.8
Kamran	Boy	4.8
Ishtiaq	Boy	4.7
Imran	Boy	4.3
Rabila	Girl	3.7
Shamaila	Girl	3.5
Shazad	Girl	3.5
Sofees	Boy	3.4

Phase 2: Collecting discourse data

Naturally occurring discourse data were collected with the use of micro-cassette recorders concealed within specially designed jerkins. Wearing protective clothing is an established practice in nursery schools. Placebo garments were worn by the other children in the classroom. The physical stature of the informants determined that the recording apparatus should be lightweight. Sanyo 6000 Micro-Talk Book recorders were used. These machines weigh 145 grammes when loaded with batteries and tape. A lapel microphone with its lead and wirings was sewn into the lining of the jerkin.

The microphone with its range of five metres (15 feet) allowed for data to be collected from the child wearing the jacket and their fellow discourse participants, together with the linguistic environment of the classroom to which the child was being exposed. The micro-recorders were concealed at the back of the jackets in a padded pocket. This location was chosen because it allowed for free access to the recording device during the recording sessions and was considered to be safely placed so as to avoid personal, accidental injury.

The children attend the nursery for two hours each day between 13.00–14.00 hours. One hour of continuous naturally occurring discourse was collected from each informant on two separate occasions between September and December. Audio-tapes were used as the preferred method of data collection for a variety of reasons. They were chosen in preference to the radio-microphones used by Tizard and Hughes (1984) and Wells (1984), or to video-recordings, because:

- they provide an instantaneous record of the linguistic events;

- the method allows for unlimited playback of the recordings, thus ensuring maximum access to the original data format for transcription, analysis and discussion;

- it is a less obtrusive method of data collection, allowing the unfettered movement of the informants both indoors and outside; and

- the age and hence size of the informants made them a more practical choice.

Of course it would have been possible to use video-recorders, but these were considered to be more obtrusive within the confined space of the classroom, and radio-microphones can be heavy for very young children to carry around for long periods of time.

Observation schedules

The linguistic data were complemented by contextual observations. As a starting point, observation schedules used in previous research were considered and two were trialled before the final version was achieved. The observation schedule used by Sylva *et al.* (1980) was considered inappropriate because the closed categories of this schedule did not allow for the full range of contextual behaviour observed to be recorded. Observation Schedule Version 1, used during the pilot phase of the project, was based on the one devised by Tough (1977) for individual child observations. In light of the need to amalgamate thick data with discourse data, amendments were made and Observation Schedule Version 2 (Figure 4.3) was trialled. It was considered necessary to adopt a more open observation schedule based on the observed behaviour of this particular group of children. The refined observation schedule that was finally adopted and used is shown in Figure 4.4.

NAME:	AGE:	DATE:
TIME ACTIVITY	OBSERVATION OF TALK AND BEHAVIOUR	UTTERANCES
SUMMARY		

Figure 4.3   Observation Schedule Version 2

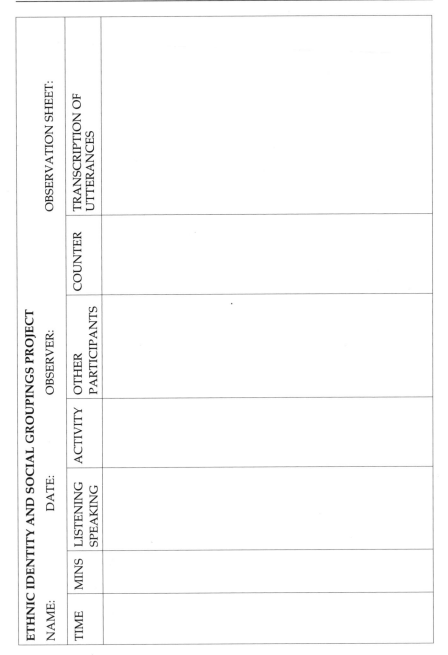

Figure 4.4   Refined Observation Schedule

The final version of the observation schedule (Figure 4.4) incorporates a number of features pertinent to *in situ* contextual observations and post-fieldwork reflections. The *in situ* observations include the time of the observation; the activity in which the child under observation was engaged; other participants present at the activity, including adults and teachers; and any other points considered to be of note or interest. Post-fieldwork reflections and notes were made in collaboration with other adults present, at the end of each observation session. The observation schedules were completed during the data analysis phase of the project when further information was added. These included information to facilitate retrieval of data for further scrutiny, like the number reading on the tape-recorder and transcriber, as well as detail more pertinent to the data analysis, such as the language used (Panjabi or English) by individuals for specific interactions.

Summary

This chapter outlines the conceptual rationale for the Box Hill Nursery Project, together with some of the practical considerations and constraints encountered in its planning and implementation. A discussion of the project has been presented, together with a suggested framework for ethnolinguistic descriptive analyses. It is important to acknowledge the constraints of ethnographic study and the onus that they place on the researcher. Some of these demands are almost contradictory. The researcher is required to collect data that are simultaneously natural occurring behaviours, rigorous and yet representative. The researcher is required to adopt a role within the observed context that is *bona fide* and yet which provides opportunities for recording the data. This requires the researcher to be simultaneously part of the community under observation and to remain sufficiently detached. Real-life situations demanded by ethnographic researchers are vulnerable to the everyday events of the world in which we live; informants are living their real lives, but for the ethnographic researcher the informants are the data. Whatever happens to the informants during the course of their daily lives impacts on the data. This can mean that if informants move away from the research site, data are lost. This is inevitable, but one consequence is that ethnographic data take much longer to collect. Researchers need to be prepared (psychologically and practically) to cope with unplanned and unforeseen events. Using dual sets of recording equipment may guard against loss of data through technical fault, but nothing can protect against families moving house (and hence school); or against children becoming ill, or the myriad other human experiences that arise to separate the ethnographer from the data. A final thought: the primary function of the researcher is to make choices. The best available option is to ensure that these choices are as fully informed as current thinking allows. There is of course always scope for development.

Chapter 5

ToTs – A Time-on-task Analysis

The Hopi, an Indian tribe, have … no tense for past, present and future. The division does not exists. What does that say about time? (Jeanette Winterton, *Sexing the Cherry*, 1989: 8)

Levels of Data Analysis

This section of the book focuses on the analysis of the data. In Chapters 5 to 10, five levels of descriptive analysis, ranging from the macro-level of contextual setting to the micro-level of an individual speaker's language use, will be presented. This chapter will present a quantitative analysis of the children's use of time in the form of a time-on-task analysis. Chapter 6 will present a second level of data analysis of the children's use of space within the nursery. Chapter 7 is a social network analysis of relationships between the children in the nursery. The data analysis is concluded in Chapters 8 and 9 with a descriptive analysis of the children's use of language. Chapter 8 addresses patterns of English language use within the social networks and Chapter 9 outlines the specific uses of Mirpuri-Panjabi, the home language, in the nursery setting. Each level of analysis presented will be described using data from the corpus as exemplar. These data have been drawn from all of the informants participating in the study.

Introduction to Level 1 of Data Analysis

This chapter begins with the first level of descriptive analysis. It is a quantitative description of how children spend their time in the nursery school. By focusing on individual children and their movements within the nursery, the aim is to demonstrate, at the macro-level, the ways in which these children spend their time on selected learning activities. Time and space are important aspects of the enculturation process in a number of ways. Lubeck (1985: 35) suggests that the study of time, space and activity enables the researcher to examine how adults organise a way of life that has subsequent effects on children. She also suggests (1985: 36) that time and space delimit 'the reality which participants of a particular cultural group experience', and cites Durkheim (1933, 1956) to support her view that the organisation of time and space reflect wider social organisation: 'the differential conception and use of time, space and activity suggest that there are cultural differences in the structuring of reality'.

Different languages also use different referents to time and space (Crystal, 1987). Lee (1980) in a re-codification of Malinowski's fieldnotes and observation manuscripts notes that the Trobriander Island people whom Malinowski describes did not use linear referents in their language. She postulates that there are both linear and non-linear codifications of reality and suggests that individuals in any society pattern their thinking and behaviour in accordance with the codes of their own culture. This behaviour is learned and forms an important part of the socialisation process. Individuals use this learned pattern for understanding all subsequent patterns of behaviour. They interpret all experiences in terms of the codes of their own culture and behaviour.

Birdwhistell (1971) in his pioneering work on kinesics reinforces the importance of non-verbal communication. He suggests that spoken language is not of equal importance in all cultures, and that even in highly verbal cultures a large part of an individual's time is spent in non-verbal interactions. The view is reinforced by Hallowell:

> The cultural patterns of different societies offer different means by which spatial perceptions are developed, refined and ordered. The spatial concepts of different societies also vary with the degree of abstraction attained ... the variability is correlated with the fact that one set of conditions may demand very little in the way of spatial discrimination of a certain order (for example, measurement), but considerable refinement in other respects (for example, directional orientation). (Hallowell, 1955/77: 147)

There are numerous examples of the ways in which different languages reflect a community's conceptualisation of time (Crystal, 1987). Thus it can be seen that the concept of time is culture-bound, and that the ways in which people use their time is behaviour that is learned, in part, during the socialisation process. For this reason the study of how the children spend their time in the nursery seemed an appropriate starting-point for this research. It also links with other studies of classrooms that will be outlined in the following section.

Previous Observational Studies of Classrooms

Observational studies *in situ* are not entirely novel, but they are a good starting-point for scrutinising what children actually do in school, how they spend their time, and for noting patterns of behaviour. There are a number of observational studies which aim at providing a descriptive analysis of young children's learning experiences (for example Bennett, 1976; Sylva *et al.*, 1980; Tizard & Hughes, 1984; Tizard *et al.*, 1988). These researchers claim that significant educational advantage is to be gained by pupils who spend sustained periods of time on teacher-structured tasks: 'Since two thirds of the activities with long spells of concentration contain clear goal structure, we conclude that children stick at activities that challenge the mind' (Sylva *et al.*, 1980: 65).

These studies all share the view that the amount of time an individual child spends on a learning activity is a significant factor in the learning processes that are taking place. This phenomenon has come to be known as 'time-on-task' or TOT, and examples of these studies can be found in both the USA and the UK. Perhaps one of the best known is Bennett's (1976) study of UK primary school classrooms. Bennett (1976: 158–9) cites a number of previous studies and sources to support his view on the importance of time-on-task in the learning process. These include Rothkopf (1970) who contends that 'in most instructional situations what is learned depends largely on the activities of the student' (cited in Bennett, 1976: 158). Bennett also cites Anderson (1970) to support his general thesis that 'the activities the students engage in when confronted with instructional tasks are of crucial importance in determining what (s)he will learn' (1976: 158).

These propositions all conform to an earlier model of school learning described by Carroll (1963) who suggests that everything else being equal, attainment is determined by the opportunities provided by the teacher in a given context, and the subsequent use that the individual pupils make of those opportunities. The relationship between teacher provision and pupil take-up has been investigated by a number of educational researchers cited in this chapter who have studied pupils at different stages in their school lives. In their conclusions, all support the view that the teacher plays a central role in structuring and sequencing learning activities for pupils and that the periods of time the child spends engaged in particular activities is a determinant of the quality of learning that takes place.

Samuels and Turnure (1974) studied the school behaviour of six-year-olds, McKinney *et al.* (1975) studied eight-year-olds, Cobb (1972) 11-year-olds and Lahaderne (1968) 12-year-olds. The findings of all of these studies are distilled in the portrait of the 'competent child' presented by McKinney *et al.* (1975) as one who is attentive, intelligent and task-orientated. All of these studies support the view that time-on-task is a crucial factor in pupil attainment. Bennett (1976) suggests two reasons for this. The first (1976: 159) is that 'the total amount of active learning time on a particular instructional topic is the most important determinant of pupil achievement on that topic', and the second (1976: 159) that 'there is enormous variation in time for learning for different pupils, their time devoted to specific learning topics, and their total amount of active learning time.'

Although Bennett's study, and those cited by him, do not include observations of children learning in nursery schools, *Childwatching*, a study by Sylva *et al.* (1980) did include children of this age. The Sylva *et al.* study went beyond the observations made by previous researchers in stating that time-on-task is central to pupil learning. It identifies a number of specific factors said to account for an individual's sustained engagement in learning activities. These influencing factors include the cognitive challenge of the task; whether it is high, complex, ordinary or low challenge. In response to the question on their observation schedule 'What keeps a child at a particular activity?' (Sylva *et al.*, 1980: 254) the coded response allows for the presence of an adult to be registered as an influential factor. This is a point that will be explored in the later levels of analysis.

Contextual Observations

This first level of data analysis addresses time-on-task. Using the semi-structured observation schedule already presented in the previous chapter (Figure 4.4), data were collected on individual pupils during their time in the nursery school. The observation schedules were only semi-structured, in the sense that pre-coded behaviours were not the focus. Instead a range of questions had been formulated to provide a semi-structured framework for the one-hour-long periods of observation. The first level of analysis addresses the following questions:

(1) How does each child spend time?

(2) Which learning domains are selected by each child?

(3) How much time is spent on these selected activities?

(4) How does each child spend time when not engaged in learning activities?

(5) How does this experience vary from day to day and change over time (the first term in the nursery school)?

Box Hill Nursery school is organised into a number of separate learning domains. The domains are referred to by teachers and by children according to the nature of the activity they house, for example 'the painting table', 'the clay area'. A more detailed description of the nursery and the educational rationale for its organisation can be found in Chapter 6. For ease of reference these domains have been numbered as shown in Figure 5.1.

Domain 1	Children's Cloakroom
Domain 2	Office
Domain 3	Library
Domain 4	Staff Cloakroom
Domain 5	Home Corner
Domain 6	Books
Domain 7	Dry Sand
Domain 8	Outside Play Area
Domain 9	Paints
Domain 10	Craft Design Technology (CDT) Bench
Domain 11	Junk Table
Domain 12	Wet Sand
Domain 13	Clay
Domain 14	Water Area
Domain 15	Washbasins
Domain 16	Sink
Domain 17	WCs
Domain 18	Kitchen
Domain 19	Food
Domain 20	Staff Kitchen
Domain 21	Construction Area
Domain 22	Train Set[+]
Domain 23	Music[+]
Domain 24	Drawing Table
Domain 25	Games
Domain 26	Book Corner
Domain 27	Building Bricks
Domain 28	Corridor Areas

[+] After 24th November Domains 22 and 23 merge as a Christmas tree. Domains 22 and 23 are also used for story times and for whole-class activities.

Figure 5.1 Box Hill Nursery learning domains

Graphs of Time-on-task during the First Hour in Box Hill Nursery School

This section outlines responses to the first three research questions posed in the previous section. The findings are presented diagrammatically in graph form. The graphs demonstrate the ways in which individual children spend their time in the nursery. The discussion begins with an analysis of the children's first hour in the nursery. A later section will compare these findings with end-of-term behaviours.

Using a time axis (in minutes) and a space (domain) axis, the graphs show which learning domains were visited by individual children and the time spent by the child in each domain. Periods of less than one minute were recorded as one minute. Three minutes was considered a benchmark time since this was the duration noted in previous studies (Sylva *et al.*, 1980) as sustained for children of this age in a nursery school. Periods of time-on-task longer than three minutes were considered significant and therefore worth more detailed scrutiny. The following sections will present time-on-task analyses of five children: Imran, Ishtiaq, Rabila, Sabia and Ammara.

Imran's first hour in Box Hill Nursery

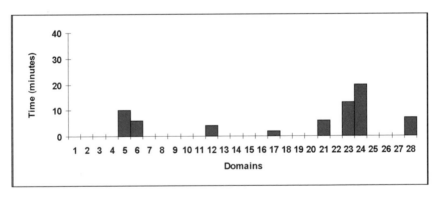

Figure 5.2   A graph of the time-on-task analysis for Imran's first hour in Box Hill Nursery

From the graph it can be seen that Imran visits a total of eight domains during his first hour. He spends significant periods of time (a total of 55 minutes) in six of the eight domains:

Domain 5   Home Corner   10 minutes

Domain 6	Books	6 minutes
Domain 12	Wet Sand	4 minutes
Domain 21	Construction Area	6 minutes
Domain 23	Musical Instruments	13 minutes
Domain 24	Drawing Table	10 + 10 minutes (2 visits)

Imran spends only short periods of time (less than 10 minutes in total) in the corridors (Domain 28). He also made one visit to the children's toilet (Domain 17). However, the corridors and the WC are not necessarily areas where he would be expected to spend long periods of time.

There are two ways of recording these observations. Imran visits eight domains but engages in a total of 10 activities. The nature and type of activity will be categorised and discussed in a later section. However, points emerge that serve to illustrate the importance of continuous observations. In a time-sampled observation, some details could be lost. The significance of Imran's profile can only fully be understood when it is compared with the profiles of the other children in the nursery.

Ishtiaq's first hour in Box Hill Nursery

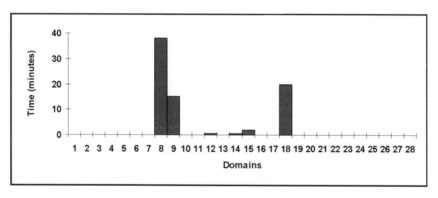

Figure 5.3   A graph of the time-on-task analysis for Ishtiaq's first hour in Box Hill Nursery

Figure 5.3 is a graph of how another boy, Ishtiaq, spends time during his first hour in the nursery. Ishtiaq visits a total of six learning domains. Again it can be seen that he spends different amounts of time in each, but with significantly longer periods of time in the following three:

| Domain 8 | Outside Play Area | 38 minutes |

Domain 9   Painting Table   15 minutes

Domain 18   Pretend Kitchen   20 minutes

Imran and Ishtiaq are both boys, but similar profiles can be observed for girls, as the following three graphs demonstrate.

Rabila's first hour in Box Hill Nursery

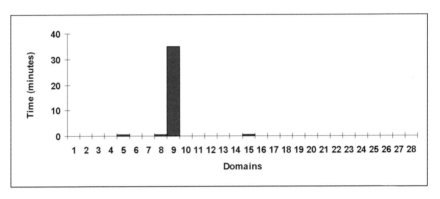

Figure 5.4   A graph of the time-on-task analysis for Rabila's first hour in Box Hill Nursery

During her first hour in the nursery (Figure 5.4) Rabila visits a total of five learning domains, spending only short periods of time at three, Domain 5 (the home corner); Domain 8 (the outside play area); and Domain 15 (the washbasins). She spends a more sustained period of time (35 minutes) at the painting table (Domain 9). She spends the first 20 minutes in school with a teacher on a visit to the main school building. This is not included in Figure 5.4. By comparing Rabila's profile with another girl, Sabia, a similar pattern of behaviour can be observed.

Sabia's first hour in Box Hill Nursery

Sabia visits a total of six domains during her first hour in school, at four of which she spends sustained periods of time (Figure 5.5). Sabia's profile is interesting because she chooses to return to one of the activities, the book corner. The first time she spends 15 minutes there; then she returns some time later and spends a further five minutes. A return visit to a domain has also been observed for other children. Sabia spends the longest time at the story session in Domains 22/23 (20 minutes). Her first hour can be summarised in the following way:

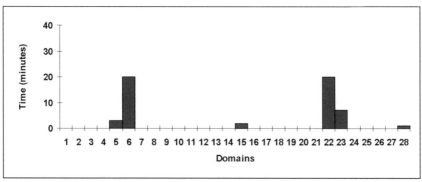

Figure 5.5 A graph of the time-on-task analysis for Sabia's first hour in Box Hill Nursery

Domain 5	Home Corner	3 minutes
Domain 6	Book Corner	15 + 5 minutes (2 visits)
Domain 23	Music	7 minutes
Domains 22/23	Story Time	20 minutes

Ammara's first hour in Box Hill Nursery

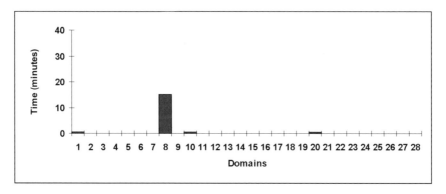

Figure 5.6 A graph of the time-on-task analysis for Ammara's first hour in Box Hill Nursery

From Figure 5.6 it can be seen that Ammara visits a total of four learning domains during her first hour in the nursery. She spends only short spells of time at three of them: Domains 1 (the children's cloakroom), 10 (CDT bench) and 20 (the staff kitchen). However, she spends significantly longer (15 minutes) in Domain 8 (the outside play area).

Table 5.1 presents a comparative overview of all eight children observed and the number of activities in which they engaged during their first hour in the nursery. Further, it identifies the total number of activities where individuals spent sustained periods of time, periods longer than the three minutes identified as significant by previous researchers, Bennett (1976) and Sylva *et al.* (1980). The table contains data on all of the informants observed during the first hour in school. However, practical constraints (illness and change of school) prevented the collection of complete data sets for two girls, Ammara and Sumera. End-of-term data are not available for these two and will therefore not be included in the discussion of other levels of data analysis. However, they have been included here because their inclusion broadens the data base and helps to confirm the general pattern of behaviours observed on the first day in school as typical of bilingual children from similar home backgrounds.

Table 5.1   A summary of first-day activities for 10 informants observed during their first hour in Box Hill Nursery

	First-day activities	
Name	*Sustained*	*Total*
Ammara*	1	5
Imran	7	10
Ishtiaq	3	7
Kamran	3	4
Rabila	2	6
Sabia	5	8
Shamaila	6	13
Shazad	4	12
Sofees	5	8
Sumera*	2	11

(* indicates no end-of-term data available)

Discussion of Time-on-task Data

A number of features worthy of comment emerge from Table 5.1. All of the children in the sample visit more than one of the learning domains on their first day in the nursery. However, the total for each individual varies from a minimum of four (Kamran) to a maximum of 13 (Shamaila). The second point to note is that of the 28 domains potentially available, not all were actually selected. So, in response to the first question posed at the outset of the observations, 'How do children spend their time in the nursery?' the graphs provide a detailed overview for each informant. There is no significant difference noted between the profiles of boys and girls. The highest number of domains recorded are for girls, Shamaila, Shazad and Sumera. Kamran, a boy, has the lowest. There is therefore little to support the findings of previous research (Clarricoates, 1987) that suggests boys are adventurous and more likely to explore and move around than girls. However, to balance this, it should be noted that both Rabila and Ammara spend more sustained periods of time engaged in one particular activity.

Perhaps the most significant feature from the data analysis is the duration of time-on-tasks that was noted. This varied from mere seconds to several minutes. All of the children in the sample spent sustained periods of time in at least one domain. Significantly, periods are longer than the three minutes reported in Sylva *et al.*'s (1980) *Childwatching* study of children of similar age in a comparable setting. The maximum period of sustained time-on-task is recorded for Ishtiaq who spends 38 minutes in Domain 8, the outside play area. Thirty-eight minutes is a considerable period of time and is not a usual feature. However, all of the children are observed spending periods longer than three minutes on selected activities.

The next section addresses the fourth and final question posed at the outset of the observations, how do the ways in which the children spend their time in the nursery school vary from day to day? Graphs comparing first-day and end-of-term observations will be presented to demonstrate the differences between first day and end of term behaviours in school.

Graphs Comparing First-day and End-of-term Observations

The data from one girl, Shazad, and one boy, Kamran, will be presented to make a comparison between the first and last observations of the term.

The graphs in Figures 5.7 and 5.8 illustrate the ways in which Shazad's behaviour changes as the term progresses. On Day 1 she engages in a total of 12 activities in nine domains. By the end of term she has reduced the number of learning activities to eight. This decrease in the number of

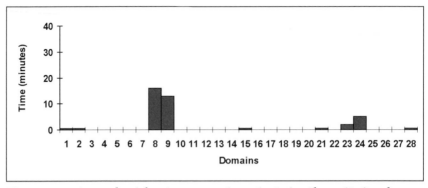

Figure 5.7 A graph of the time-on-task analysis for Shazad's first hour in Box Hill Nursery

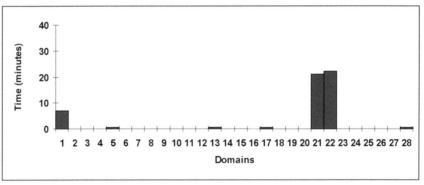

Figure 5.8 A graph of the time-on-task analysis for Shazad's end-of-term activities

activities is accompanied by an increase in the time she spends on selected tasks. She spends longer periods of time in fewer domains. On Day 1 she spends sustained periods of time on four of the seven activities. By the end of the term she spends sustained periods of time on three of the seven activities. Shazad's first- and last-day profiles exemplify this general trend across the informants.

A different profile can be seen in Figures 5.9 and 5.10 for Kamran.

From Figure 5.9 it can be seen that Kamran visits a total of four learning domains during his first hour in the nursery. He spends short spells of time in the corridors (Domain 28) but sustained periods in three other domains:

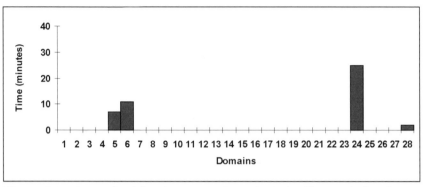

Figure 5.9   A graph of the time-on-task analysis for Kamran's first hour in Box Hill Nursery

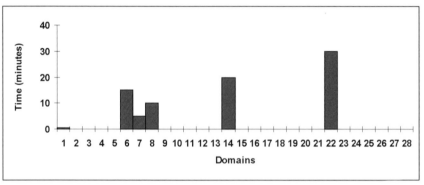

Figure 5.10   A graph of the time-on-task analysis for Kamran's end-of-term activities

Domain 5   Home Corner   7 minutes

Domain 6   Books   11 minutes

Domain 24   Drawing Table   25 minutes

Kamran's profile shows an increase in the number of learning activities. At the end of term he visits six domains, spending sustained periods of time in five.

The changes in first-day and end-of-term activities are summarised in Table 5.2. The table presents a comparison between first-day and end-of-term behaviour for eight informants.

From Table 5.2 it can be seen that Shazad's profile, indicating a decrease in the number of learning activities at the end of term, is representative of the general trend noted. Kamran's profile stands in contrast to this. An increase in the number of learning activities at the end of term is recorded in only one other profile (Rabila).

Table 5.2   Comparison between first-day and end-of-term activities

Name	First Day		End of Term	
	Sustained	Total	Sustained	Total
Imran	7	10	4	5
Ishtiaq	3	7	5	6
Kamran	3	4	5	9
Rabila	2	6	3	7
Sabia	5	8	5	7
Shamaila	6	13	6	10
Shazad	4	12	3	8
Sofees	5	8	2	2

Comparison between First-day and End-of-term Activities

The findings from the Box Hill Nursery Project both concur with and differ from findings of previous studies. The findings can be summarised to demonstrate general trends and patterns of behaviour. These are:

(1) All of the children in the sample select more than one learning activity, even on their first day in the nursery.

(2) For six of the informants the total number of learning activities selected each day *decreases* as the term progresses.

(3) For only two informants (Kamran and Rabila) the total number of learning activities selected each day *increases*.

(4) All children spend some of their time on sustained activities, even on their first day.

(5) For all of the informants, over the course of the observation period of one term, there is an increase in the duration of time spent on sustained activities.

(6) Not all of the learning domains in the nursery are visited.

(7) Finally, and perhaps most significantly, the time that these children spend on sustained tasks is significantly longer than the times recorded in previous observational studies.

The data suggest patterns of behaviour common to all children on their first day in school and there is strong evidence to suggest that these behaviours change as the term progresses.

Observations and Comments on the Data Analysis

Firstly, there are a number of comments to be made that relate to the research methods appropriate for observational studies of young informants in classroom settings. The individual child profiles presented here demonstrate the benefits to be gained from sustained periods of observation. The difference in the times spent on tasks reported here in comparison with the findings of other studies referred to, such as Sylva *et al.* (1980), could in part be explained by the time-sampling methodology favoured by these other studies. It could be said that time sampling is an approach that can lead to partial insights which may distort the information gathered. By using continuous (one-hour) observations for this study a different profile of the individual's behaviour emerges. Also, the pre-coded observation schedules used in previous observational studies by Tough (1977) and Sylva *et al.* (1980) did not prove suitable for this study because they did not allow all observed behaviour to be recorded. These established schedules did provide a useful starting point for the research design. It should be stated that it is unlikely that any pre-existing observation schedule could be used without some modification to suit the specific context (and children) that are being observed.

The second point relates to the presentation of data gathered. To present data on time-on-task in graph form is useful for a number of reasons. It provides a profile of individual children in a format which is reasonably accessible and easy to read. It also allows for comparisons to be made between individual children and for individual children on different days. It is also an easy way to record findings. It is not without limitations, however. Graph format imposes practical constraints. For example, from Figure 5.2, the graph of Imran's first hour in school, it can be seen that although he was observed engaging in 10 different activities, this information is recorded on the graph as only eight activities. This is because the graph format, without the benefit of colour graphics, does not allow easily for return visits to a domain to be recorded separately. Nor does it allow for separate time-spans to be recorded within a re-visited domain. In addition, the graph format does not allow for the order of these visits to be recorded.

On one level these limitations may not seem significant. However, when attempting to look for explanations for specific patterns of individual behaviour they do assume a significance. Hence it should be noted that, although graphs of time-on-task are a useful form for presenting records of children's behaviour, there are factors which they do not reveal and hence they must be viewed as partial. Therefore graphic representation alone cannot provide a full account of an individual's behaviour and in this sense it may be regarded as potentially a distortion.

The second set of comments relate to the analyses undertaken and the subsequent findings presented.

> Different uses of time suggest different conceptualisations of time. Traditionally educational research has assumed that schools are educational rather than social institutions and that teachers and pupils are individuals rather than social beings. That meanings are created inter-subjectively and that history and culture help to orient individuals in time and space are basic premises of ethnographic enquiries but ones quite new to educational research. (Lubeck, 1985: 69)

The assertion that history and culture help to orientate individuals in time and space have important implications in a nursery setting where the teachers and pupils come from different cultural, linguistic and religious backgrounds and traditions. It is reasonable to assume that the expectations of appropriate uses of time spent in the classroom may not be the same for the teachers and their newly arrived pupils, even when they share a common culture and background. The disparity in expectations may be even wider when the teacher and the pupils come from different cultures.

> The organisation of time and space is of enormous significance in most cultures, making it one of the most frequent areas for cross-cultural conflict or misunderstandings, in large because it is so often unconscious. (Saville-Troike, 1982: 140)

Summary

Time-on-task analysis is a useful quantitative structure from which to form impressions of children's experience of school. However, there are aspects of detail which it is not possible to include in this level of data analysis and which may serve to provide a greater understanding of the observed behaviours. The cognitive complexity of specific learning tasks has been suggested by Bennett (1976) and Sylva *et al.* (1980) as one reason for the sustained periods of time spent on task by individual learners. However, this would not seem to account fully for the time-on-task data from the Box Hill Nursery Project. If cognitive complexity were the crucial factor, one would expect to find a pattern to emerge in the range of tasks selected. However this is not the case. Neither is there a set pattern of tasks for individual learners. Some domains remain unvisited. Occasionally a learner returns to a particular task on a given day. It seems therefore that there are other factors which influence the duration of time spent on selected learning activities.

These findings raise a number of questions: what are the factors that hold the interest of one child for sustained periods yet do not attract even a short visit from another? What sustains the attention of one child for several minutes and another for just seconds? It is the answers to these and similar questions that cannot be delivered by time-on-task analyses alone. However, they are precisely the questions that educational researchers need to explore if we are to come closer to understanding the motivations of learners. In an attempt to explore them Chapter 6 will present a second level of data analysis.

Chapter 6
Children Creating Social Contexts

Children do quite like to gather together, in fits and starts, to enjoy one another's company, to find out how others live. (Fay Weldon, *Darcy's Utopia*, 1990: 54)

Introduction to Level 2 of the Data Analysis

This chapter presents a second level of data analysis in the form of a qualitative analysis of the children's use of space within the nursery. The case studies of five children, three girls and two boys, will be presented in a descriptive analysis that complements the time-on-task data analyses presented in Chapter 5. It will show how the physical organisation of the nursery and the other people present influence the children, their behaviour and their activities. The chapter begins with a description of Hymes' (1972a) 'ethnography of communication'. This is followed by a summary of previous studies of the spatial and physical layout of classrooms. The data from the Box Hill Nursery Project will be presented in the form of maps to show five children's movement around the nursery during their first term in formal education. Their observed behaviours have been analysed and four types of behaviour that characterise first term activities in the nursery school will be described. The chapter begins by outlining Hymes' mnemonic for the 'ethnography of speaking' which links individual's choice of language to contextual features of setting.

The Ethnography of Communication – Speaking

The 'ethnography of communication' provides a framework, defining five aspects of context, that influence an individual's language use. For Hymes, the basic unit of analysis is the speech community. He outlines (1967: 8–28) a descriptive model for researchers to use when describing language use within the speech community. He calls this the 'ethnography of speaking'. It aims to provide an explicit set of components included in a description of communicatively competent language use. Hymes (1972b: 52) outlines the following descriptive ethnography of speaking:

Macro level

- Speech community: the basic unit of sociolinguistic analysis. It is a community in which the rules for the conduct and interpretation of at least one language (linguistic variety) must be shared.

- Speech situation: the context or environment in which speech events occur.

- Speech event: the activity in which the rules or community and situation norms for interactions operate.

- Speech act: the minimal unit of a speech event which implicates both social norms and linguistic form. The speech act mediates between aspects of grammar and a speech event or situation.

Individual Speech Style

This refers to the contrastive choices that people make when selecting the ways they speak from their personal linguistic repertoire, the languages and varieties that they can speak and understand.

Micro level

- Ways of speaking: these describe the rule-governed behaviour that allows for a variety of individual choices to be made while still maintaining mutual intelligibility between speakers of the same language.

Hymes (1968) outlines eight components of speech acts, events and situations in the mnemonic SPEAKING, which covers aspects from the macro organisation of 'setting' to micro features of speakers' texts or 'genre'. These are described thus:

Setting and scene	The setting is the physical context.
	The scene can be the psychological frame of the participants.
Participants	The people present.
Ends	The goals or outcomes.
Act sequence	The order of the message, its form and content. The generic structure of some speech acts and events

have already been described linguistically, for example, adjacency pairs, service encounters and teacher-pupil discourse within the classroom.

Key   The tone or manner (for example serious, mocking) of the utterance.

Instrumentalities   The channels and forms of speech, for example written or spoken texts, emails and telephone interactions.

Norms of interaction Discourse rules of silence, interruptions that govern the status of the speakers, their roles and relationships in a particular context.

Genres   The form or style appropriate to the type of text, for example a poem, letter, casual conversation or public speech.

The Social Context of Language Development

Halliday's conceptual framework of language as socio-semiotic acknowledges that language is learned through an ongoing exchange of meaning with significant others (parents, peers, siblings, caregivers). This coterie of significant others constitutes a meaning group for a child who is learning a language. Language learning is thus not a discrete activity, independent of social context: learning language *is* a social activity. While the child is learning a language, other significant learning is taking place simultaneously, through the medium of language. The child is thereby constructing an internal and an external reality to which the coterie of significant others with whom interaction is taking place are also contributors. Hence as Halliday (1978: 1) says, 'The construal of reality is inseparable from the construal of the semantic system in which the reality is coded'. For a child, therefore, learning a language requires more than learning the lexis, the syntax, and the phonology of a language system. Learning a language requires learning how to mean, and how to construe a reality or understanding of the speech community of which he or she is striving to become a member.

Consequently, when learning a language it is insufficient for a child to be merely grammatically competent, to have learnt merely the grammatical rules which govern that language; a child must also learn to be 'communicatively competent'. In order to do this the learner must learn the appropriate accompanying rules of social and linguistic behaviour. This behaviour was termed 'communicative competence' by Hymes (1972b). He defined it as knowing 'when to speak, when not to, what to talk about and with whom, when, where and in what manner to interact' (1972b: 277). In other words, children must learn the sociolinguistic behaviour appropriate to a given cultural context and the particular social situation within that context. Appropriate behaviour in the playground may not be appropriate behaviour in the classroom, and vice versa, even between the same participants.

Halliday (1975: chap. 6) states that although learning a language and learning the culture are different, they are interdependent:

> This is true not only in the sense that a child constructs a reality for (her) himself largely through language, but also in the more fundamental sense that language is itself part of this reality. The linguistic system is part of the social system. Neither can be learned without the other. (Halliday, 1975: 120)

Halliday presents the conceptualisation of socio-semiotic which combines the social system with the linguistic system; together these two, in a relevant relationship with one another, create a developmental context. He suggests that the child's construction of a semantic system takes place alongside the construction of a social system. The two are dual aspects of a single process. The child, learning a language, builds up a social semiotic, the network of meanings that constitute the culture. Through this process the child is becoming a member of the speech community. It is a process of socialisation. The child builds a semiotic of the community or society through interaction with others, peers, family members or significant others (Halliday, 1978: 143). Halliday (1978: 144) further identifies the school as one of the influential forces in contributing to the development of a semiotic network of meanings.

Hence it can be seen, from the theoretical frameworks described by Halliday and Hymes, that learning a language is a complex process that combines linguistic and contextual parameters. It is through language that cultural norms and values are learned and taught.

Previous Studies of the Structure of Classrooms

There have been a number of studies of the spatial organisation of classrooms. Previous ethnographic research includes Sommer's (1967) study on the ecology of classroom participation. This is based on the implicit assumption that increased pupil participation correlates with more learning. Rist's (1972) study of an American ghetto kindergarten goes beyond this, to argue that the actual spatial arrangement of the classroom setting reflects the kinds of social distinctions that develop later between teachers and pupils. He claims that spatial arrangements are based on a number of social class criteria, predetermined by the teacher and independent of any measure of the child's cognitive capacity or ability to perform academic tasks. He argues that spatial organisation based on these assumptions actually contributes to inequality and that it leads directly to pupil underachievement. A study by Hitchcock (1982) focuses on the social organisation of space and place in an urban, open-plan primary school in the north-east of England. It reports that with the absence of walls and other delineating boundaries teachers create elaborate boundaries of their own. His study reveals the discrepancies between the intended uses of locations and the ways in which they are actually used by the people within them. Lubeck's anthropologically informed study sought to 'look at the day-to-day processes by which adults teach children to adapt to the reality which they themselves experience' (Lubeck, 1985: 1). Collectively these ethnographic studies contribute to an understanding of how the behaviour of children and teachers can be influenced by place, space and time. This study adds a further perspective.

Space and Place in the Nursery Setting

Level 2 of the descriptive analysis is founded in the theoretical tradition of systemic linguistics. It accepts Malinowski's (1923/66) position of context as integral to linguistic description (as outlined in Chapter 3) and the Hallidayan description of language as social semiotic. Further, it includes Hymes' ethnography of communication which identifies a number of components of what it means to be communicatively competent, linking an individual's language choice with social, cultural and contextual factors. These descriptions combine to illustrate the ways in which language is not merely a feature of the interpersonal contact, but that it actually creates those social contexts through personal encounters.

Human orientation towards, and interaction within, the visible and invisible boundaries referred to as space and time of the environment are culturally determined. Hall (1959) refers to an individual's use of space as a 'specialised elaboration of culture' and suggests that space is a socio-cultural phenomenon, with different settings creating different codes and rules of permitted behaviour including varying degrees of permitted proximity between the participants in the setting. These ideas have been acknowledged and expanded by other studies by, for example, Gumperz, who acknowledged (1964) the importance of domains for social interactions and later (1975) examined aspects of cross-cultural communication in specific domains to illustrate this view.

Classrooms are specific social settings with their own codes and rules of appropriate behaviour. Chapter 3 discussed the ways in which the physical organisation of classrooms can be understood as one example of Vygotsky's object-regulation. The spatial arrangement of the classroom, the activities that take place there, and the influence that the specific organisation exerts on the individuals present has been acknowledged and discussed in educational circles since the influential Plowden Report *Children and their Primary Schools,* published in 1976 (DES, 1976). Schools and their classrooms may be conceived of as 'arenas of interaction', their spatial organisation providing the structural framework of possibility and constraint for the verbal and non-verbal behaviours that can take place within the boundaries. In the UK, discussions about primary school classrooms and the curriculum (Alexander *et al.,* 1992) have made the organisation of space within classrooms a philosophical and pedagogic statement of teachers' values, assumptions and expectations.

Space is also a crucial aspect of wider human interaction. The physical features of a setting contribute to (or even determine) the nature of the social interaction which can take place there. Spaces and places contain social information, signs or semiotics. Teachers organise a particular spatial arrangement within a classroom to present and reinforce intrinsic symbolic messages. In this way the classroom assumes social properties which signal to participants (pupils, parents, other teachers and professionals) a predetermined range of possible permitted and appropriate social interactions and behaviours that can take place within that setting. These organisational features can also signal expected patterns of permissible behaviours. They contain 'signals of expectation', that is, they signal to the new pupils the teacher's expectations of appropriate behaviours within the nursery.

The Box Hill Nursery Setting

The structure of the nursery setting where the study was undertaken is significant in nurturing particular types of individual and group behaviour. The organisation is deliberate, intended to signal, nurture and reinforce expectations of appropriate pupil behaviour. The large open-plan room is divided into a number of learning domains, each containing learning activities designed to address a specific aspect of social, cognitive, physical, moral or aesthetic development. Each learning domain is delineated by the positioning of furniture and 1.2-metre-high screens, thus allowing supervising adults an overview of the room while simultaneously providing maximum seclusion to the children inside the individual domains. The domains are deliberately small, allowing only a few children (between four and six) to be in each at any given time. There are 26 structured learning activities, each with its own apparatus, learning materials and carefully planned learning activity. The domains are created by the nursery staff and remain constant for about one term. Towards the end of the first term Domains 22 and 23 were combined to form one larger domain. This accommodated a seasonal Christmas tree which the children helped to decorate and which became the focus of new learning activities throughout the month of December. This area was also used for whole-class activities, for example story-time and singing, which took place at the beginning and end of each nursery session.

The educational rationale underpinning the layout and design was explicit. The aim was to encourage learner autonomy. Pupils were expected to select their own learning activity and to be responsible for the collection and storage of all learning materials they required for their activities. Materials were available within each domain, stored in labelled units. This helped to introduce the children to routines of preparation. The written labels were an informal but meaningful introduction to reading. Figure 6.1, a plan of Box Hill Nursery, identifies the learning domains by name and number. The numbering of the domains on the map is for purposes of identification only and has no other significance. In addition to these self-selected activities, the teachers gathered the children together as a class, twice each day, for activities such as story-time, singing, physical education and games. Each nursery session followed a predictable pattern, allowing the children to become familiar with the layout and learning activities. Some changes were introduced, for example the type of group activities and the focus of the structured activities within domains.

The Data

Maps of five informants, three girls, Rabila, Shamaila, and Shazad, and two boys, Ishtiaq and Imran, and their movements around the nursery will be presented as case studies. In order to understand the maps a brief explanation of the information they contain is required. The movements of each child around the nursery setting during one hour of continuous observation have been recorded on an outline map of the nursery setting. The organisation of the floor space into learning domains, as well as functional areas such as toilets, washbasins, cloakroom and teachers' office, are also marked on the map. The individual child's movements are recorded using

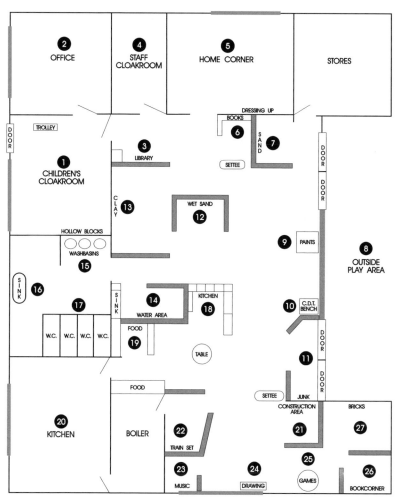

Domain 1	Children's Cloakroom	Domain 11	Junk Table	Domain 21	Construction Area
Domain 2	Office	Domain 12	Wet Sand	Domain 22	Train Set[+]
Domain 3	Library	Domain 13	Clay	Domain 23	Music[+]
Domain 4	Staff Cloakroom	Domain 14	Water Area	Domain 24	Drawing Table
Domain 5	Home Corner	Domain 15	Washbasins	Domain 25	Games
Domain 6	Books	Domain 16	Sink	Domain 26	Book Corner
Domain 7	Dry Sand	Domain 17	WCs	Domain 27	Building Bricks
Domain 8	Outside Play Area	Domain 18	Kitchen	Domain 28	Corridor Areas
Domain 9	Paints	Domain 19	Food		
Domain 10	CDT* Bench	Domain 20	Staff Kitchen		

* Craft, Design & Technology
[+] After 24 November Domains 22 and 23 merge – Christmas tree

Figure 6.1 A plan of Box Hill Nursery

two types of dotted line: the bold lines show determined movement from one area to another; the lighter lines denote a transient movement. Together with each map, a table will be presented. This will offer a summary of the domains visited and the number of activities in which the child was engaged during the one hour of observation. These maps complement the time-on-task data presented in Chapter 5. Each map contains the following information for each child:

(1) The order in which the child visited each of the learning domains.

(2) The period of time (to the nearest minute) spent by the child in each do-main.

(3) A summary of the activities in which the child was engaged.

(4) A categorisation for each of the activities in terms of the characteristic features of behaviours identified in the following section.

There are ways other than mapping in which it would also be possible to record these data. Graphs, bar charts and whisker graphs could also be used to report the children's movements. However, it is felt that the maps presented capture something of the essence of the children's movements around the nursery site in a more naturalistic way than could be conveyed using these other means. It was also felt that recording and reporting data in this way is more in keeping with the spirit and philosophy of ethnographic study.

Four Types of Pupil Behaviour during the First Term in the Nursery

From these hour-long observations it is possible to identify four distinct patterns of behaviours that characterise the first term in the nursery. The first two can be defined in terms of the nature of the activity.

Functional activities are those which serve a utilitarian need or necessity. Examples include toilet visits, getting a drink, changing into or out of the appropriate clothing for a given task. The significance of functional activities cannot be gauged by their duration. They are typically short-term. However, they can be seen as necessary, purposeful and highly significant. When functional behaviour is appropriate it can be evidence of the child's enculturation into the norms of classroom behaviour. It is important because it demonstrates the child's independence within this new context. Functional behaviour also demonstrates that the child is learning appro-priate classroom behaviour, for example wearing the appropriate protective clothing for sand and water play or for painting and junk modelling activities, and putting the apparatus away afterwards into the correct storage boxes. Functional behaviour differs from related activities in that each activity can be regarded as self-contained, for example tidying away one activity's apparatus before moving on to the next.

Related activities are defined not in terms of time-span, but by their connection to a previous activity and behaviour. Examples are when a child moves from one domain to another in order to get materials or apparatus specifically for the activity in which they are already engaged, or when the child visits the washbasins to wash their hands and tidy up after a junk modelling, gluing or painting session. These activities are categorised as 'related' because of their connection to the previous activity. They are usually connected with, and consecutive to, other activities, including sustained activities. However, it has been decided to identify them as separate to emphasise the importance of the connections that the children make between the activities in which they are engaged. They are also indicators of a child's enculturation into appropriate classroom behaviour. In addition, identifying these activities as separate illustrates the point that activities of short-term duration may be as challenging for the young child as the sustained activities. They may present an equivalent cognitive challenge, but in a different way.

It is important that activities of short duration are understood within the context in which they occur. Viewed separately they could be regarded by the observer as less significant. Indeed, some related and transient behaviours, if observed in isolation, may give the impression that the child is not very engaged. This may be because the activities involve the child in moving around the nursery to find something or someone. Related behaviours are similar to transient behaviours in that they may last for only short periods of time.

Two further activities can be more specifically defined in terms of their duration or time-span (usually in minutes).

Sustained activities are characterised by a sustained period of time on one activity. Behaviour has been categorised as 'sustained' if it lasts for more than three minutes (as previously discussed in Chapter 5), the duration identified by Sylva *et al.*'s (1980) study as significant for time-on-task in the nursery context.

Transient activities describe any momentary behaviour observed. They are characterised as short. Such activities usually last less than three minutes, but can and frequently do last mere seconds. Transient activities are not obviously related to the previous activity in which the child was engaged. They are similar to the 'cruising behaviour' identified in the Sylva *et al.* (1980) study, but differ in one important respect: the periods of time registered for transient behaviour are considerably shorter than for cruising. Sometimes these activities last mere seconds. Transient behaviours include moving from one activity to another; or walking around the nursery searching for someone or something specific, to find a friend or teacher, or to fetch a piece of apparatus. Transient activities are short but frequently purposeful, with a very specific focus or intent. They are frequently found when the child is moving on to a new activity, having just completed a task. They are short but significant periods, because the course of the child's afternoon can be altered as a result of chance encounters and happenings during these times. It is the serendipity of transient time that makes it influential for the child. It also provides the researcher with insights into how the new pupil is coping and learning to respond when faced with a new and unfamiliar experience.

These are the four types of pupil behaviour that have been observed during the children's first term in the nursery school. The characteristic features of pupil behaviour during these activities can be summarised as Functional, Related, Sustained and Transient, which combine to form the acronym (FiRST). These four types of behaviour provide the descriptive framework for categorising how the children use their time (Chapter 5) and the space within the nursery school. The following sections present the case studies of five children, Rabila, Shamaila, Shazad, Ishtiaq and Imran, demonstrating their use of space and how language and the physical organisation of the nursery play a part in structuring events. On the maps, the behaviours of the children have been categorised in terms of the four behaviours just described.

Rabila's Story

Most of the children arrive at the nursery via the children's cloakroom. It is used as a greeting area as well as storage for coats and outdoor wear. It adjoins the teachers' office. Rabila begins at the nursery when she is aged three years and seven months (3.7). On the first day she arrives at the nursery with her mother. She is met at the door by the head of the nursery. After the usual routines of hanging up her coat and registration, her mother leaves. Rabila immediately becomes very upset and begins to cry. Instead of taking her into the nursery, the teacher picks her up and tries to comfort her. When this fails to calm her, the teacher, who was on her way to the main school building on business, takes Rabila with her. Figure 6.2 is a map of Rabila's movements around the nursery on her first hour in school. This

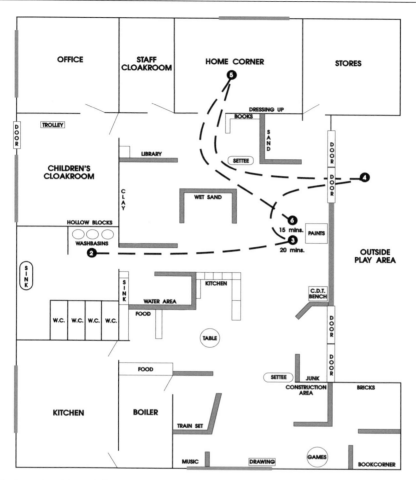

Activity 1   Main School   *Not on map*   Sustained behaviour for 20
                                                   minutes

Activity 2   Domain 15   Washbasins   Functional behaviour

Activity 3   Domain 9   Paints   Sustained behaviour for 20
                                                   minutes

Activity 4   Domain 8   Outside Play Area   Related behaviour

Activity 5   Domain 5   Home Corner   Related behaviour

Activity 6   Domain 9   Paints   Related behaviour for 15
                                                   minutes

Figure 6.2   A map of Rabila's movements on her first day at Box Hill
Nursery

first activity with the teacher is not represented on the map. However, it is included in the summary of the day's activities, as Activity 1. Rabila and the teacher return to the nursery 20 minutes later. Rabila is more settled and has stopped crying. She goes to the washbasins to wash her face and freshen up after the crying, Activity 2 (Domain 15). This is where the mapping begins. The teacher arrives at the washbasins to wash some paint-brushes. Rabila then follows her back to the painting table (Activity 3, Domain 9). She joins a number of other children in a teacher-directed painting activity, where she stays for 20 minutes. The painting table is near a large window overlooking the outside play area (Activity 4, Domain 8) and the exit to it. This gives teachers (and children) a clear view of the outside area. When the teacher goes outside briefly to talk to some chil-dren, Rabila again follows her. Rabila continues to follow the teacher to the home corner (Activity 5, Domain 5) and then finally back to the painting table (Activity 6, Domain 9), where she continues with the painting activity. Rabila's profile is both unique to her and yet in some ways also representative of the first day experiences of other children. It is representative in that she visits only a small number of the learning domains available, and she spends varying amounts of time ranging from just seconds to a sustained period of 20 minutes on one of the activities. She makes a return visit to the painting table to continue with a familiar activity. Rabila's attachment to a particular teacher is significant in deter-mining how she spends her time. Rabila's first-day activities are summarised in map form in Figure 6.2.

In order to assess how representative Rabila's first day behaviour is, it is necessary to compare her profile with those of other children.

Shamaila's Story

Shamaila is aged three years and five months (3.5). Shamaila, like Rabila, visits a number of learning domains during her first hour in the nursery. However, her behaviour is dissimilar in a number of ways. Figure 6.3 pres-ents a overview of Shamaila's first hour in school as 'action-packed'. It can be seen that she travels around the nursery a good deal. She arrives in school and spends two minutes in the children's cloakroom (Activity 1, Domain 1) going through the rituals of hanging up her coat, with the help of her grandfather, registering herself present on the attendance board and then saying goodbye to him and hello to the teachers. This has been cate-gorised as functional behaviour because she is actually going through a number of routines which she will need to remember and repeat each day on her arrival at the nursery. From the outset she is confident and independent. She is quite happy when her gandfather leaves her at the nursery. She seems more independent of teachers than the other children in the study. During her first hour in school she experiences a number of different play activities. These start in the dry sand area (Activity 2, Domain 7) where she stays for seven minutes. She then spends a short time in the corridor with another girl, Sabia.

Like Rabila (and the other children) her behaviour can be seen to be influenced by adults. At the suggestion of a teacher who says: 'Well, you go and find somewhere to play, then,' Shamaila moves from the corridor to a learning activity. Shamaila then goes to the pretend kitchen (Activity 4, Domain 18) where she stays for just two minutes, and spends a similarly short time (two minutes) playing with the clay in Domain 13 (Activity 5). She then progresses through a number of sustained activities: junk modelling (Activity 6, Domain 11) for five minutes; playing with the train set (Activity 7, Domain 22) for four minutes; the drawing table (Activity 9, Domain 24) for nine minutes and dry sand (Activity 10, Domain 7) for a further four minutes. These periods of play activity are punctuated by general movement around the nursery and some functional visits to the children's cloakroom (Activity 11) and the washbasins (Activities 8 and 12). Shamaila ends her first hour in the nursery with a sustained activity of four minutes (Activity 13, Domain 14) playing in the water area.

A profile of this first hour in school can be summarised by noting that a number of different play activities are experienced, but not all domains of the nursery were visited and that different periods of time were spent on a variety activities. Figure 6.3 presents an overview of Shamaila's first hour in the nursery. It captures something of the flurry of her activity. Shamaila's profile and use of space is interesting because it stands in contrast to Clarricoates' (1987) study which suggests that boys dominate the space available in classrooms; they move around a great deal more and create territory for themselves. In the observations presented here, Shamaila is observed moving around the nursery and is recorded as visiting more domains than any other child in this study, boy or girl, on the first day in school. From Table 5.1 it is noted that one other girl, Shazad, also visits a wide range of domains (a total of 12) on her first day in school (Figure 6.4).

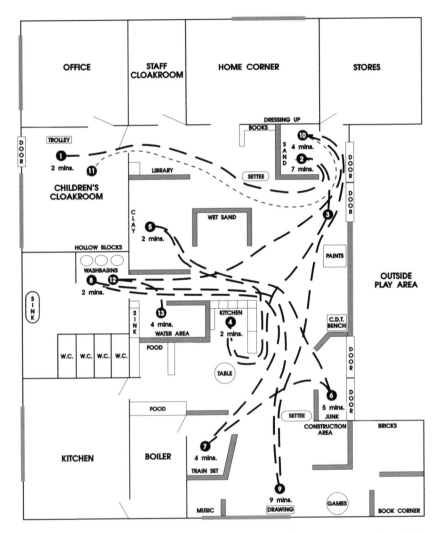

Figure 6.3 A map of Shamaila's movements on her first day at Box Hill Nursery

Activity 1	Domain 1	Children's Cloakroom	Functional behaviour for 2 minutes
Activity 2	Domain 7	Dry Sand	Sustained behaviour for 7 minutes
Activity 3	Domain 28	Corridor	Transient behaviour
Activity 4	Domain 18	Pretend Kitchen	Related behaviour for 2 minutes
Activity 5	Domain 13	Clay	Related behaviour for 2 minutes
Activity 6	Domain 11	Junk Table	Sustained behaviour for 5 minutes
Activity 7	Domain 22	Train Set	Sustained behaviour for 4 minutes
Activity 8	Domain 15	Washbasins	Related behaviour for 2 minutes
Activity 9	Domain 24	Drawing Table	Sustained behaviour for 9 minutes
Activity 10	Domain 7	Dry Sand	Sustained behaviour for 4 minutes
Activity 11	Domain 1	Children's Cloakroom	Related behaviour
Activity 12	Domain 15	Washbasins	Related behaviour

Figure 6.3   *(cont.)*

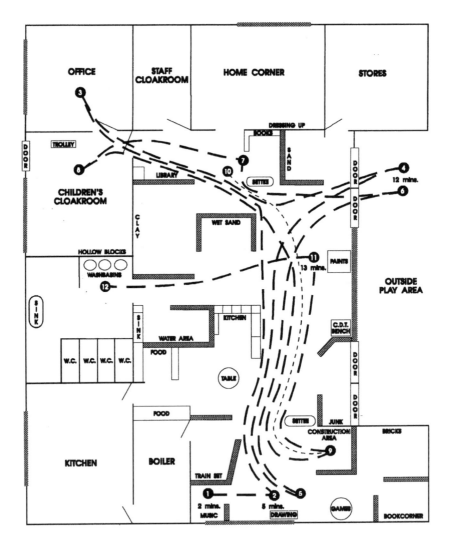

Figure 6.4   A map of Shazad's movements on her first day at Box Hill
Nursery

Activity 1	Domain 23	Music	Sustained behaviour for 2 minutes
Activity 2	Domain 24	Drawing	Sustained behaviour for 5 minutes
Activity 3	Domain 2	Office	Related behaviour
Activity 4	Domain 8	Outside Play Area	Sustained behaviour for 12 minutes
Activity 5	Domain 24	Drawing	Transient behaviour
Activity 6	Domain 8	Outside Play Area	Sustained behaviour for 4 minutes
Activity 7	Domain 28	Corridor	Transient behaviour
Activity 8	Domain 1	Children's Cloakroom	Transient behaviour
Activity 9	Domain 21	Construction Area	Transient behaviour
Activity 10	Domain 28	Corridor	Transient behaviour
Activity 11	Domain 26	Book Corner	Sustained behaviour for 5 minutes
Activity 12	Domain 8	Outside Play Area	Sustained behaviour for 2 minutes
Activity 13	Domain 9	Paints	Sustained behaviour for 13 minutes
Activity 14	Domain 15	Washbasins	Related behaviour

Figure 6.4   (*cont.*)

Ishtiaq's Story

Ishtiaq is a little older than Rabila, Shamaila and Shazad when he starts at the nursery; on his first day he is aged four years and seven months (4.7). He arrives at school at 13.00 hours with his aunt. He is met by the bilingual classroom assistant who greets him in Mirpuri-Panjabi and takes him to play in Domain 18 (Activity 1), the pretend kitchen. There he meets three other Mirpuri-Panjabi speaking children, two girls, Shazia (SA) and Rabila (RN), and a boy, Mushtifaq (MI). All four role-play together with the bilingual classroom assistant for a sustained period of 20 minutes. The role-play takes a variety of forms. They pretend to read a menu; they play at preparing food, cutting up a banana; while they are doing this their talk covers a variety of topics, including the names and properties of the fruit, and more general news, about their families and their homes. The language throughout is Mirpuri-Panjabi. The bilingual classroom assistant plays an active role, encouraging individual children to participate in the conversation and directing the topic of the discourse with questions and prompts. Her dominance in the discourse and her influence on the children's behaviour is evident when the pretend play activity ends because she moves away to another domain. Ishtiaq, Mushtifaq and Shazia all follow her to Domain 12, the wet sand area (Activity 2). She eventually leaves them in this domain. Although they remain in the wet sand domain, the nature of their interaction changes. Once alone and no longer under adult supervision and guidance the children no longer interact with each other. They stop playing in the sand. However, they remain within the domain.

The interaction then takes a different turn. Ishtiaq pushes Mushtifaq and then without speaking he leaves the sand domain and moves away to the play area opposite, Domain 14, the water area (Activity 3). Without comment, all of the other children follow him. After only one minute Ishtiaq moves again. This time he goes to the outside play area (Activity 4). He goes without his coat and since it is cold, he returns almost immediately. As he passes the painting table (Domain 9) a teacher says, in English, 'You're all going to paint.' From the tape-recording we know that Ishtiaq overhears this directive and we can presume that he thinks that the teacher is addressing him and including him in the activity. He joins the painting group where he stays for a sustained period of 15 minutes (Activity 5), mixing paints on a palette and painting a pattern. The teacher is showing the children how to wash their paintbrushes after using each colour and how to mix the paints to create new shades. When Ishtiaq has finished his painting he goes to the washbasins with the other children to wash his

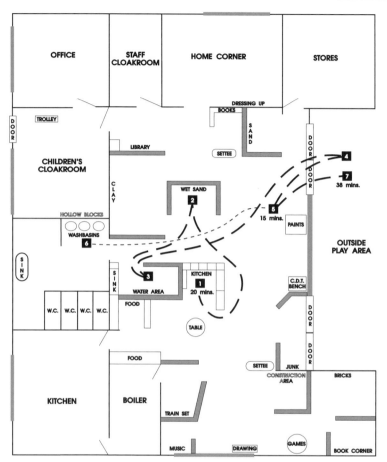

Activity 1	Domain 18	Pretend Kitchen	Sustained behaviour for 20 minutes
Activity 2	Domain 12	Wet Sand	Transient behaviour
Activity 3	Domain 14	Water Area	Transient behaviour
Activity 4	Domain 8	Outside Play Area	Transient behaviour
Activity 5	Domain 9	Paints	Sustained behaviour for 15 minutes
Activity 6	Domain 15	Washbasins	Related behaviour
Activity 7	Domain 8	Outside Play Area	Sustained behaviour for 38 minutes

Figure 6.5 A map of Ishtiaq's movements on his first day in Box Hill Nursery

hands and his paintbrush and to help with the general tidying up (Activity 6). All children are expected to help with the tidying up at the end of each activity. Ishtiaq then hangs up the painting overall that he has been wearing for the activity. This is expected and appropriate pupil behaviour.

Ishtiaq next goes outside to join another teacher who is with a large group of other children. He stays there playing on a variety of apparatus for 38 minutes (Activity 7). He leaves to go home when a relative calls to collect him, before the afternoon officially ends. Ishtiaq has spent his first day at the nursery on a total of six different learning domains, three of which he sustained for significant periods of time. Some of the activities Ishtiaq chose for himself and some were chosen for him by teachers. Most of his interactions with peers and adults were in Mirpuri-Panjabi. The language of these interactions will be discussed in detail in Chapters 8 and 9. Ishtiaq spent some of his time in the company of others, both teachers and peers. This will be discussed in detail in Chapter 7. Only six of the 28 domains were visited. Figure 6.5 presents the map of Ishtiaq's first hour in the nursery school.

Imran's Story

Imran is aged four years and three months (4.3). Like Ishtiaq he is a little older than the three girls when he starts at the nursery. On the first day he arrives a little late, a few minutes after the official start of the school session. All of the afternoon's activities have begun and all of the teachers are already working with children in small groups. He arrives with his mother and she leaves him in the cloakroom, almost immediately. He is left alone. He walks along the corridors leading from the cloakroom where two other boys, Geoffrey and Michael, are playing with building bricks (Activity 1). From the tape-recording we know that he can hear Geoffrey and Michael talking to each other. There is also the sound of banging in the background. A bilingual classroom assistant walks by and says to the boys in English, 'Come on, all play together.' However, Imran does not join them, he continues walking around the corridors. The reason for this is unclear. Perhaps he has not understood the instruction in English, or perhaps he is unsure about his new classmates or how to join in their activity. The same bilingual classroom assistant is sitting on the sofa in Domain 6, reading a story in Mirpuri-Panjabi to a small group of bilingual children. Imran hears her voice, moves towards it and then stops. He continues to stand within hearing distance of the story but does not actually go into the domain (Activity 2). Although this activity lasts for some five minutes, it has been categorised as transient behaviour because he does not actually enter the domain where the storytelling session is in progress. Imran stays outside the domain, walking around the screens. However, it is clear from his audio-tape for this session that he can hear the story quite clearly throughout. Why he does not join the group is again unclear. Perhaps it is the same reticence that prevented him from joining Michael and Geoffrey earlier. He seems very shy and is clearly unsure. He continues to move slowly around the corridor but is still listening to the story. The teacher cannot see him because she is sitting down inside the domain. He is shielded from her view by the screens around the domain. There is the general classroom hubbub all around him. He whispers to himself in Mirpuri-Panjabi. His utterance is barely audible, he is repeating part of the story he has overheard. This utterance can be interpreted as evidence of what Vygotsky terms 'private speech' or 'speech for oneself'. Azia, one of the girls sitting inside the domain listening to the story, suddenly gets up and leaves the domain. She goes to the outside of the screen where Imran is standing and takes him by the hand. They do not speak but they continue to stand outside the book corner, listening to the story (Activity 2).

As they stand there together another teacher calls to Azia from Domain 21, the construction area. Hand-in-hand, Imran and Azia walk across to Domain 21 to join her. Imran stays in the construction area with Azia for six minutes (Activity 3). He is playing with the apparatus. They are not talking to each other, but Imran is making playing sounds to himself (further evidence of Vygotsky's private speech). The construction area is positioned next to the musical instruments. There are some children playing there and the sound of the musical instruments is quite clear. Imran begins singing quietly to himself. Azia then speaks to him in Mirpuri-Panjabi, explaining how to build up the blocks on top of each other so that they do not fall over. They continue talking in their home language. They then go to the toilets (Activity 4, Domain 17). They move on when prompted by the teacher, 'Come on you two, out you come.'

Imran and Azia continue talking to each other in Mirpuri-Panjabi and return to Domain 6, the book corner (Activity 5). They sit down and Imran picks up a picture book, *The Bad-tempered Ladybird*, and pretends to read it. He is demonstrating appropriate early reading behaviour, holding the book correctly and turning over the pages. From the audio-tape we can hear that he is not actually reading the text from the book. However, his intonation and language rhythm sound like a story, even though the utterances do not actually make sense. He is using intonation patterns and his voice to pretend to read a story to himself. Azia is also in the book corner. She is tidying the bookshelves. After three minutes at this activity they are

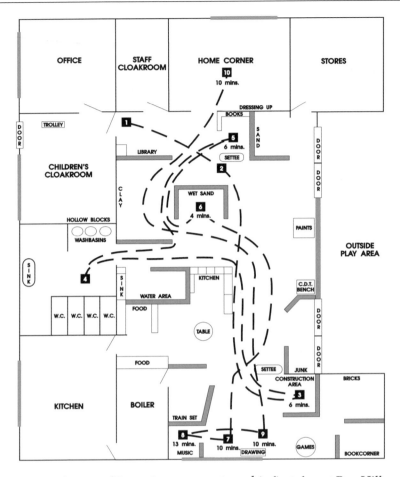

Figure 6.6   A map of Imran's movements on his first day at Box Hill Nursery *(details shown opposite)*

interrupted by a teacher who suggests, 'Go and play in the sand or in the water.' Immediately Azia replies in English, 'I want to do.' She is keen to co-operate and please the teacher. Imran remains silent.

Azia and Imran then go off together. They choose the wet sand area (Activity 6, Domain 12). Azia does not go into the domain with Imran. Imran, seeming to have gained confidence as the afternoon has worn on, enters the domain and stays there playing alone, talking to himself and making playing sounds quietly. After four minutes he leaves the domain and spends a few minutes walking slowly around the nursery, stopping from time to

Activity 1	Domain 28	Corridor	Transient behaviour for 2 minutes
Activity 2	Domain 28	Corridor	Transient behaviour for 5 minutes
Activity 3	Domain 21	Construction Area	Sustained behaviour for 6 minutes
Activity 4	Domain 17	WCs	Functional behaviour for 2 minutes
Activity 5	Domain 6	Books	Sustained behaviour for 6 minutes
Activity 6	Domain 12	Wet Sand	Sustained behaviour for 4 minutes
Activity 7	Domain 24	Drawing Table	Sustained behaviour for 10 minutes
Activity 8	Domain 23	Music	Sustained behaviour for 13 minutes
Activity 9	Domain 24	Drawing Table	Sustained behaviour for 10 minutes
Activity 10	Domain 5	Home Corner	Sustained behaviour for 10 minutes

Figure 6.6   (*cont.*)

time outside domains, watching the activites and listening to the children from behind the screens but not attempting to join in any of them. Eventually he arrives at the drawing table (Activity 7, Domain 24), where he sees Azia again. She is sitting with Kamran, another bilingual child. Two teachers are talking nearby. Imran joins Kamran and Azia without speaking. He stays with them for 10 minutes, drawing, pretend-writing (scribble writing) and folding pieces of paper. The bilingual classroom assistant joins them. She initiates the following interaction in English (see Chapter 8 for an explanation of the chosen method of dialogue transcription):

Bilingual classroom assistant   nearly finished.

[classroom noise]

Azia   *[repeats teacher's utterance in Mirpuri-Panjabi]*

Imran   *[repeats teacher's utterance in Mirpuri-Panjabi back to Azia]*

Bilingual classroom assistant   can you write 'Kamran', this is the way I write it, can you go over this ...

Again we have here evidence of Imran's private speech, with some modification. It is as if he is repeating utterances that he has overheard in the classroom to himself as a way of practising and familiarising himself with the sounds and patterns of the language. The interaction is terminated when Imran makes an inaudible response and then leaves quickly. He walks back to the music domain, where after a short time he is joined by Azia and Kamran (Activity 8). One possible interpretation of this exchange between the bilingual classroom assistant and this small group of children is that they thought she was expecting them to have finished at the writing table, and so to comply, they move on to another activity. The three then stay together in the music domain for 13 minutes in sustained play activity with a variety of musical instruments. As a group all three then go back to the drawing table where the bilingual classroom assistant is working with another girl. They continue with drawing activities for a further 10 minutes (Activity 9) before moving again as a group to the final sustained activity of the afternoon, Domain 5 the home corner (Activity 10), a pretend play area designed as a sitting-room with chairs and home furniture.

These case studies focus on the children's first afternoon in the nursery. The descriptions show how the children differ in their activities. They also show how other people present, children as well as adults, can influence an individual. The observations also suggest that each child experiences the common context of the nursery in uniquely different ways. The next section describes how the children's behaviour changes over the first term in the nursery.

Changes in Behaviour during the First Term in the Nursery

From the observations of these children it is noted that a number of changes take place in observed behaviour over the first term in the nursery. These can be illustrated more clearly by comparing maps of the children on their first day in the nursery with those made on the last day of the term. Figure 6.6 is a map of Imran's first day in Box Hill Nursery and Figure 6.7 a map of his movements around the nursery at the end of the term. These observed differences typify those of the other pupils. Using Imran's maps as an example, it is possible to summarise the differences between the pupils' beginning- and end-of-term behaviours in the following ways:

- There is a reduction in the amount of time spent on transient movements around the corridors and learning domains.

- The number of transient activities observed is also reduced as the term progresses.

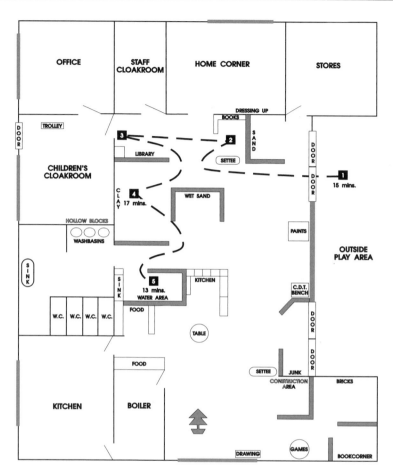

Activity 1	Domain 8	Outside Play Area	Sustained behaviour for 15 minutes
Activity 2	Domain 6	Books	Related behaviour for 5 minutes
Activity 3	Domain 3	Library	Functional behaviour
Activity 4	Domain 13	Clay	Sustained behaviour for 17 minutes
Activity 5	Domain 14	Water Area	Sustained behaviour for 13 minutes

Figure 6.7 A map of Imran's movements at the end of the first term in Box Hill Nursery

- There is a consolidation of interests. Fewer learning domains are visited. For Imran this is reduced from a total of 10 activities on the first day, to five at the end of term.

- More time is actually spent on each of the sustained activities.

This pattern can be observed across all of the children in the study. It is not considered useful to offer averages for the time spent on tasks because this alters the record of time that individual children actually spend on sustained activities by reducing it. An average would also present a very different profile of behaviours.

Summary

The following summarises the main points of this chapter:

(1) The data from the Box Hill Nursery Study have shown that individual children spend varying amounts of time on selected learning activities and that this behaviour changes during their first term in the nursery school. Four types of behaviours have been observed and described. These are: Functional, Related, Sustained and Transient. They can be represented by the acronym FiRST.

(2) By tracking and mapping the individual pupil's movements and recording time-on-task in this way, it can be seen that accounting for the time spent engaged in learning activities is complex. It is not merely dependent on the cognitive complexity or other inherent qualities of the structured learning activities available within the nursery; there are extraneous influential factors.

(3) There is a social dimension to the children's behaviours which encourages individual children to spend sustained periods of time on selected learning activities.

(4) Analysis suggests contextual features can influence the time children spend on activities. These contextual features offer a number of plausible explanatory factors for the time an individual child spends engaged in a particular learning activity. They include the physical structure of the nursery which can provide a supportive context for nurturing particular types of movements and personal behaviour and the presence of certain individuals, a teacher, adult or other children, as possible influencing factors. These can act as attraction factors and result in the child spending more sustained periods of time-on-task.

(5) The teachers are a key influence on the children.

(6) Children influence each other.

(7) There is wide variation in the children's experiences within the nursery. Children have unique experiences of a common context.

(8) Children adapt very quickly and soon become enculturated and socialised into appropriate school behaviour.

(9) The physical organisation of the nursery influences the children's individual and collective behaviours.

In summary two suggestions are offered. Firstly, that time-on-task is not *per se* the only indicator of the validity of a learning activity. Secondly, that the cognitive complexity of the learning activity is not the only reason for a child to spend a sustained period of time-on-task. It is suggested that there is a social dimension to learning activities. This social dimension to interactions with teacher and peers provides a reason for some children spending different amounts of time on selected learning activities in the nursery. It is equally plausible as an explanatory factor as the cognitive complexity or challenge of the learning activity in which they are engaged. This feature will be explored and developed in later chapters.

Finally, it has been suggested that continuous observation has certain advantages over time-sampling as a method of data collection. Hour-long observation periods, complemented by other contextual information, provide a description of the total classroom environment, as experienced by the individual carrying the recording equipment. This includes a number of contextual details, such as information about the other people present in the nursery and the sounds as heard by each child. This enables the researcher to gain a better understanding of individual children's behaviour. The next chapter will present a third level of the descriptive analysis.

Chapter 7
Social Networks and the Process of Enculturation

The Soul selects her own Society (Emily Dickinson, Poem No. 303)

Introduction to Level 3 of Data Analysis

This chapter addresses a third level of data analysis. Using social network analysis as a research method, discourse and 'thick' (Geertz, 1975) contextual data will be combined to demonstrate the ways in which the children in the study establish contact with each other (and other pupils) during their first term in the nursery setting. These first-day contacts will be compared with end-of-term contacts to demonstrate the ways in which an individual's ties become established as the term progresses. Analysis will trace the emergence of two types of network, *pupil networks* and *friendship networks*. It will be suggested that the presence of adults (teachers and bilingual classroom assistants) exerts an influence on the establishment and consolidation of these networks, and that the basis of the children's developing ethnicity can be found in these emerging networks. The chapter begins with an overview of social network analysis as a theoretical framework for data analysis.

The Concept of Social Network Analysis as a Research Method

Social network analysis is an established paradigm within sociolinguistics and anthropology. The idea of the social network as an analytic concept was originally introduced by Barnes (1954) to describe an order of social relationship which he considered to be important for understanding the behaviour of the inhabitants of the Norwegian village of Bremnes. He felt that a great deal of social behaviour could not be accounted for by concepts based on an individual's status, territorial location or economic activity alone.

A number of researchers have since used the concept of social network analysis. The social network has been defined by Milroy (1980: 174) as 'quite simply ... the informal social relationships contracted by an individual', and by Le Page and Tabouret-Keller (1985: 116) as 'those structural complexes within communities made up of chains and criss-crossings of friendship, relationship and acquaintanceship to which each of us belongs'. A social network may be regarded as a boundless web of ties which reaches out through a whole community, linking people to one another. The individual remains the locus of the network, hence social networks are anchored to individuals. Tajfel (1981: 135) suggests that this 'social categorisation is a cognitive tool which allows individuals to define and organise their social world into meaningful units'. Individuals use social categories to order their social environment, as a means by which to make sense of the world around them and their experiences within it. This view corresponds with a general view of learning held by others such as social psychologists, including for example Bruner (1986) and Bruner and Haste (1987), who claim the social dimension is an important and central factor in young children's learning processes. Systemic linguists (cf. Halliday, 1978) also support the view that young children learn to mean by engaging in conversation with others.

There are specific reasons that make social network analysis a particularly suitable research method for the Box Hill Nursery Project. Milroy (1980) suggests that the network concept is a principle capable of universal application and hence less ethnocentric than other descriptions of social groupings such as class or caste. This reinforces it as a research method that is particularly suitable for describing the social behaviour of a group or community when the researcher is not a member of that community. It also makes it appropriate for the study of clearly definable communities, like the major linguistic and ethnic minority ones now established and permanently settled in Britain. A fundamental postulate of network analysis is that individuals create personal communities which provide them with a meaningful framework for solving the problems of their day-to-day existence (Mitchell, 1989: 74). This focus makes social network analysis useful for observing the enculturation process as experienced by individuals in new social settings.

Established researchers indicate their approval of social network analysis. Although it was not the research method used by Le Page and Tabouret-Keller in their description of Creole-based languages and ethnicity, in retrospect they state: 'Had we been familiar with the concept of networks when we planned our survey, we might well have used [social network analysis] ourselves' (Le Page & Tabouret-Keller, 1985: 116).

From the numerous studies to use social network analysis as a research method to date, two types of network ties have been identified. Boissevain (1974) describes and exemplifies procedures used to analyse personal networks in terms of *dense* or *multiplex ties*. These correspond approximately to the *first order zones* and *second order zones* described by Barnes (1954). These dense or first order zone ties are those which individuals make through direct, personal contact. By comparison with dense, first order zones, the multiplex, second order zones are more loosely formed. They typically involve larger numbers of individuals; they include fewer personal contacts, and are usually made for a variety of functional purposes, for example, negotiating transactions and getting things done.

Social network analysis is also an established methodology in socio-linguistics. A number of studies have adopted it. Apart from the early studies by Gumperz (1976), Milroy's (1980) Belfast study is perhaps the most widely known. Agnihotri's (1979) sociolinguistic study of Sikh children in Leeds is a rare example of the method being used to describe young children's networks. Hence it can be seen that social network analysis is an established methodological paradigm in sociolinguistic and anthropological studies. It is regarded as an acceptable alternative to the social or economic groupings used by other researchers including Labov (1981) and Bernstein (1971).

There are a number of ways already established for quantifying social network ties. Milroy (1980: Chapter 1) outlines a six-point scale, indexed from nought to five, in which each individual is assigned a score at some point on the scale. The scale is constructed with reference to key indicators of relative multiplexity and density. This is a method that has also been used by Li Wei (1994). Using this index, individuals are assigned a numerical score, called a 'network score'. In comparison to Milroy's approach, Gal (1979) uses a much more straightforward measure based on the actual number of contacts a speaker makes within a given observation period. Her approach is endorsed by Gumperz (1976: 14) who points out that personal network structure is influenced by a very large number of factors and that it is very unlikely that any investigation will be able to identify all of these, let alone measure them. His view suggests that the numerical approach favoured by Milroy (1980) can only be partial. The analytical approach adopted for this study, therefore, is closer to the less complex numerical approaches favoured by Gal (1979) and Gumperz (1976).

Previous studies have established a number of ways for presenting an individual's social networks. Two examples of these diagrammatic representations are presented. Figure 7.1 shows the approach favoured by

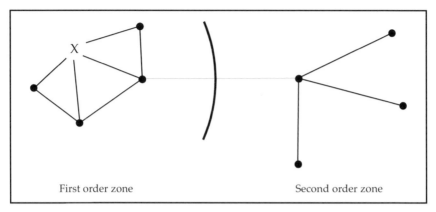

First order zone   Second order zone

Figure 7.1   High-density personal network structure, showing first and second order zones with X as the focal point of the network (Milroy, 1980: 48)

Milroy for demonstrating high-density personal network structures with first and second order zones, while Figure 7.2 shows a different approach, used again by Milroy, for illustrating an individual's social network ties. Figure 7.2 is a portion of the data (a Clonard network) from Milroy's Belfast study (Milroy, 1980).

The Box Hill Nursery data have been collected with a focus on individual behaviour. Social network analysis has been selected in preference to other available methods (cf. Kenny & La Voie, 1984, as reported in Dunn, 1993: 8), because it makes the individual, rather than the group, the focus of the observations. It should be stated, however, that this method, although established as a research paradigm within a number of disciplines, is not without its limitations and constraints. Neither quantification of the number of interpersonal contacts, nor qualification of the stability of these ties, can fully explain the nature of the contacts or their durability. There are other factors inherent in these links that are less accessible to the observer. Social network analysis cannot, for example, demonstrate the relative status of the contacts, nor the extent to which this may contribute to the fragility or durability of the tie. Nor can it quantify the power relationship that exists between contacts and any subsequent inequality that this may introduce. But these shortcomings aside, social network analysis does provide a more detailed description of the social context of the nursery, and the human relationships that are formed therein, than the time-on-task analysis can do.

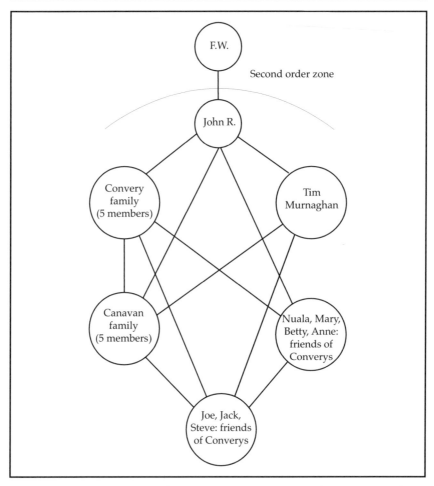

Figure 7.2   A social network analysis from Milroy's Belfast study (Milroy, 1980: 58). Reproduced by permission of Blackwell Publishers Ltd.

Analysis of the Social Networks in Box Hill Nursery

This third level of analysis continues towards a micro-level analysis with a description of the contacts or ties formed by the children during their first days in nursery school and the ways in which these ties become established during the first term. The aim is to describe, in greater detail, the characteristic features of the formal and informal situations in the learning domains where individual informants spend a sustained period of time-on-task (as presented in Chapters 5 and 6), with a view to under-standing their observed behaviour more fully. This level of description will enhance the previous analyses of time-on-task which suggest that the inherent cognitive complexity of learning activities cannot alone account for some children spending sustained periods of time engaged in these tasks. It will be suggested that there is a social dimension to the time-on-task phenomena. Further, it will be suggested that certain individuals act as what will be termed an *attraction factor* for some children. The presence of specific individuals at a particular learning activity will attract learners to that activity and their continued presence will account, in part, for a period of sustained engagement on the task. Analysis will demonstrate that the presence of specific individuals acts as an attraction, thus ensuring sustained engagement in selected learning activities for some of the children. It will be argued that this represents a social dimension to sustained time-on-task activities. The presence of an attraction factor can in part account for the sustained periods of time spent on selected tasks as presented in the time-on-task data analysis (Chapter 5).

Analysis of the data has been carried out in the tradition of grounded theory (Glaser & Strauss, 1967). Recurring patterns of behaviour, or 'codes', have been identified from close scrutiny of the data from two of the children, a girl (Shamaila) and a boy (Ishtiaq). These codes have been used as the analytical framework for the data from all eight informants. Case studies of these two informants will be presented to exemplify the patterns of observed behaviour. Analysis focuses on two aspects:

- The individuals who are in close proximity to the child being ob-served, i.e. those people (adults and children) who are nearby and available for interaction. These are termed *potential participants*.

- Those individuals with whom interaction(s) are observed and re-corded. These individuals have been selected from the group of po-tential participants for interaction. They are therefore regarded as *preferred participants*.

Previous studies have established conventions for demonstrating social network ties. These have been illustrated in Figures 7.1 and 7.2. For this study, an alternative method of diagrammatic representation has been devised in an attempt to illustrate more clearly the membership of the types of networks identified. By presenting the data in this new way it is also possible to illustrate the (small) degree of individual movement between the networks. This movement helps to show the ways in which new contacts are made and how they are developed in the new social situation of the nursery classroom. The diagrammatic representation devised also makes it easier to demonstrate the place of the developing networks described in the nursery setting, within the hierarchy of Bronfenbrenner's ecological framework. This will be presented in detail in Chapter 10.

For two of the eight informants included in this study, Ishtiaq and Shamaila, social networks will be presented for each of the activities in which they were observed during their first day in school. A comparative set of data will be presented for the informants at the end of their first term in the nursery. This will add a further level of analysis to those previously presented and discussed in Chapters 5 and 6.

Ishtiaq's social networks

Analysis begins with a description of Ishtiaq's social networks. Figure 7.3 shows a diagrammatic representation of Ishtiaq's first encounters in the nursery school.

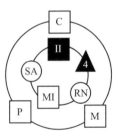

Figure 7.3   A social network analysis for Ishtiaq's first activity in Box Hill Nursery

For each activity two social networks are shown. The inner circle corresponds to Boissevain's (1974) multiples ties and Barnes' (1954) first order zones. The informant being observed, Ishtiaq himself, is represented at the centre of this network by the symbol ■. The outer circle corresponds to what Boissevain (1974) calls multiplex ties and Barnes (1954) calls second order zones.

The inner circle will be termed the *dense network* and the outer circle the *loose network*. The loose network represents individuals, pupils and teachers, who are present in or near a particular learning domain and who by their presence and proximity are available for interaction. These represent a group of potential participants, defined as those individuals who are present and potentially available to participate in activities and/or interactions. They are available both to initiate interactions with Ishtiaq and/or to respond to his.

In the social network diagrams, girl participants are represented by the symbol ○ and boys by □. Individual children are identified by their initials, for example Ishtiaq is II. Teachers (and other adults) are represented by triangular symbols △ numbered 1 to 7. Bilingual teachers are shown as ▲. Not all are necessarily present in the nursery on each day of observation. Figure 7.4 presents the social network analysis for Ishtiaq's encounters during his second learning activity.

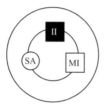

Figure 7.4 A social network analysis for Ishtiaq's second activity in Box Hill Nursery

The inner circle represents the dense network of participants with whom verbal interaction(s) are recorded on the audio-tapes and/or non-verbal interactions recorded on the observation schedule. These individuals (⒮, Ⓜ) are drawn into the dense network from the loose network of potential participants either because they initiate verbal or non-verbal interaction with Ishtiaq or because he initiates (or attempts to initiate) interaction with them. To be included in this dense network, therefore, individuals have to interact verbally or non-verbally with the informant.

This level of data analysis enhances the previous analysis of discourse presented in Chapter 6 by identifying specific individuals, including both teachers and fellow pupils with whom interaction takes place. Chapter 5 provided a comprehensive overview of one hour in the nursery: this analysis focuses more specifically on the micro-level activities within individual learning domains.

Figure 7.5 presents the analyses for each of the learning activities in which Ishtiaq is engaged during his first hour in the nursery. Analysis illustrates the emergence of two types of social network: the loose, outer *pupil network*, and the dense, inner *friendship network*.

Loose pupil networks

These loose networks, *pupil networks*, are those in which pupils come together for specific group activities which are often teacher-led. Examples of pupil networks include occasions when all of the children in the nursery come together in a joint activity. Story-time and singing activities are just two examples. However, pupil networks are not always large groupings. The painting activity with Teacher 1 (Figure 7.5, Activity 5) and playing in the pretend kitchen (Figure 7.5, Activity 1) are just two examples of smaller groupings of pupil networks. All the teachers feature as key participants in the networks of the children. However, they have not been included in the dense networks, because child–teacher interactions differ in a number of ways from child–child ones. It can be seen from the data from all informants that the teachers play a significant role in maintaining interest in a learning activity. (Detailed analysis of the language within the social networks will be the focus of Chapter 8 and 9.)

In the pupil network individuals participate in a common learning activity, for example painting, making a calendar, listening to a story. They participate as pupils. Characteristic features of the pupil network include the nature of the recorded interactions. These usually reflect their participation in the learning activity in their role as pupils. Interactions are made for functional rather than for social purposes. The following extracts of interaction between members of a pupil network illustrate this functional interaction:

Shamaila   tidy up

Kamran   brown, move your hand

The topic of their exchanges relates to their participation in the learning activity as pupils. They talk about the activity in which they are engaged. They interact for the purpose of getting things done.

These interactions are interesting in their own right as evidence of interaction between children within the pupil network. However, they are also of further significance: they are evidence of the individual's developing communicative competence. They demonstrate the ways in which the children are learning to behave appropriately as pupils. But these initial

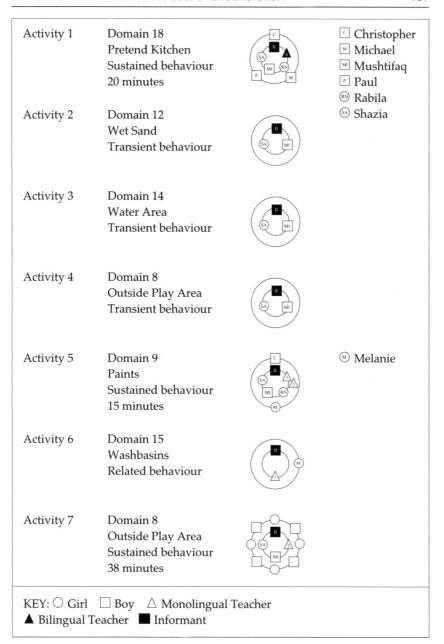

KEY: ○ Girl   □ Boy   △ Monolingual Teacher
▲ Bilingual Teacher   ■ Informant

Figure 7.5   A social network analysis for Ishtiaq's first hour in Box Hill Nursery

contacts are important for other reasons: they are significant because they frequently form the basis of more enduring contacts between individuals. For example, Ishtiaq's friendship ties with Mushtifaq and Shazia are begun in the very first hour in the nursery. Initial ties were formed through participation as pupils in a teacher-directed learning activity (Figure 7.5 Activity 1) in the pretend kitchen (Domain 18). During the first hour in the nursery, it can be seen from Figure 7.5 that these contacts are maintained as the three children, Ishtiaq, Mushtifaq and Shazia, move from one activity to another together in a small group. In this way it can be seen that children come into initial contact as pupils, and these initial contacts with selected individuals become consolidated into friendship ties over a period of time (that is, during the first term in the nursery).

The focus of the pupil network groupings is frequently a teaching function. It can be seen that these groupings are strongly teacher-influenced. On arrival in the nursery the first encounter for most of the pupils is with a teacher, as the following extracts from the transcripts demonstrate (MT: monolingual teacher, BT: bilingual teacher).

MT5   what a pretty coat

BT7   come and leave it here, is that all right like that

MT3   Shamaila, hang your coat up please,

             you put this one on …

From these initial greetings, the children are initiated into the routines of the nursery with the person who brings them to school. They are shown where to hang their coats, how to register and collect their name cards from a board, as well as a number of other activities that they are expected to perform on their arrival in the nursery each day. Sometimes engagement in these activities leads to encounters with other pupils or teachers. Teachers are alert to the arrival of newcomers and are constantly on the look-out for ways of involving them in ongoing activities. Teachers will also deliberately select individuals for inclusion in a particular activity, as in the following extracts:

BT4   sit down here, Natalie, you sit down here

MT1   *[to Rabila]* come on let's go for a walk

MT3   come on you play as well, come on Kamran, all play together

There is a second type of grouping observed, a dense network.

Dense friendship networks

Children's membership of these dense networks, *friendship networks*, is defined in terms of three factors:

(1) the number of interactions recorded between individuals;

(2) the initiator of the interaction; and

(3) the topic of the exchange.

In Figure 7.5 it is possible to observe an emerging pattern of selected individuals who move from the loose pupil network into the dense inner network to become preferred participants. Attention is drawn to Activities 1, 5 and 7, all of which are periods of sustained time-on-task . During these activities the recurring presence of two participants, a boy (Mushtifaq [MI]) and a girl (Shazia ⊗), is observed. These two preferred participants have emerged from the loose, pupil network to enter Ishtiaq's dense network of close ties. Preferred participants can be described as those individuals with whom interactions (as previously defined) are sought and maintained. This dense network of close ties, the friendship network, thus differs from the pupil network where the children come together (or more accurately are brought together by a teacher) for the purpose of a particular learning and/or teaching activity.

Figure 7.6 shows the social network analysis for Ishtiaq at the end of his first term. The recurring presence of the same two participants, Mushtifaq and Shazia, confirms their position in Ishtiaq's dense friendship network. They have moved from the loose pupil network to the dense network of close ties. They have become friends. The friendship network comprises close ties with only a small number of preferred participants. These are the individuals with whom interaction is preferred and even sought. The movement from the pupil network to the friendship network occurs over the first term in the nursery. However, it can be seen from the data that the origins of the dense friendship network can actually be traced back to the very first hour in the nursery, when the teacher brings these children together in a group as pupils on a joint learning activity.

Not all contacts progress from the loose pupil network to the dense friendship network. It can therefore be inferred that a selection process is operating. Individuals select preferred participants from the loose pupil network for inclusion in their dense friendship network. This pattern of an emerging dense friendship network, comprising selected individuals from the loose pupil network, can be observed across the data from all eight informants. The significance of this selection, the choices the children

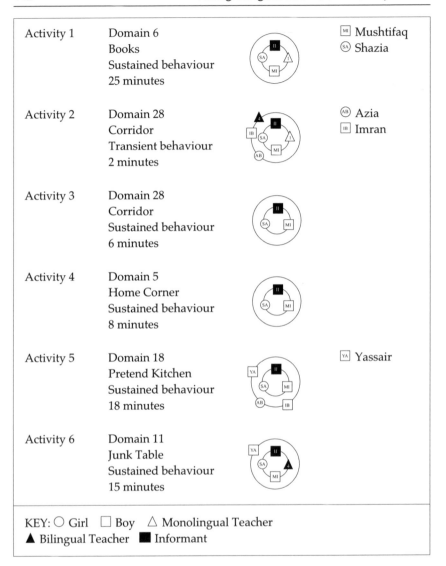

Activity 1	Domain 6 Books Sustained behaviour 25 minutes		▣ Mushtifaq Ⓢ Shazia
Activity 2	Domain 28 Corridor Transient behaviour 2 minutes		ⒶⒷ Azia ▣ Imran
Activity 3	Domain 28 Corridor Sustained behaviour 6 minutes		
Activity 4	Domain 5 Home Corner Sustained behaviour 8 minutes		
Activity 5	Domain 18 Pretend Kitchen Sustained behaviour 18 minutes		▣ Yassair
Activity 6	Domain 11 Junk Table Sustained behaviour 15 minutes		

KEY: ○ Girl   □ Boy   △ Monolingual Teacher
▲ Bilingual Teacher   ■ Informant

Figure 7.6   A social network analysis for Ishtiaq at the end of his first term in Box Hill Nursery

make, will become apparent when an overview of the data from all eight is presented in Table 7.1, a table of preferred participants.

Shamaila's social networks

Figure 7.7 presents a social network analysis of those present during the activities in which Shamaila was engaged during her first hour in school. Patterns observed in her social networks confirm the emergence of two types: the pupil network, and the friendship network.

Closer examination of the individuals in the friendship network reveals the recurring presence of specific individuals, Sabia ⓩ and Sofees ⓢ. This friendship network comprises boy and girl peers as well as teachers. The presence of the adults and peers can be explained in different ways. Upon arrival at school Shamaila encounters a group of three children, all boys, Geoffrey Ⓖ, Michael Ⓜ and Sofees ⓢ, and also a monolingual teacher △. The teacher is the only one with whom interaction occurs and, not surprisingly, the interaction is teacher-initiated. English is the language of the interaction:

MT3   Hello Shamaila, hang your coat up please,

you put this one on,

you go and play.

At this point, I should like to focus on the peers present in the friendship networks. Sofees ⓢ and Shamaila Ⓢ move to the dry sand domain together to work with another monolingual teacher △ on a structured play activity which lasts for seven minutes. When they have completed this task they leave together. In the corridor (Activity 3) Shamaila meets Sabia ⓩ. Here again we see an initial contact begun within the loose pupil network. However, it soon progresses and becomes established as a dense friendship network tie.

From Day 1, these two children, Sofees and Sabia, are frequently found in Shamaila's dense network. This emerging network begins within the first hour at school and is consolidated over the first term. This is presented in Figures 7.8a and 7.8b, the social network analyses for Day 2 activities at the end of the first term in school. A similar pattern can be observed for all of the other informants in the study.

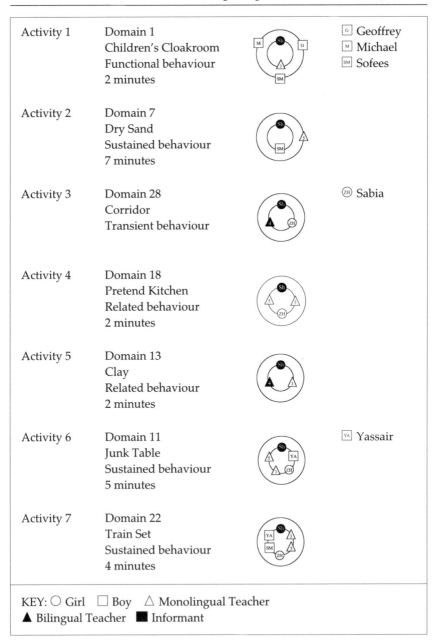

Figure 7.7a A social network analysis for Shamaila's first hour in Box Hill Nursery (Part 1)

Activity 8	Domain 15 Washbasins Related behaviour 2 minutes	⊡ Michael
Activity 9	Domain 24 Drawing Table Sustained behaviour 9 minutes	ⓒ Clare ⓖ Gemma ⓐ Amy ⓢ Susan
Activity 10	Domain 7 Dry Sand Sustained behaviour 4 minutes	ⓏⱧ Sabia
Activity 11	Domain 1 Children's Cloakroom Related behaviour	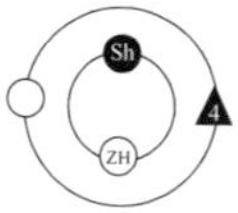
Activity 12	Domain 15 Washbasins Related behaviour	⊡ Yassair
Activity 13	Domain 14 Water Area Sustained behaviour 4 minutes	

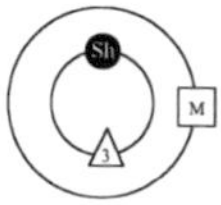

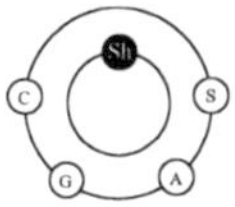

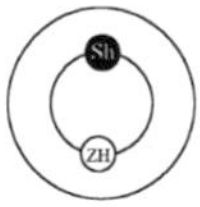

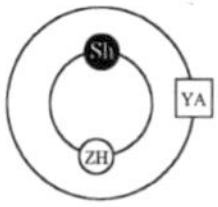

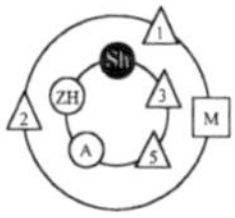

KEY: ○ Girl □ Boy △ Monolingual Teacher
▲ Bilingual Teacher ■ Informant

Figure 7.7b A social network analysis for Shamaila's first hour in Box Hill Nursery (Part 2)

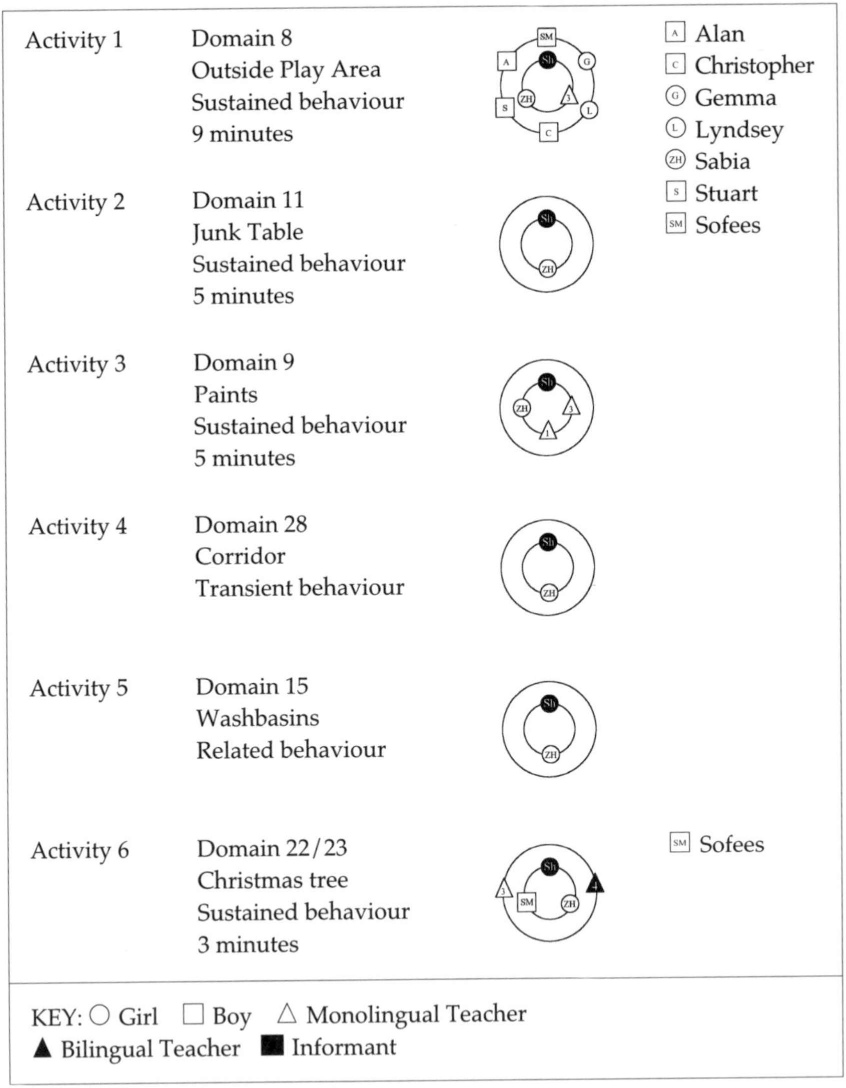

Activity 1	Domain 8 Outside Play Area Sustained behaviour 9 minutes		Ⓐ Alan Ⓒ Christopher Ⓖ Gemma Ⓛ Lyndsey Ⓩ Sabia
Activity 2	Domain 11 Junk Table Sustained behaviour 5 minutes		Ⓢ Stuart ⓈⓂ Sofees
Activity 3	Domain 9 Paints Sustained behaviour 5 minutes		
Activity 4	Domain 28 Corridor Transient behaviour		
Activity 5	Domain 15 Washbasins Related behaviour		
Activity 6	Domain 22/23 Christmas tree Sustained behaviour 3 minutes		ⓈⓂ Sofees

KEY: ◯ Girl   ▢ Boy   △ Monolingual Teacher
▲ Bilingual Teacher   ■ Informant

Figure 7.8a   A social network analysis for Shamaila at the end of her first term in Box Hill Nursery (Part 1)

One of the stated aims of the Box Hill Nursery study is to observe and record the process of enculturation which the pupils experience as they begin formal education in the nursery as a linguistic minority group. Enculturation has been described as:

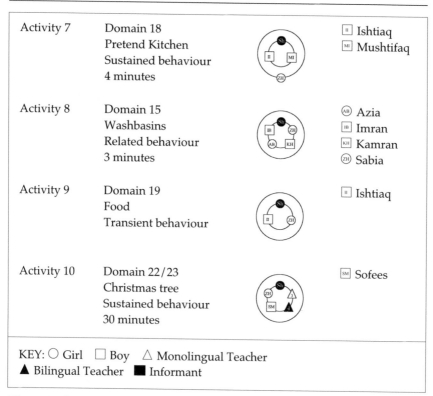

Activity 7   Domain 18   [II] Ishtiaq
     Pretend Kitchen   [MI] Mushtifaq
     Sustained behaviour
     4 minutes

Activity 8   Domain 15   (AB) Azia
     Washbasins   [IB] Imran
     Related behaviour   [KH] Kamran
     3 minutes   (ZH) Sabia

Activity 9   Domain 19   [II] Ishtiaq
     Food
     Transient behaviour

Activity 10   Domain 22/23   [SM] Sofees
     Christmas tree
     Sustained behaviour
     30 minutes

KEY: ○ Girl   □ Boy   △ Monolingual Teacher
▲ Bilingual Teacher   ■ Informant

Figure 7.8b   A social network analysis for Shamaila at the end of her first term in Box Hill Nursery (Part 2)

learning one's place within the group, learning one's rights and responsibilities; it is the process of learning the whole complex of meanings that defines the social reality of the group and the rules which allow a newcomer to function. (Lubeck, 1985: 13)

The concept of social network analysis is important for the Box Hill Nursery study in two ways. The method provides, firstly, data on each individual's pattern of friendship and other ties, and secondly, an analysis of the social context in which these interactions are taking place. From these data it is possible to identify the pattern of preferred participants within individual emerging networks. Table 7.1 presents an overview of the emerging friendship networks for each of the eight informants.

Table 7.1   A table of pupils' emerging friendship networks

Informant	Girls in dense network	Boys in dense network	Preferred participants
Imran (IB)	Azia (AB) Shamaila (Sh)	Kamran (KH) Yassair (YA)	Azia (AB) Kamran (KH) Yassair (YA)
Ishtiaq (II) Kamran (KH)	Shazia (S)	Mushtifaq (MI) Imran (IB)	Mushtifaq (MI) Imran (IB)
Rabila (RN)	Sabia (ZH)		Sabia (ZH)
Sabia (ZH)	Sumera (SK)	Sofees (SM) Sufyaan (SA)	Sumera (SK)
Shamaila (Sh)	Sabia (ZH)	Sofees (SM) Sufyaan (SA)	Sabia (ZH) Sofees (SM)
Shazad (SH)	Sumera (SK) Rabila (RN)	Kamran (KH) Yassair (YA)	Rabila (RN) Yassair (YA)
Sofees (SM)	Shamaila (Sh)	Yassair (YA)	Shamaila (Sh) Yassair (YA)

There are a number of observations to be made about the composition of these networks. Two types of social network have been identified: the children's dense self-selected ties, and the loose, teacher-influenced groupings. The dense network of preferred participants, the friendship network, comprises, firstly, a very select number of preferred participants, usually only one or two individuals. Imran (IB) is the only informant to select three preferred participants for his friendship network. Secondly, the friendship network comprises both boy and girl ties except where there is only one preferred participant, when the selection of same-sex preferred participants applies. This is the case for both the boys and the girls in the study. For example, Mushtifaq (MI) is the preferred participant in Ishtiaq's (II) friendship network; Imran (IB) in Kamran's (KH); Sabia (ZH) in Rabila's (RN); and Sumera (SK) in Sabia's (ZH). So it can be seen that when the friendship network comprises only one participant, then that individual is always of the same sex. However, when the friendship networks comprise two (or less usually, three) members, then the same-sex option is different. These larger friendship networks are mixed, including both boys and girls as preferred participants. This is the case for three of the informants: Imran (IB) selects Azia (AB), Kamran (KH) and Yassair (YA) for his friendship ties; Shamaila (Sh) selects Sofees (SM) and Sabia (ZH); Sofees (SM) selects Shamaila (Sh) and Yassair (YA).

Inclusion in a friendship network is not automatically a reciprocal arrangement between children. For example, Rabila (RN) is a member of Shazad's (SH) friendship network while Shazad (SH) only features in Rabila's (RN) loose, outer pupil networks. This could be accounted for by suggesting that the friendship bond is asymmetrical, stronger on one side than the other. The differences in the roles played by these girls in each other's network system are, in part, determined by the nature and topic of the exchanges that take place between them. Shazad and Rabila assume different participant roles in each other's networks. However, it should be noted that Rabila is not Shazad's only preferred participant. There is another member of Shazad's friendship network with whom she has formed a stronger bond, a boy, Yassair (YA).

There are examples from the data of reciprocal inclusion in friendship networks. For example, Imran (IB) features in Kamran's (KH) friendship network as the only preferred participant and Kamran (KH) features as one of the three preferred participants in Imran's (IB) friendship network. There is no example of two children selecting only each other as sole preferred participants. Further, this group of observed children does make contacts with other children who are not in the sample group. However, one striking pattern can be observed across the data sets from each of the informants, namely that the preferred participants who form the dense ties of the friendship networks are exclusively same ethnic group peers. This is the chief significance of the individuals who form the friendship networks: they are predominantly members of the same ethnic group of Mirpuri-Panjabi speakers. They carry a number of emblems of their ethnicity: their style of dress (shalwar-kameez, for the girls), jewellery (nose-pins, earrings and glass bangles), and hairstyle. As Mirpuri-Panjabi speakers they also share a linguistic repertoire which includes both Mirpuri-Panjabi and English, to varying degrees of competence. These markers of ethnicity have been identified by Le Page and Tabouret-Keller (1985) as significant in helping groups and individuals to identify themselves and each other as same-group members. They suggest (1985: 209) the following criteria for an individual's self-allocation to an ethnic group:

- Physical features

- Provenance

- Language

- Family descent or race

- Nationality

- Culture

- Traditions

- Religion

It is suggested, therefore, that these markers of ethnic identity may also act as attraction factors for the newly arrived pupils at the nursery and serve to help them identify each other within the new social setting. It may be that they actively seek to establish contact with those whom they perceive as similar to themselves. This is a recurrent pattern of behaviour across all the children in the study.

Based on these observations from the Box Hill Nursery Project, it is suggested that there is mutual recognition of at least some of the characteristic features of ethnic identity (as described by Le Page & Tabouret-Keller, 1985) in children as young as three years. This concurs with the findings of Milner (1984) who suggests that children at the ages of three and four years can identify members of their own ethnic group, distinguishing them from other groups. It is clear that the informants in the study are making choices. The children are making friends and forming friendship networks based on a selection from a wider group of children. The emerging pattern of preferred participants in the friendship networks suggests that these choices are not random. Deliberate choices are being made. Specific individuals are identified for contact. Once identified, these selected individuals may become the preferred participants for joint activities. As the term progresses these contacts become consolidated as friendship ties.

It is further suggested that these preferred participants, whose company is sought and with whom interaction is frequently observed, correspond to Halliday's (1973) coterie of significant others; that is, a small group with whom language and appropriate social behaviour is learned. The selection of this group of preferred participants begins from the very first hours in school and is consolidated over time. However, the extent to which individual children are aware of their choices, or are conscious of making them, remains unknown.

From the data it can be seen that clear friendship networks emerge and that while these are different for each child, they share common features. It is suggested that these dense networks of preferred participants, the friendship networks, have an influential role to play in the developing communicative competence of newcomers to the nursery. It should also be noted that members of the friendship network are always present with the informant during periods of sustained time-on-task. It can be said, therefore, that the presence of some individuals acts as an attraction factor in sustaining interest in particular activities. It is also proposed that there is a social dimension to classroom activities that can (in part) account for some children spending sustained periods of time on selected learning activities.

Characteristic Features of Friendship Networks

A number of key characteristic features emerge from the analyses of the dense friendship networks at Box Hill Nursery.

(1) The friendship network is based on same ethnic groupings. All are Mirpuri-Panjabi speakers of ethnic Pakistani background. They carry the physical emblems of their ethnic background as previously described, as well as intrinsic features such as skin and eye colour. These features, identified by Le Page and Tabouret-Keller (1985) as distinguishing markers of ethnic identity, have a dual function: firstly, they help individuals to recognise each other; secondly, they confirm and reinforce group boundaries. The findings presented here suggest that the children in this study recognise these features of their own ethnicity. Furthermore, it is suggested that they form friendship ties on the basis of Le Page's (1978/80) distinction of 'same as each other' rather than 'different from each other' criteria. The children select their friends from those who are like themselves rather than from those who are different.

(2) The friendship networks comprise only a small number of potential others. Kamran, Rabila and Sabia each have only one participant in their friendship network. Shamaila, Shazad, Ishtiaq and Sofees each have two, and only one informant, Imran, has three.

(3) When the friendship network comprises only one preferred participant, this is termed the *key participant*. Only three children, Kamran, Rabila and Sabia have just one key participant. Key participants are always of the same sex. For example, Kamran's key participant is Imran; Rabila's key participant is Sabia; and Sabia's key participant is Sumera.

(4) When the friendship grouping comprises two or more individuals, then both girls and boys are to be found in the network. This suggests that the exclusive same-sex friendship groupings reported by other studies (Roffey *et al.*, 1994) perhaps represent learned behaviour that occurs as children get older. It may also suggest that the social structures of school and the wider community influence the individual's

behaviour. This is a point that will be explored in more detail in Chapter 10 in a discussion of Bronfenbrenner's (1977, 1979) ecological systems theory.

(5) Children spend longer, more sustained periods of time-on-task, engaged in learning activities, when they are working with members of their friendship network.

(6) The language of interactions within the friendship network is predominantly (but not exclusively) Mirpuri-Panjabi, the language spoken by the children in their homes. It is also one of the community languages spoken in the Cleveland region.

(7) Teachers (and other adults) play an instrumental role in making initial introductions between children. These are usually made on the basis of groupings for teaching purposes when the children come together as pupils on a learning task. Once these contacts have become established, teachers continue to play an important role in allowing emerging ties to flourish. They do this by providing structured opportunities for the consolidation of these ties and the initiation of others.

(8) Friendship networks are not necessarily mutual or reciprocal. For example, Shamaila is a key member of Rabila's friendship network, but Rabila only features in Shamaila's loose pupil network. Friendship bonds can therefore be asymmetrical, stronger on one side than the other. The participant roles assumed in each other's network is determined by the nature and purpose of the exchanges that take place between individuals. Language use within the networks plays an important role in the consolidation and reinforcement of network ties. It is a feature that will be discussed in further detail in Chapters 8 and 9.

(9) There is no observed situation where two individuals select only each other as preferred participants. For example, Imran and Kamran both feature in each other's network but not as the sole participant. Imran features as the sole participant in Kamran's network, but Kamran is only one of three participants in Imran's friendship network. This observation concurs with those of Roffey *et al.* (1994: 2) who suggest that true reciprocity is not a usual feature of pre-schooler friendships.

(10) The findings presented here support Dunn's (1993: 117) suggestion that children's relationships are dynamic. It has been seen that the friendship networks emerge and become consolidated during the children's first term in school. Further studies are required to determine in detail the rate and extent of change in these networks as the children

get older and their experiences of school and other social situations broaden. Dunn (1993: 117) further suggests that the development of social understanding can be influenced by the quality of close relationships, but determining the extent to which this could be achieved through introductions with other children from outside the ethnic group, and the role that adults and teachers could play in encouraging such inter-ethnic groupings, would also require further studies.

In summary it can be said that the children in Box Hill Nursery make friends through the formation of dense friendship networks, and that teachers influence pupils through the composition of the loose pupil networks. However in retrospect it is also important to reflect on the chosen research method and the possible influence of this on the data gathered. In their analysis of ethnicity and friendship patterns among older schoolchildren, those aged between seven and 11 years, Denscombe *et al.* (1993) note the contrast in findings yielded from two different methodological approaches: sociometric tests using the Cresswell Index, and ethnographic observations. They note:

> While there is no inherent contradiction between ethnographic research and the quantification of data, there are complexities vital to our understanding of inter-ethnic friendship patterns which exclusive reliance on quantitative research methods cannot hope to unravel. (Denscombe *et al.*, 1993: 142)

Contextualising Social Network Analysis

It is important to establish that, while individual personal networks can be described in detail, they can only be fully understood when contextualised within a broader social framework. Bronfenbrenner (1979: 226–230) suggests that the patterns of social interchange carry an inherent value system that is embedded in an ecological paradigm. He suggests that social contexts and their inherent value systems can influence individuals and the learning that takes place within these contexts. This is an idea that will be explored more fully in Chapter 10.

There is support from social psychologists (Vygotsky, 1962; Bruner & Haste, 1987) to suggest that children learn through social interaction with others. This is a view supported by systemic linguists (for example Halliday, 1973) who suggest that language plays an instrumental role in this process:

The closest of the child's relationships, that with the mother, is partly, and in time, largely mediated through language ... interaction with other people, adults and children, is very obviously maintained linguistically. (Halliday, 1973: 13)

The central role played by language in the creation of social contexts has already been discussed in detail in Chapters 4 and 7. In addition, there is clear support (Halliday, 1973) for the view that language is central to developing relationships:

Language in the maintenance of permanent relationships, the neighbourhood and the activities of the peer group, provide the context for complex and rapidly changing interactional patterns which make extensive and subtle demands on the individual's linguistic resources. Language is used to define and consolidate the group, to include and to exclude, showing who is 'one of us', and who is not. (Halliday, 1973: 13)

Dunn's (1993: 117) findings suggest that children's relationships are dynamic and that the development of social understanding can be influenced by the quality of these relationships. The findings from the Box Hill Nursery Project support the notion of social networks as dynamic. Analysis demonstrates the ways in which individuals identify each other during their first day in the nursery and how these initial contacts are developed during the first term to become consolidated social networks. Further studies are needed to ascertain the durability of these networks, to investigate how they change, and to offer possible reasons for this evolution.

Summary

Analysis of the data presented in this chapter suggests the emergence of two types of social network within the nursery setting: loose pupil networks, and dense friendship networks. The former are characterised by the presence of teachers, who can be seen to play an influential role in the composition of the cluster and on the activities and behaviour of individuals that take place within the groupings. As the term progresses, key individuals emerge from the pupil network and move to form dense friendship networks. The friendship networks are characterised by the dominance of same ethnic group peers. Membership of these emerging pupil and friendship networks is seen to be a significant influence in accounting for the time an individual child spends engaged in a particular learning activity.

A number of attraction factors (as described by Le Page & Tabouret-Keller, 1985) have been identified. These help to illuminate further understanding of the time-on-task phenomena and to clarify why some children spend more sustained periods of time on selected tasks. Two suggestions are offered: firstly, that the cognitive complexity of the learning activity is not the only reason for a child to spend a sustained period of time-on-task; and secondly, that there is a social dimension to learning activities and the time spent on tasks. This social dimension is offered as a factor to explain why some individuals are observed in sustained periods of time-on-task that differ markedly from those of previous studies (Sylva *et al.*, 1980; Bennett, 1976). This is a view supported by Clark (1988) who suggests that the pairings of the bilingual children in Tough's (1977) study of language assessment influenced their language performance. The grouping or organisation of children for classroom teaching and assessment activities is therefore highly significant for teachers. Clark (1988) suggests that some pairing and groupings may lead some pupils to underperform. Educational underachievement is a recurring theme in the discussions of the academic performance of ethnic minority pupils (Swann Report, DES, 1985; Troyna, 1991).

In summary, the membership of emerging pupil and friendship networks can be seen as significant in accounting for bilingual children's social and linguistic behaviour in the nursery setting. The establishment and consolidation of social networks is also an important influence on bilingual children's enculturation into mainstream education. Social network analysis offers insights which illuminate these processes. As Roffey *et al.* (1994: 21) state, 'an important part of developing a sense of self is identifying with the groups to which we feel we belong'. Heller (1988: 180) makes a similar claim, that 'the basis of ethnicity can be found in the social networks within which an individual forms relationships and carries out activities', while Milroy and Li Wei (1991: 235) suggest that 'network analysis offers a basis for understanding the mechanisms that underlie this process of language maintenance, and the converse, language shift'.

Language use within the social networks is the focus for the fourth and fifth levels of descriptive analysis presented in Chapters 8 and 9.

Chapter 8

The Children's Language Choice: English Utterances

You have to learn it all over again,
The words, the sounds, almost the whole language
Because this is a time when words must be strict and new
Not concerning you,
Or only indirectly,
Concerning a pain
Learnt as most people some time or other learn it
With shock, then dark

(Elizabeth Jennings, *Let Things Happen*, 1972)

Introduction to Level 4 of the Data Analysis

This chapter and Chapter 9 should be considered together. They represent the final levels of data analysis. The focus of these analyses is the informants' preferred language use or language choice. Using Hymes' (1972b) taxonomy as a guide, discourse data from the corpus will be presented to demonstrate the ways in which individuals are learning to be communicatively competent in their new social setting of the nursery. The focus of the analysis is the individual's choice of language for their interactions. Analysis addresses:

- when individuals chose to speak;

- preferred interlocutors; and

- preferred language for the interaction(s).

The audio-tape recordings of the naturally occurring discourse provide the data. By focusing on aspects of the situation, the interlocutors and the topic of the interaction, explanations will be sought for the individual informant's particular choice of language, English or Mirpuri-Panjabi. This chapter will focus on the use of English for selected utterances, and begins with a description of the processes involved in the transcription of the audio-taped data, a discussion of the methodological considerations and a description of the key and codes included in the transcripts. Chapter 9 will describe specific features of the utterances where the two language systems are combined for interactions.

Transcribing the Discourse Data

There are a number of established conventions for transcribing audio-taped recordings. Some of these are discussed critically in Edwards and Westgate (1987: Chapter 3), who emphasise the inevitable relationship between the purpose of the analysis and the choice of codes and the procedure for analysis. Edwards and Westgate (1987: 56) state that 'there are many possible ways to transcribe language data ranging from the minimally helpful to the complicatedly tedious'. Discourse data for the Box Hill Nursery Project were gathered using candid audio-tape recorders. Pre-coded schedules were not used for the analyses. In the tradition of 'grounded theory' (Glaser & Strauss, 1967) retrospective analysis was favoured.

The transformation of the audio-tapes into a form that allows for analysis and comparisons across the informants began with the production of verbatim transcripts. These were compiled using the standard orthographic alphabet. In an attempt to avoid the imposition of idealised sentence structures, features of written language including punctuation and capitalisation have been avoided and used only to facilitate the reading of the transcripts. Some critics of ethnographic studies (Milroy, 1987; Stubbs, 1983) claim that the transformation of data in this way actually distorts the data by imposing meaning. An alternative view, however, is that the inclusion of basic punctuation and other conventions more usually associated with written forms of language facilitates reading, making the data more accessible and hence available to a wider, less specialist audience. This is an important consideration for ethnographers who need to involve participants in data analysis and interpretation.

Coding the Transcripts

Once the data have been transcribed, the next stage in the preparation of the discourse data is to add the coding features identified as central to analysis and interpretation. Codings have been added to help answer the research questions posed:

- which language(s) are spoken;
- the interlocutor(s) with whom they interact; and
- to whom.

By combining the fieldnotes and contextual descriptions with the transcribed data it is possible to construct transcripts carrying the following information:

(1) The participants (who said what).

(2) The actual site in the nursery setting where utterances were made (where they spoke).

(3) The child participants, who have been identified by pseudonyms and initials, for example Azia (AB), Kamran (KH). Their given names and initials can be found in Table 8.1.

Table 8.1 Key to the informants

Imran	(IB)
Ishtiaq	(II)
Kamran	(KH)
Rabila	(RN)
Sabia	(ZH)
Shamaila	(Sh)
Shazad	(SH)

(4) Adult participants (teachers, bilingual classroom assistants and others, including researchers) are identified as monolingual or bilingual and then as numbers 1 to 7:

   MT1   Head of the Nursery

   MT2   Nursery Nurse

   MT3   Monolingual Classroom Assistant

   BT4   Bilingual Classroom Assistant (BCA)

   MT5   Researcher (experienced, qualified primary school teacher)

   MT6   Experienced, qualified primary school teacher

   BT7   Bilingual Classroom Assistant (BCA)

(5) The language of each utterance is marked P for Mirpuri-Panjabi and E for English. In some instances it has not been possible to attribute an utterance to a particular language. Examples of these utterances include:

Imran	brrr *[playing noises]*
Imran	*[making car noises]*
Ishtiaq	*[humming and murmuring to himself]*
Ishtiaq	brumm, brumm
Shamaila	*[playing noises]*
Shamaila	*[laughing]*
Shazad	*[mimicking crying as if hurt]*
Shazad	beep, beep, beep
Shazad, Rabila	*[making sounds together]*
Rabila	*[crying]*
Shazad	*[singing to herself during story-time]*

It is possible that phonological analysis would be able to categorise these utterances within one of the language systems, and this would tell us more about the simultaneous acquisition of the children's languages. However, for the purpose of this study these utterances have not been allocated to a particular language system and hence have not been included in the quantification of the individual informant's preferred language use.

(6) The type of utterance, where this is ambiguous. It has not, of course, been possible to allocate codings to every utterance recorded. This is partly due to the difficulties researchers face in approaching naturally occurring language data. These include features such as inaudible utterance and the inability to recognise a particular participant's voice, two of the difficulties encountered in the transcription process and in collecting language data from very young informants. Some of these features have been identified using the following symbols:

/ / /   inaudible utterance

?   for a speaker who is difficult to identify

(7) Codes that represent particular types of language behaviour. Idiosyncratic uses have not been noted, but the following two codes have been included because they represent language behaviour recorded as used by more than one of the informants:

(echoes)   similar to Vygotsky's (1962) private or self-regulated speech

codeswitching   a feature of bilinguals' utterances

These specific features will be defined and described in a later section on the descriptions of individual language use. Other information from the audio-taped recordings and from the observational schedules have also been included. These include details of background sounds and the many contextual features that are a feature of busy classrooms. These have been included because they represent the *linguistic environment* as experienced by each child. These sounds are significant for a number of reasons. Some represent sounds that are unique to the school environment, bells ringing, whistles, the teachers clapping their hands to attract the children's attention or as a signal to stop the present activity and turn attention to the teacher for further instructions. The child has to distinguish between sounds that are meaningful to them and which need to be responded to, for example the teacher's whistle in the playground, or the school bell that signals the divisions in the school day (break- and lunch-times, home-time); and environment sounds, those which are just part of school life. The sounds recorded on the children's audio-tapes include:

- the sound of building bricks falling down;
- music in the background;
- footsteps;
- classroom noise;
- the sound of crying;
- the sound of the glockenspiel and other musical instruments,

Not all sounds, or even utterances are necessarily addressed to an individual child. Sometimes teachers address a small group within the classroom, or even speak privately to an individual child. These utterances can be overheard by those other than the intended addressee. Children each have to adjust to being a member of a large group (or a small crowd). They have to learn to become members of the class group. Learning to distinguish between the sounds and utterances that they hear in the classroom is all part of that process. New pupils must learn to distinguish between those sounds and utterances to which they are expected to respond, verbally or non-verbally, and those to which they are not. This is a frequently ignored aspect of language development. Young bilingual learners need to learn which language they can ignore, as well as which language they need to be seen to respond to, if they are to be perceived as fully communicatively competent in their new social setting.

Information on ambient sounds appears in the transcripts in brackets. It has been included (though not always used in subsequent discussions of social and language behaviour) because it helps to provide information about the child's total linguistic environment and to convey the impression of that environment as experienced by the child. Everyday life in the nursery is often noisy, boisterous and full of sounds and noises. The new pupil is learning which of the sounds are significant and to be responded to and which can be ignored.

The focus of the study is not a detailed description of all possible levels of language use; the phonological, phonemic realisations and syntax have not been included. The informants are very young children. Their utterances are therefore typical of children at the early stages of language development. Not all utterances are fully formed or standard. The children in this study are also learning more than one language. Their utterances in English have been transcribed as they were spoken. No attempt has been made to mark non-standard or unformed utterances. Sometimes information has been included about the manner in which an utterance was spoken (using Hymes' key). Examples of this level of detail include:

- whispering;

- laughing;

- voice fades away;

- upset;

- singing;

- mimicking reading, being happy, being upset, etc.

This information has been included because it is considered important to the understanding of an individual's behaviour and their developing linguistic competence. Silences have not been quantified. For ease of reference, line numbers have been inserted in the left-hand column of the transcripts. Counter readings relating to the audio-tapes have also been included. These were used extensively during the various stages of the transcription process; they are helpful to researchers during analysis but may not be necessary in the presentation of the final transcripts, partly because they are no longer of immediate significance and partly because they leave the transcipt over-detailed and less immediately comprehensible to the reader.

Data from only seven of the eight informants will be presented in this chapter on the children's use of English throughout the term. Technical difficulties with recording equipment have resulted in incomplete data sets for one of the children, Sofees. Dealing with these occurrences is all part of learning to be a researcher!

There is no claim that this process of transcription is value-free. Milroy (1987: 117) reminds us that 'transcription of any kind is invariably a selective process, reflecting underlying theoretical goals and assumptions'. There are nevertheless ways of minimising the impact of the researcher's subjective bias, without denying its existence and possible influence. Edwards and Westgate suggest that one option is to make information about the research methods used available to other researchers. They note:

> The researcher's highly problematic task remains therefore [one] of devising ways of capturing and displaying for analysis in the first place, enough evidence from the relevant channels of communication for the observers' interpretations to approach the reliability of those originally made by the participants and upon which they acted. (Edwards & Westgate, 1987: 70)

This is a view endorsed by Stubbs (1983). An attempt has been made to meet his call for a 'principled approach'. The transcripts, prepared in the way described, are the basis for all analyses and descriptions.

Finally it should be noted that the process of transcription is a time-consuming one. It has been suggested that each hour of tape recording may take 15 hours or more to transcribe (Edwards & Furlong, 1985; Westgate *et al.*, 1985). In the Tizard and Hughes (1984) observational study of 30 four-year-old girls at home and in the nursery school, five transcribers were employed to prepare the transcripts. They warn:

> Researchers considering a similar study should note that this process of transcribing and editing is very time-consuming. One hour of tape took nine hours to transcribe, and a further three hours to check over and add context notes … This adds up to approximately four thousand hours of work involved in collecting data, transcribing it, checking it and adding context notes, before the analysis could even begin. (Tizard & Hughes, 1984: 34–35)

My own view is that these estimates are conservative! In the Box Hill Nursery study the task of transcription was even more time-consuming than usual due to the age of the informants. The process was further complicated because the informants were using more than one language for their interactions.

Despite the extra time involved, a further stage in the preparation of the transcripts was undertaken. In an attempt to reduce the claim that transcription can distort the data, the transcriptions, together with the original audio-taped recordings, were presented back to the adults who had been in the nursery at the time of the data collection. Their comments, views and interpretations have been distilled and combined with contextual fieldnotes. Some of these details have been used to interpret the recordings. The audio-tapes were also made available to the families of the informants for comment and interpretation. Invaluable insights were gained from these procedures. A full discussion of the research methods can be found in Chapter 4.

In total there were five stages involved in the preparation of the transcripts:

Stage 1 The transcription of the audio-tapes.

Stage 2 Combining the transcriptions of the audio-tapes with the contextual information from the observation schedules and other sources.

Stage 3 Adding the codes to the transcripts.

Stage 4 Providing feedback from those present in the nursery at the time of the data collection and from the families of the informants.

Stage 5 Refinement of the transcripts in light of Stage 4.

The transcripts, prepared in the way described above, are the basis for the analyses and comments which follow.

The Children's Use of English on their First Day in Box Hill Nursery

Many sociolinguistic studies of the classroom have focused on the teacher's use of language (see, for example, Edwards & Westgate, 1987 for an overview of the most important studies). While this is of some interest, the primary focus here will be the language used by the children. Using the transcripts prepared in the way described, the fourth and fifth levels of data analyses will explore the questions:

(1) When do the children speak ?

(2) Whom do they speak to?

(3) What language do they use for their interactions?

Pre-observation interviews with the families of the children provided information about each individual's linguistic repertoire. All families reported that to the best of their knowledge, their children had little or no knowledge of spoken English prior to attending the nursery. English was not used extensively in the home, where the language of family interactions was reported as almost exclusively Mirpuri-Panjabi, the community language. This was a comment common to the families of all of the children in the project. Yet despite this, there is evidence from the audio-tape recordings that some English was spoken by the children even on their first day in the nursery school. Analysis begins with a description of these utterances recorded in English.

Imran's linguistic repertoire

During his first hour in the nursery Imran speaks Mirpuri-Panjabi almost exclusively. There is only one recorded instance of his use of English. This takes place when he is seated at the drawing table, Activity 9, a sustained activity lasting 10 minutes. He is with Azia (AB), Kamran (KH), a bilingual classroom assistant and a monolingual teacher. He is heard to say 'brown' when he is talking to Kamran. The boys are drawing, using different coloured crayons, and although there are teachers present, they are not leading the activity. They are merely present, sitting alongside the children. The children are engaged in making their own drawings. All other interactions between Imran and Kamran throughout this activity, and indeed throughout the subsequent activities, are in Mirpuri-Panjabi. Imran's utterance of 'brown' is very quiet, almost inaudible. It is therefore taken as further evidence of the children using language as a mean of internalising or clarifying things for themselves. Earlier in the day the children had been listening to teachers talking, giving instructions and directions. Knowledge of colours figures significantly in the nursery setting. Children need to be able to recognise colours and to know the names of the primary colours pretty quickly because they are used constantly for grouping and categorisation. Activities using paints, crayons and other art materials are found in a number of the structured learning activities. Knowledge of the names of colours is therefore considered to be important early learning that has a very practical function in the nursery. It is possible, that having heard the word 'brown' several times, Imran is now privately practising his previous learning and the sounds of the new language, English. The volume of his utterance suggests that he was not attempting to communicate with anyone else present. It is doubtful that his utterance would have been audible, except for the power of the lapel microphone that he was wearing. It is unlikely that he was heard by the adults present, or by the children he was sitting alongside.

Kamran's linguistic repertoire

In contrast to Imran, the preferred language used by another boy, Kamran, during his first hour in the nursery is English. A total of 103 utterances are recorded in English. This compares with only 48 in Mirpuri-Panjabi. The following extracts are from his conversation with a monolingual teacher, during his very first encounter of the afternoon:

Kamran   he [pointing to Geoffrey who is playing with a gun nearby] got his got [picking up a toy gun]

Teacher   I hope you're not playing with a gun
           we don't have guns here in the nursery
           go and put it away

Kamran   guns … put in car
           [trying to explain to the teacher what Geoffrey is doing with a toy gun]

Teacher   [moving to a bowl of plastic fruits and vegetables and beginning a pretend play activity with fruit in an attempt to attract Kamran's attention away from the toy gun and Geoffrey]
           I like this pear, I like pears, do you eat pears? What fruits do you like?
           [sound of musical instruments in the background]

Kamran   apples, green apples and red apples

Teacher   very nice, I like strawberries as well

Kamran   [to the teacher] he has a … [moving closer to Geoffrey]
           if you don't give it me … I'll …

Teacher   [to the boys]
           come on you play as well, come on Kamran, all play together, what are you doing Geoffrey?

During this sustained interaction Kamran uses English for his utterances. From this relatively short exchange it is possible to conclude that Kamran is displaying a number of competencies in his English repertoire. His use of English in this context is significant not only because it demonstrates a competence in the language but also because he is demonstrating a sense of appropriate language use within the context of the nursery school, and in the presence of a monolingual teacher. He chooses English as the language of interaction with the teacher because he recognises that she only speaks English and hence this is the only appropriate language for interaction with her. He is also demonstrating his ability to protect his own interests when he threatens another pupil, Geoffrey, who, like the teacher, is monolingual. When Kamran says *'if you don't give it me ... I'll ...'* he is using the formulaic 'if you ... I'll ...' as a threat. Again, while his choice of English for this utterance is appropriate, his competence does not (at this stage) include the ability to issue the full threat. He seems unable to complete it. This utterance is not grammatically standard. However, Kamran is demonstrating communicative competence in two ways: firstly, through his choice of English, since Geoffrey speaks and understands only English; and secondly, because the utterance carries communicative force. As a threat it succeeds in safeguarding Kamran's interests (whatever these might be). How he would have terminated this exchange is difficult to say. In the event the intervention of the teacher, with the directive 'come on you play as well, come on Kamran, all play together', removes the linguistic responsibility for terminating or resolving the situation he has created.

Imran's use of language can be taken as evidence of his developing communicative competence in another way, too. He is trying to alert the teacher to Geoffrey's inappropriate classroom behaviour; guns are not allowed as toys in the nursery, but Geoffrey is playing with one and has just put it in the toy car. From the contextual observations, we know that Geoffrey was trying to hide the gun from the teacher and it is possible that Kamran was trying to report this to the teacher. Before starting at the nursery the children had been informed, during the home visits, what toys and other belongings were permitted there. There is a certain division emerging between the two boys. This becomes more apparent when Kamran puts a physical distance between himself and Geoffrey, and moves away to join a small group of Mirpuri-Panjabi speakers who are quickly establishing themselves as a friendship group. The physical move coincides with a linguistic move. Kamran simultaneously switches from English to Mirpuri-Panjabi as he leaves Geoffrey. This choice of language and switch from one to another can be described in terms of boundary maintenance. The preferred use of one of the two languages in his linguistic repertoire, English and Mirpuri-Panjabi, can be understood as a linguistic mechanism for including or excluding specific interlocutors. The use of

English for Kamran's threat to Geoffrey followed by the switch to Mirpuri-Panjabi excludes Geoffrey from further interactions and activities.

This is one example of preferred language use demonstrating a communicative competence that serves to reinforce the membership of the social networks. This interpretation is further expanded in Chapter 7. For all of the other activities of the afternoon Kamran is with his bilingual friends and a bilingual teacher. His language for interactions in those contexts is, appropriately, sometimes English and sometimes Mirpuri-Panjabi. Thus he demonstrates appropriate knowledge of both languages.

In addition to linguistic and communicative competence, Kamran is demonstrating conversational competence. He is participating in exchanges with adults and peers in a variety of ways. In the extract above he is *initiating* the interaction with the teacher. He initiates interaction with Geoffrey. He is also recorded as responding appropriately to others' interactions in both English and Mirpuri-Panjabi. There is less evidence of his ability to resolve disputes or negotiate the termination of an exchange. This is seen from his exchange with Geoffrey. However, he is developing conversational competence in both languages.

Rabila's linguistic repertoire

The pattern of Rabila's preferred language use is quite different from that of the other children. She is recorded using English for a total of 14 utterances. These utterances are unlike Kamran's use of English in that they occur in isolation rather than during the course of sustained interactions with others. The following discussion presents the utterances recorded during Rabila's first activity of the afternoon when she is upset and being comforted by the teacher. When she is left in the nursery she protests in English, saying 'no, no, no'. A monolingual teacher attends to her and attempts to console her but Rabila rebuffs her with the same utterance, 'no, no, no'. Although somewhat limited, there are points to note about these similar utterances. The repetition serves as emphasis and adds communicative force. She is clearly distressed, so in both cases the enunciation, the emphasis through repetition and the choice of the word 'no' are all appropriate. So too is the choice of English, since this conveys her feelings appropriately to the teacher and to a wider audience of listeners.

Despite her protest the teacher does take Rabila out of the nursery, partly to give her individual attention, and partly not to distress the other new arrivals. She takes her to the main school building, talking to her, pointing out the playground and the school hall, as well as other children playing. The teacher frequently uses the filler 'mmm' between utterances. After visiting the main school building together, they both arrive back in the nursery where the following exchange with the teacher is recorded:

Teacher	what are you going to play with mmm
Rabila	mmm

A little later at the washbasins there is a further exchange between the same monolingual teacher and Rabila. The teacher initiates an exchange with Rabila by saying: 'I've got paint all over my hands, that was blue, now I've found red, I've got blue and red paint on my hands'; to which Rabila replies, with seeming conversational sophistication, *'mmm'*. It is clear that the teacher and her style of speaking have influenced Rabila after only a short time of their being together. Rabila identifies aspects of the teacher's repertoire and demonstrates the ability to use these in her own utterances.

This particular teacher's influence on Rabila's language use becomes further apparent in a later activity when the teacher is working with a small group which includes Rabila. The children are all colouring in pictures that require them to match colours on their own drawing with a master copy that the teacher is holding and talking about. The children are required to name the colour on the template, select that colour from a box of assorted crayons and then colour in their own copy appropriately.

Teacher	do you know what colour this is? *[talking to all of the children in the group]* do you? it's red Now would you all like to find a red crayon
Rabila	*[echoes, barely audible]* a red
Teacher	*[pointing to the part of the picture coloured red and addressing the group]* let's have a look at the picture what colour is this? altogether, 'red'
Rabila	*[echoes, barely audible]* red, red, *[singing to herself, barely audible]* re, ra, re, ra, red
The group (except Rabila)	red
Teacher	now would you all like to find a red crayon *[all of the children begin looking in their crayon boxes]*
Christopher	I need a red one *[reaching for a crayon]*

Teacher	*[to Christopher]* yes, that's red
Rabila	*[echoes, barely audible]* red yes

Echoing

It is worth considering this extract in some detail. If we consider Rabila's actions and responses, to an observer or a busy classroom teacher it may seem that she is not behaving appropriately within this group activity. For example, when the teacher asks the group to name a particular colour, none of the children replies. In this Rabila's response is in keeping with that of the rest of the group. However, unlike the other children, she does not look up from her own drawing. The teacher points to the relevant section of the master picture and says 'it's red'. She then prompts the rest of the group with a clue, 'would you all like to find a red crayon'. At this point that Rabila's response again differs from that of the other children. While the rest of the group respond to the teacher's directive, 'now would you like to find a red crayon', Rabila does not attempt to look for a red crayon. Instead she continues colouring with the blue crayon that she is already using. However, without looking up at the teacher or the template picture she is heard, in a barely audible voice, to repeat the last part of the teacher's utterance and say '*a red*'. The teacher continues to talk the group through the colouring-in activity, moving from one part of the template picture to another, testing the children's knowledge of the names of colours, and directing them to colour in the corresponding section of their individual pictures appropriately. Rabila continues in verbal play, repeating to herself, very quietly, the word 'red' and alternating the first phonemes of the word re with rc. The other children continue to colour their pictures.

From these utterances it can be seen that Rabila is already influenced by the teacher. She tries to mimic her and is quick to repeat her utterances. She is following the teacher rather than the language and behaviour of the other children. Throughout the transcripts Rabila's utterances 'mmm' have been coded as English because they are so similar to the teacher's style of speaking. These utterances (and the extract above) demonstrate the important role that monolingual teachers play in providing a model of language for children in their care. There are a number of instances where the pupils seem to copy, mimic or repeat the utterance(s) that they have just heard. This behaviour has been termed *echoing* and is coded in the transcripts. It is difficult to offer definitive explanations for echoing. The reasons for it are not entirely clear. It may be that the child is trying out the utterance to see what response (if any) can be evoked. Equally, it may be that the child is intrigued by the sound pattern(s) of the language that they have heard and are using the utterance because they are attracted to its sound. It could be that the word or phrase is already familiar to them; that they are repeating it out of familiarity. (It is not often clear whether a child is sure of the meaning and appropriate usage of the words and phrases that they are echoing.) All of these are possible explanations; none can be claimed with surety.

Echoing is a pattern of verbal behaviour that has been observed across all the informants in the study. It differs in a number of ways from the straightforward repetition of an utterance that they have just heard. It differs in volume. Echoing is usually very quiet and barely audible. It is as if the child is speaking to him- or herself. It is almost as if they are trying out what they have just heard. Because it is so quiet, in the study it was barely distinguishable, even on the audio-recordings. Hence at first it did not seem significant. It was only with repeated listening during the transcription process that it emerged as noteworthy behaviour. Echoes would not be heard in the buzz of everyday classroom noise. Even teachers close to the child heard to echo were aware of it only on hearing the tape-recordings during Stage 4 in the preparation of the transcripts. Although echoing demonstrates the significant ways in which teachers can be said to influence children's behaviour, the children do not only echo the teachers' language. Examples of Rabila echoing other children can also be found. For example, when Shazad says to a teacher, 'I've finished' and hands the teacher her finished painting, Rabila can be heard to echo 'I've finished', although she is still engaged in her painting.

Echoing corresponds to the language behaviour that Vygotsky (1962) terms self-regulated speech or a means of commenting on behaviour. It is suggested that it is a stage in development that becomes redundant when internalised as thought processes. However, it is proposed that the echoing recorded here differs from self-regulated speech in terms of specific linguistic features; for example, the volume of the utterance. Echoes are very quiet, almost inaudible. Self-regulated speech is not always quiet. Echoing is a particular linguistic behaviour observed amongst this group of young bilingual children.

There is another general trend to note among all of the informants. Comparisons are not always useful, but Table 8.2 presents an overview for the informants and the number of utterances recorded in English for each child during the first day in the nursery. Although the actual number of utterances varies across the informants, it can be seen that all choose to speak English for some interaction, even during the first hour in the nursery. The two children who are recorded using English for the most utterances are Kamran (103 utterances) and Sabia (41 utterances). There does not appear to be a gender difference between those who speak most English. Boys (Kamran the most and Imran with only one recorded utterance) feature at both the top and the bottom of the table.

Table 8.2 Number of informants' utterances recorded in English during the first hour in Box Hill Nursery

Informant	Total number of utterances in English
Imran	1
Shamaila	3
Shazad	9
Rabila	13
Ishtiaq	14
Sabia	41
Kamran	103

The choice of English for some utterances is interesting. It suggests that all of the children have a level of linguistic competence unrecognised and unacknowledged by members of their families. Further, to speak English as they do means they have a degree of understanding of this, too, as is evident from the appropriateness of their utterances. It may be that the children's passive knowledge of English and their understanding of English speakers is even more extensive than their utterances suggest, though this cannot be judged since there is no evidence beyond the audio-taped recordings. It can be seen, however, that the children do have an active, if limited, command of (at least) two linguistic systems: English and Mirpuri-Panjabi.

It is important to note that the number of utterances *per se* is not necessarily significant. Other factors can influence the amount of talk. These can include personality traits, as well as the linguistic and communicative competence of the individual, including knowing when to talk, what to talk about and the manner and extent of the interaction. All these factors can be highly significant in determining the amount that a child talks and the number of the utterances recorded for each. Some children are talkative, others are not. Contextual features, including the specific linguistic and cultural setting of the school and classroom, can also influence children's behaviour, particularly the amount they talk. Two unrelated studies of child language development (Wells, 1984; Tizard & Hughes, 1984) both note the small number of utterances spoken by some monolingual children during their first experiences in school. The Wells' study of 32 children reported that they talked significantly less in the classroom than at home and addressed a considerably smaller proportion of their utterances to adults. By contrast, the amount of talk addressed to other children did not differ significantly between the home and the school settings. Both studies suggest that the context of the classroom and its prevailing rules of discourse limit the contribution that children, as pupils, are permitted to make to ongoing interaction:

> Compared with homes, schools are not providing an environment that fosters language development. For no child (in the Bristol Language Project) was the language experience of the classroom richer than that of the home. (Wells, 1984: 87)

While these comments were made about monolingual children, it seems reasonable to speculate that the contextual features that monolingual children find constraining in classrooms will also impact on bilingual children, perhaps to a greater degree. So it is not the actual number of utterances in English that are significant when describing each child's linguistic repertoire and communicative competence. A fuller picture emerges when comparing the number of utterances recorded in English with those recorded in the home language, Mirpuri-Panjabi. This helps to put the utterances in English into a relative perspective. Table 8.3 presents a comparison between the informants' utterances recorded in Mirpuri-Panjabi and in English during the first hour in Box Hill Nursery.

Table 8.3   A comparison between the number of informants' utterances recorded in Mirpuri-Panjabi and in English during the first day in Box Hill Nursery

Informant	Total number of utterances in Mirpuri-Panjabi	Total number of utterances in English	Total number of utterances
Kamran	48	103	151
Sabia	66	41	107
Shamaila	65	3	68
Shazad	22	9	31
Imran	24	1	25
Ishtiaq	4	14	18
Rabila	3	13	16

The Children's Utterances during their First Hour in the Nursery

From Table 8.3 it can be seen that there are clear differences between the children in their choice of language. Kamran talks most, with a total of 151 utterances (48 in Mirpuri-Panajbi and 103 in English). Sabia comes next with 107 utterances, but the composition of her profile differs. She has a similar number of utterances in both languages (66 recorded in Mirpuri-Panajbi and 41 in English). Of the seven children this is probably the most balanced profile. The children who talk a lot in Mirpuri-Panajbi, their home language, for example Sabia (66) and Shamaila (65), have very different overall profiles. Sabia has a balanced profile with 41 utterances in English, while Shamaila chooses English for only 3 of hers. Ishtiaq (a total of 18 utterances) and Rabila (16) speak least. Yet in both profiles, English is the most recorded language, with 14 utterances for Ishtiaq and 13 for Rabila. The uniqueness and individuality of the children is clear. Some children talk a lot, while others do not talk much. Although both Rabila and Kamran use English for the majority of their utterances, the pattern of language use is different for each. It has already been seen that Kamran uses English during one sustained interaction with a monolingual teacher, while Rabila uses English for shorter contributions on a number of different occasions. The common element in her choice of English is that it is always with the same monolingual teacher.

A closer examination of specific utterances in English offers insights into the developing communicative competence of the children. A summary profile of Ishtiaq's preferred language use across all the networks which emerged on Day 1 shows that within each setting, Mirpuri-Panjabi is the dominant language. The preferred language is determined on the basis of the number of turns spoken in that language and the discourse function which each turn fulfils. The only occasion when English is the preferred language is during Activity 5 on Day 1, the painting activity in which he is participating with three members of his friendship network, two girls, Sabia (SA) and Rabila (RN), and a boy, Mushtifaq (MI). The difference, however, within this setting is the presence of two monolingual teachers. Consider the following sample of data from the corpus.

Teacher 1   first wet your paintbrush with the water like this
[demonstrates]
then dip the tip of your brush into the paint, just the end of the brush

like this
yes, good, that's the way

Ishtiaq   *[sees his friend Mushtifaq just outside the domain and picks up an apron for him]*
you can do

Teacher 1   What's that for Ishtiaq? You've got an apron, haven't you? Come over here, come over here, Mushtifaq.
here we go. I don't think you'll reach the paint if you don't. Come, come around here. Come around here
look dip the brush into the water
yes, good
then into the paint
that's red it's a lovely colour, it's red.
[aside to another teacher] come and see what's going on here, look at this, the little ones can't reach very well, it's too far for them to reach, what can we do?

Teacher 2   you could

Child   *[holding up her painting for the teacher to see]*

Teacher 1   yes that's right that's lovely

The interaction (in bold) between Mushtifaq and Ishtiaq is particularly noteworthy. This is the first time, using the data as evidence, that Ishtiaq chooses English as the language of interaction with Mushtifaq. The utterance '*you can do*' is unformed grammatically and may be described as non-standard, but it carries the communicative force to include Mushtifaq in the painting activity and in turn in Ishtiaq's dense friendship network. The utterance, combined with the act of getting an apron (appropriate painting clothing) achieves this. However, both action and utterance (probably unheard) are misinterpreted by the monolingual teacher, who is clearly focused on talking the children through the painting activity and the practicalities of this for some of the children who are too small to reach across the table to the paint pots.

Ishtiaq's choice of English for this interaction could be explained by his desire to remain consistent with the others in this particular setting. There is an equally plausible factor that can explain Ishtiaq's use of English for this utterance, namely the presence of the monolingual teachers. This concurs with the findings of previous researchers, for example Sylva *et al.* (1980) who suggest that the presence of an adult can influence child behaviour, and Wells (1984) who, like Tizard and Hughes (1984), identifies the constraints that institutional discourse norms exert on pupils' linguistic behaviour during their early days in school.

The following sample from the data demonstrates the way in which Shazad is anxious to conform as a pupil and to comply with teacher requests and expectations. The teacher is trying to get all of the children seated, in a circle, on the carpet for the story-time that signals the end of the nursery session. She wants them all to be together and seated so they can see the pictures. She is walking around the nursery directing children to sit down.

Teacher	Carpet time, carpet time, come on everybody on the carpet
Shazad	**Rabila back**
Teacher	Come on Shazad on the carpet please
Shazad	/ / / *[inaudible]*
Teacher	on the carpet please
Shazad	Rab ...
Shazad	Rabila
Teacher	*[in the distance]* come on everyone to the carpet please, Melanie come on
Shazad	Teacher, teacher teacher
Teacher	Shazad please, sit down there *[pointing to a place on the carpet]*
Shazad	Rabil ...
Teacher	you won't be able to see the story if you don't move a little bit

There then follows a sustained activity, story-time, which lasts for 10 minutes. In the above extract Shazad chooses English to try to tell the teacher that her friend Rabila is not there. Of course the utterance '*Rabila back*' does not achieve this goal. Indeed it is not understood by the teacher, whose main concern at that moment is getting all of the children seated in a circle on the carpet so they can see the book and enjoy the story session. One interpretation of Shazad's utterance is that it was unsuccessful. However, despite the obvious breakdown in the communication between Shazad and the teacher, there is evidence of developing communicative competence in Shazad's utterance. She has chosen English as the preferred language for this interaction. This shows a developing sense of linguistic awareness, since the teacher is monolingual. The fact that Shazad's utterance is ineffective is less significant than her appropriate choice of language for the interaction. She is persistent in pursuing her interaction with the teacher. She tries five times to initiate interaction with the teacher to tell her that Rabila is not present. This is another example from the data of a bilingual pupil's choice of English for an interaction with a teacher being misunderstood. These examples from Ishtiaq and Shazad support Willes' (1983) view that children very quickly become socialised into the norms of appropriate school behaviour, linguistic and social. Children quickly learn to be pupils. If this is so, then the implications of the dominant presence of monolingual teachers in classrooms with bilingual pupils may result in a language shift (LS) towards English, the dominant language of the nursery classroom and the societal language.

Summary

This chapter has discussed the stages involved in transcribing and analysing children's naturally occurring language in the nursery setting. Data analysis shows that all seven of the children speak some English, even on their very first hour in the nursery. A number of factors have been suggested as influential in the individuals' choice of English as the language for these utterances. Echoing has been described as a particular feature of the children's language behaviour. The choice of English is only one facet of the informants' linguistic repertoires. Chapter 9 will present an analysis of the children's use of the home and community language, Mirpuri-Panjabi, and describe codeswitching, another feature of bilinguals' language behaviour.

Chapter 9
Codeswitching as a Feature of Bilingual Children's Language

> Maybe he had different words in his language; the only one she and her
> mother had wouldn't do, they weren't meant for a situation not pro-
> vided for in their lives. (Nadine Gordimer, *Some are Born to Sweet
> Delight*, 1991: 80)

Introduction to Level 5 of the Data Analysis

This chapter continues the data analysis with a description of the informants' choice of language for interactions with selected interlocutors.
Analysis will reveal a pattern of language use that is specific to bilingual
children. This is termed *codeswitching*. Analysis will also identify generic
patterns of language choice and the subsequent impact these choices exert
on the development of the discourse. The chapter begins with a definition
of codeswitching and the features that distinguish it as language
behaviour.

Codeswitching as a Feature of Bilingual Interactions

Chapter 8 examined the children's use of English in the nursery setting.
The focus on their use of English is valid. However, it remains only one
facet of their linguistic repertoire. A unique feature of bilinguals' linguistic
repertoire is their ability to draw on more than one language for their interactions with others. Bilinguals have a choice of languages that they can use
for interactions. For the informants in this study the choice available to
them is English, Mirpuri-Panjabi or a combination of the two. Bilinguals'
combined use of both of the languages in their repertoire is an established
linguistic phenomenon. It is described in the literature and three types of
linguistic behaviour of this kind have been identified. These have been
termed 'codeswitching', 'code-mixing' and 'borrowing'. It is important to
distinguish between these three types of language use.

The term code-mixing refers to the use of one or more languages for the
consistent transfer of linguistic units from one language into another,

and by such a language mixture developing a new restricted – or not so restricted – code of linguistic interaction. (Kachru, 1978: 28)

Codeswitching, by contrast, has been defined by Heller (1988: Introduction) as 'the use of more than one language in the course of a single communicative episode' and by Sankoff *et al.* (1991) as 'the combination of two or more languages in ... discourse'.

Some scholars of bilingualism distinguish between speakers' codeswitching and the borrowing of lexical items, idioms, phrases or terms from another language. Treffers-Daller (1991) provides cogent theoretical arguments for regarding codeswitching and borrowing as the same language behaviour. This position is reinforced by Myers-Scotton (1990) who has advanced a model of language behaviour which treats codeswitching and borrowing together, along with a number of other linguistic features which distinguish the specific use of language(s) in contact situations. The difficulties of distinguishing codeswitching and borrowing as separate linguistic behaviours have also been detailed by Schatz (1989) and Nortier (1989).

The essential difference between codeswitching and borrowing can be better understood by examination of the assumptions that underpin the two terms. *Borrowing* adheres to the prevalent assumption that speakers use only one (dominant) language and complement it by borrowing from one or more others. *Codeswitching* offers an alternative to this one-speaker-one-language description of language behaviour. The notion of the exclusive use of one language as the norm is prevalent not only among researchers. Heller (1988) suggests that the assumption is so powerful that speakers who codeswitch can remain unaware of their own behaviour and can even vigorously deny it. In contrast to borrowing, code-switching is viewed as language behaviour that integrates both language systems. This integration takes place at all levels in both language. It is argued (cf. Genesee & Bourhis, 1982; Pfaff, 1979) that codeswitching derives from a universal pattern of relationships between the form, function and context of language use and therefore representing a structurally unified use of both linguistic systems, distinctly different from borrowing behaviour. For the purposes of the descriptions of language use that follow, codeswitching (together with its inherent assumptions) will be the preferred term.

Types of Codeswitch

Codeswitching studies have adopted a variety of foci. Some researchers have focused on linguistic features, others on social and contextual aspects. Poplack (1980) identified three types of codeswitching: lexical (at word level), intra-sentential (the use of both languages within the same sentence), and inter-sentential (switches that coincide with sentence boundaries). Extracts from the transcripts of the audio-taped discourse data from the Box Hill Nursery study will be presented to demonstrate the range of codeswitching behaviour observed in the nursery classroom. The types of switch observed will be described and the range of discourse and communicative functions which they perform will be outlined. Analysis will focus on the children's utterances, rather than the teachers'.

The most frequently occurring types of codeswitch identified from the data are lexical. These follow a particular pattern. Lexical codeswitches into English occur in sustained utterances in Mirpuri-Panjabi and can be observed across all informants, as the following extracts from the data demonstrate:

Imran   good girl

Azia   good girl

Kamran   Teacher *[used as a form of address]*

Shazia   bye bye

I suggest that these utterances be coded as lexical rather than inter-sentential codeswitches because of their functions within the discourse. They are utterances that are formulaic in their function. The teachers and parents can frequently be heard to say 'good girl' and 'good boy' as terms of encouragement and even endearment. These words combine to form a unified string, almost a form of address. The words 'boy' and 'girl' are not used alone in the same way by the adults. However the word 'teacher', by comparison, is used by both parents and children as a form of address, in place of the more formal 'Mrs' or 'Miss' + name, or the equivalent form of address in Panjabi ('Aunty' is also frequently used as an option in English). It is further suggested that the utterance 'bye-bye' is similar in structure to 'good boy' and 'good girl' and so this too can be regarded as a lexical switch.

There is also evidence of a second type of codeswitch, the intra-sentential. Some examples (P stands for Panjabi; English is in brackets) include:

Sabia   *[in conversation with bilingual teacher]* (look) P just come here, just come here, I'll show you something P (look)

Rabila   *[engaged in a painting activity with other children with Teacher 1 and Teacher 2 present]* (like this) P round and round P (round and round)

Further extracts from the transcripts illustrate more examples of inter-sentential and lexical switches into English. Kamran, during a storytelling session with a bilingual teacher and two pupils, Azia and Imran, repeats the line of the story that he has just heard read by the teacher.

Kamran   the mouse ... drip, drip, drip

Another example, from Shazia, is when she is at a painting activity with a monolingual teacher, Ishtiaq and other children when her mother arrives at the nursery. She says 'bye, bye' to the group with whom she has been painting, before leaving the activity to go over to greet her mother. The group includes both bilinguals and monolinguals. Her choice of English can be explained as the language that she thought would be understood by all participants in the group, both monolinguals and bilinguals.

Again, Kamran is in the book corner with Imran. They are speaking Mirpuri-Panjabi. He calls 'Teacher' as a form of address to attract an adult's attention. The conversation continues in the community language. Later on the same day Kamran is with Imran and a bilingual classroom assistant (BT4) in the home corner, Domain 5. They are looking at a book and the assistant is reading it to them:

BT4   *[reading from a book]* mom give him cheese and he just won't have that, mammy starts to cry, he won't have anything, I'm so worried about him, then the children go, I know, why don't you give him *[pause]* a mango

Kamran   P mango P

Similarly, Rabila is at a painting activity with two monolingual teachers and some children. She is speaking Mirpuri-Panjabi to herself and laughing. She codeswitches into English to say 'round and round' (with an intonation that suggests to the teachers that she is reciting a well-known rhyme, 'Round and round the garden like a teddy bear'). One of the teachers present comments in an aside to the other: 'That's familiar.'

The range of codeswitches identified from this corpus may differ in extent and range from those reported in other findings. This can be explained in a number of ways. Li Wei (1994: 151) suggests that 'it is a mistake to assume that codeswitching occurs in all bilingual communities on all occasions'. He suggests (1994: 151) that in language shift situations 'codeswitching occurs only between certain speakers in certain contexts'.

It should also be remembered that codeswitching is a sophisticated use of language which requires speakers to combine two linguistic systems. The children in this study are still very young and are at an early stage in their language development. Children aged around three years are not expected to have full command of all of the standard forms available in any one language system. The predominance of lexical codeswitches found in this corpus can therefore perhaps be accounted for in terms of the informants' age and their stage of language development at the time of the recordings.

There are other descriptions of codeswitching behaviour that focus on the social rather than the linguistic features. Scotton (1976), Heller (1982) and Gumperz (1982) all describe it as a verbal strategy that represents the ways in which the linguistic resources available to an individual speaker may vary according to the demarcation of social boundaries within a given community. From their descriptions, codeswitching can be regarded as a diverse linguistic resource from which an individual speaker may draw in order to communicate effectively. Bilingual children therefore have a choice of languages available for selected interactions. The children in the study make a choice between using English, Mirpuri-Panjabi or a mixture of the two. Codeswitching as a language choice remains the linguistic privilege of those individuals who can speak and understand more than one language.

Although there is evidence from the data of the children using some of the codeswitching behaviours described in previous studies, it is not possible for a monolingual researcher to provide a more detailed analysis of these codeswitches. However, there are aspects of codeswitching behaviour on which a monolingual researcher can comment. These include features already established but (to date) not widely reported, together with a description of codeswitching that goes beyond the actual utterances spoken by the informants to address contextual aspects of language use.

To make a link between codeswitching as language choice and the description of language as socio-semiotic outlined in Chapter 4, it is necessary to inspect more closely the role of codeswitching in the turn-by-turn organisation of the interactions between the informants and their interlocutors. Conversational analysis offers a means of doing this. The principles of conversational analysis have been outlined by Auer (1991) and the American ethnomethodologists including Garfinkel (1967) and Sacks *et al.* (1974). These approaches focus on the organisation of interactions between individuals in their exchanges and reinforce the systemic linguistic description of talk as a social activity. One important feature of conversational analysis is the significance it attaches to turn-taking within the organisation of an exchange. Discourse is organised into a sequence of exchanges, with one speaker's turn (or discourse contribution) leading to that of another speaker. This sequential organisation of conversation has been described by Schegloff and Sacks (1973). They use the term 'adjacency pair' to describe the paired utterances that occur. Adjacency pairs are sequentially constrained, in that the first utterance of the pair creates the environment for the second utterance of the exchange. Schegloff and Sacks (1973) describe a number of prototypes of adjacency pairs which include formulaic exchanges (in English) like question–answer sequences and greetings.

Central to this concept of adjacency pairs is that the first speaker establishes conditionally relevant expectations for their discourse partner(s). Interlocutors can fail to fulfil these conditionally relevant expectations by uttering inappropriate second pair parts in their exchange. This 'noticeable absence' is frequently perceived as a lack of communicative competence on the part of the second speaker. When the second speaker is a bilingual pupil, the resulting assessment can have unfortunate consequences. To date, little is known about the patterns of bilingual discourse in UK primary school classrooms. A sequential analysis of codeswitching at the level of turn-taking provides an overview of the recurring patterns of language choice based on data from the corpus.

Figures 9.1 to 9.3 illustrate the generic pattern of strategies observed in the nursery data. Speaker 1 sets the the scene with their choice of language. This will be termed the *frame language* (FL). When the frame language is English and Speaker 2 is a monolingual English speaker then there are only three discourse options available to that interlocuter. English has to be the language of the next utterance. Acceptable alternatives are silence, or a non-verbal response (Figure 9.1).

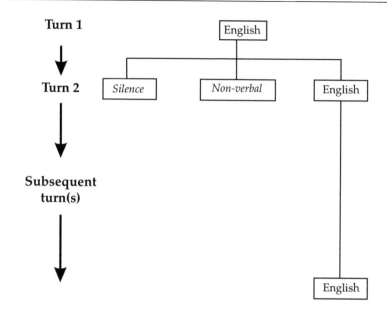

Figure 9.1 Discourse options available to monolingual speakers

However, when English is the frame language and Speaker 2 is a bilingual discourse participant, then the number of discourse options available to Speaker 2 is increased to five (Figure 9.2). These discourse options can be identified as:

Discourse Option 1   Silence

Discourse Option 2   Non-verbal response

Discourse Option 3   English

Discourse Option 4   Mirpuri-Panjabi

Discourse Option 5   English with subsequent code-switch (CS)
into Mirpuri-Panjabi

Discourse Option 6   English with two subsequent codeswitches:
CS1 into Mipuri-Panjabi; CS2 into English

Discourse Option 7   Mirpuri-Panjabi with subsequent codeswitch back
into English

Discourse Option 1, silence, is sometimes misunderstood by teachers as lack of understanding on the part of the child. This may not always be the

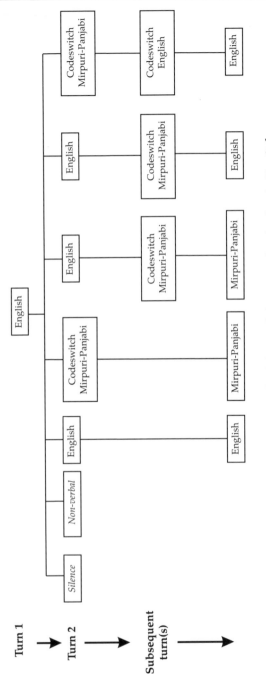

Figure 9.2   Generic patterns of adjacency pairs for bilingual discourse beginning in English

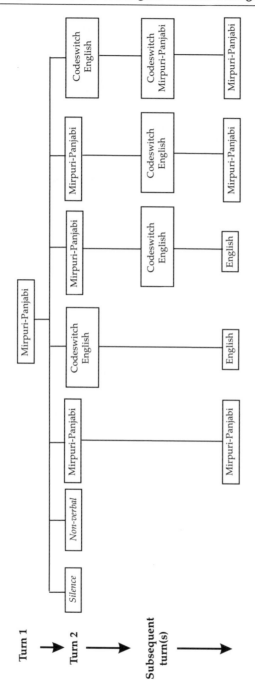

Figure 9.3   Generic patterns of adjacency pairs for bilingual discourse beginning in Mirpuri-Panjabi

case. A child may have understood what has been said by a speaker but may lack the linguistic and social knowledge of appropriate response. Discourse Option 2, non-verbal response, is equally open to misinterpretation. Gestures, facial expressions, eye contact are all examples of non-verbal responses. Non-verbal behaviours are linked to language systems and cultures. They are open to misunderstanding in cross-cultural interactions. Discourse Options 3, 4, 5, 6 and 7 all require understanding of both linguistic systems and the accompanying rules of social behaviour.

Generic patterns of exchanges that begin with Mirpuri-Panjabi as the frame language present a similar range of discourse options for bilingual discourse participants (Figure 9.3). These are:

Discourse Option 1	Silence
Discourse Option 2	Non-verbal response
Discourse Option 3	Mirpuri-Panjabi
Discourse Option 4	English
Discourse Option 5	Mirpuri-Panjabi with subsequent codeswitch into English
Discourse Option 6	Mirpuri-Panjabi with two subsequent codeswitches: CS1 into English; CS2 into Mirpuri-Panjabi
Discourse Option 7	English with subsequent code-switch back into Mirpuri-Panjabi

For the bilingual discourse participant, the frame language of an interaction is important. Figures 9.2 and 9.3 outline the generic pattern of discourse options available to bilinguals. Both Figures 9.2 and 9.3 identify a chain of possible linguistic outcomes that are available only to bilinguals. The options available to monolingual speakers are reduced. These are presented in Figure 9.1.

Li Wei (1994: 153) states that 'different bilingual communities or groups within a community … adopt different codeswitching strategies'. It is not therefore suggested that the two generic patterns of codeswitching and language choice outlined in Figures 9.2 and 9.3 are appropriate structural models to describe patterns of codeswitching behaviours in other contexts. The claim is merely that in the current corpus, it is possible to identify codeswitching that occurs at the boundaries of turn-taking. A discourse participant may, when taking the floor (or a turn) alter the development of the discourse through their particular choice of language code.

In keeping with the description of discourse offered by conversational analysis, a speaker's decision to change the discourse code at any point in the interaction impacts on the subsequent organisation and code of the ongoing exchange. If codeswitching is viewed as a linguistic resource that is only available to bilinguals, it is possible to regard it as purposeful (if often unconscious) linguistic behaviour. Closer examination of interactions where codeswitches do occur demonstrates specific communicative strategies of codeswitches that coincide with a change of speaker and turn-taking. The following examples illustrate this.

At the end of term in the nursery Imran is in conversation with Azia. It is the fourth activity of the day. They are in Domain 13 working at clay modelling. They are engaged in a sustained interaction. The language chosen for most of their utterances is Mirpuri-Panjabi. There is a monolingual teacher nearby but she is not actually working with them, nor does she talk directly to them. Another monolingual teacher passes by as they are working and talking. She does address a comment to them about the biscuits. Closer examination of the interactions where codeswitches occur demonstrates the speakers' strategies:

Imran	(P) I want it (P)
Teacher 1	Stuart, don't go outside
Azia	oh no, no, no, no, no eeh
Imran	(P) I want it for my clay (P)
Azia	*[sounds upset]*
Imran	(P) yours is finished (P)
Teacher 2	what are you making, you've made a biscuit, mm I like biscuits
Imran, Azia	*[conversation in Panjabi]*
Imran	*[Panjabi]*
Azia	*[Panjabi]*

Azia's switch into English performs the function of maintaining her interests. She is demonstrating her determination to keep the shape cutter that she is using for the modelling. There is no obvious explanation for her choice of English for this utterance. However, one possible explanation is that she is aware of the presence of the two monolingual teachers who are both within hearing distance. If she is using English as a way of attracting their attention in the hope of getting them to intervene, then there are two points to be made. Firstly, if this is the case then she is demonstrating an awareness of the norms of classroom conventions. Teachers are figures of authority and are willing to intervene. Secondly, she is successful in her utterance. Teacher 2 intervenes and indirectly stops Imran from taking the shape cutter. Viewed in this way, the above example of codeswitching confirms the view that it is not random behaviour. Codeswitching into English serves a specific social function and can therefore be viewed as a speaker's choice. It may however remain at an intuitive level of language behaviour. The second code-switch into Mirpuri-Panjabi coincides with Azia's discourse turn. It can be interpreted as exerting an impact on the second speaker, Imran, and his choice of Mirpuri-Panjabi for his utterance. Her choice of English offers an opportunity for a monolingual English speaker to become a participant in the discourse.

The ability to codeswitch requires sophisticated understanding of a number of levels of language use. Firstly, it requires knowledge of both linguistic systems. However, not all speakers use their linguistic competence in both of the languages that they speak to codeswitch. Li Wei (1994: 151) suggests that codeswitching is related to the interlocutor(s) being addressed and the context in which the utterances are spoken. If it is accepted therefore that codeswitching is context-bound and addressee-specific, it is important to note more precise details of the occurrences in the classroom. Codeswitching as a discourse choice has been noted for all the informants.

Recent research in codeswitching has addressed a broader range of anthropological and sociological issues concerning the relationship between linguistic and social processes, the individual speaker's interpretation of experience and their construction of social reality. These studies suggest that codeswitching behaviour is used by speakers to convey a range of social, discourse and referential meanings. For example, Heller (1984: 3) suggests that to focus on codeswitching as a linguistic variable can help researchers to understand the wider relationship between social processes and linguistic forms. She believes that this is possible because social and linguistic boundaries are signalled more overtly in multilingual settings, making it easier for the researcher to observe the relationship between the two. This point is further reinforced by a later observation (Heller, 1988: 81) when she maintains that observing codeswitching behaviour offers opportunities for the interpretation of social action that would not be available from observations of a single language.

Pride and Holmes (1972) also perceive the link between individual's choice of language and a broader social perspective:

The study of social meaning conveyed by different languages in a multilingual community can be undertaken at two levels, the one logically preceding the other. In the first place one can examine the way languages are used on the macro-scale, using large-scale surveys to reveal community norms of language use. Then against this background one can examine how the individual exploits ... awareness of the society's norms in order to achieve particular effects. (Pride & Holmes, 1972: 7)

This broader perspective on codeswitching as sociolinguistic behaviour is also taken by Gal in her 1988 paper 'The political economy of code choice'. In this paper she interprets codeswitching practices not only as a conversational device that can maintain or change personal relationships and ethnic group boundaries but also as a symbolic creation concerned with the construction of self and others within a broader political economic and historical context. This descriptive rationale for codeswitching provides important insights into the language choices of the informants in the nursery setting. Heller (1988) extends Gal's arguments and suggests that codeswitching behaviour can best be understood by locating it within the speech economy of the community in which it occurs.

From the data it is possible to identify patterns of preferred language use in specific domains. It is possible to identify times when an individual informant speaks English and when they speak Mirpuri-Panjabi. Using the individual informant profiles as a basis, the *dominant* language used by each of the informants in specific domains of the nursery can be identified. The dominant language of the setting will be termed the *preferred language*. It is determined by the actual number of utterances recorded in each language (English or Mirpuri-Panjabi) within each domain. It is important to stress that the language identified as the dominant or matrix one is not necessarily the sole language recorded during the interactions. Codeswitching also occurs within these domains, at these times.

By matching this level of analysis with the previous analyses of time on task (Chapter 5) and social network ties (Chapter 7) an interesting trend can be observed. In the activities where the groupings are self-selected friendship ones, the dominant language spoken is the home language, Mirpuri-Panjabi. The same trend can be noted for interactions with bilingual teachers. These are also the activities where the informants spend sustained periods of time-on-task. Figures 9.4 and 9.5 demonstrate this general trend for one informant, Ishtiaq, on his first day and at the end of term in the nursery. However, even in these situations where the dominant language is Mirpuri-Panjabi, there is evidence of codeswitching to English.

Language and Ethnic Identity

One interpretation of preferred language use and codeswitching is that language use is an explicit statement of an individual's self-perceived identity. However, identity so defined can operate on a number of levels. It can relate to an affiliation with a number of non-linguistic variables, including age, gender, or membership of a religious group. An individual's particular language choice in a given social situation will be open to a number of influences besides linguistic factors. These factors may themselves act as either constraining or enabling the range of language choices available to the speaker. However, they will not necessarily remain constant. The ability to perform a linguistic act of identity will always be dependent upon the language varieties (ideolect, accents, dialects and languages) available to an individual in their personal linguistic repertoire. Individuals may elect to perform acts of identity which make statements about themselves. The force of the statement will depend in part upon each individual's communicative competence and in part upon the competence of their audience to comprehend their act(s).

The linguistic element is only one component of the statement of self which the children are performing when they select a particular language for their interaction(s). In their use of English the children in this study are not merely demonstrating their language learning proficiency, they are also demonstrating that they are simultaneously learning the relative position of Mirpuri-Panjabi in the linguistic hierarchy of present-day British society. Gal (1988) suggests that codeswitching or preferred language use reveals the workings of social and cultural processes at a number of levels. Language use in interpersonal interactions is evidence of an awareness of the unequal power relations that exist. It represents the individual's (or group's) response to the material and cultural domination which they feel. Codeswitching, as described, can be taken as clear evidence that speakers have been enculturated into the dominant society's language, English. However, it can also be understood as evidence of simultaneous enculturation into the dominant society's values. The children have quickly learned the relative position of Mirpuri-Panjabi in the stratified linguistic structure of present-day British society.

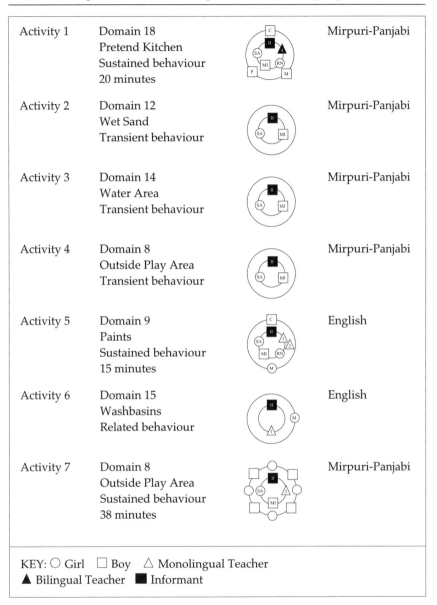

Activity 1	Domain 18 Pretend Kitchen Sustained behaviour 20 minutes		Mirpuri-Panjabi
Activity 2	Domain 12 Wet Sand Transient behaviour		Mirpuri-Panjabi
Activity 3	Domain 14 Water Area Transient behaviour		Mirpuri-Panjabi
Activity 4	Domain 8 Outside Play Area Transient behaviour		Mirpuri-Panjabi
Activity 5	Domain 9 Paints Sustained behaviour 15 minutes		English
Activity 6	Domain 15 Washbasins Related behaviour		English
Activity 7	Domain 8 Outside Play Area Sustained behaviour 38 minutes		Mirpuri-Panjabi

KEY: ○ Girl   □ Boy   △ Monolingual Teacher
▲ Bilingual Teacher   ■ Informant

Figure 9.4   Preferred language use within Ishtiaq's social networks on his first day in Box Hill Nursery

Activity 1	Domain 6 Books Sustained behaviour 25 minutes	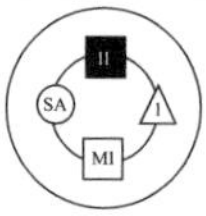	Mirpuri-Panjabi
Activity 2	Domain 28 Corridor Transient behaviour 2 minutes	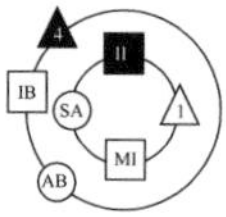	Mirpuri-Panjabi
Activity 3	Domain 28 Corridor Sustained behaviour 6 minutes	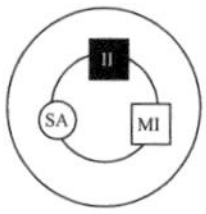	Mirpuri-Panjabi
Activity 4	Domain 5 Home Corner Sustained behaviour 8 minutes	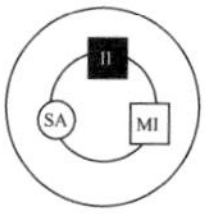	Mirpuri-Panjabi
Activity 5	Domain 18 Pretend Kitchen Sustained behaviour 18 minutes	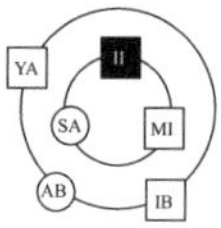	Mirpuri-Panjabi
Activity 6	Domain 11 Junk Table Sustained behaviour 15 minutes	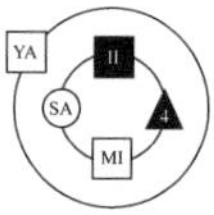	Mirpuri-Panjabi

KEY: ○ Girl   □ Boy   △ Monolingual Teacher
▲ Bilingual Teacher   ■ Informant

Figure 9.5　Preferred language use within Ishtiaq's social networks at the end of his first term in Box Hill Nursery

The formation of ethnic identity has been studied from both the psychological perspective (for an overview see Gudykunst, 1988) and the social (Gal, 1988; Heller, 1988; Milroy, 1980). The focus chosen for this analysis is the latter. This view of ethnic identity as a social construct is compatible with other descriptions foregrounded as theoretical frameworks: language as socio-semiotic (Halliday, 1973, 1975, 1978; Malinowski, 1923/66, 1935/66); social network analysis (Barnes, 1954; Gumperz, 1977; Milroy, 1980); and bilingualism as an act of identity (Le Page & Tabouret-Keller, 1985). This view of ethnic identity underlines the centrality of social organisation in accomplishing the tasks of everyday life and places the individual at the centre of a complex social organisation or ecology (Haugen, 1972). These descriptions view ethnic identity as the product of participation in social networks. This social organisation, which goes beyond the actual situation in which the interactions are taking place, also reinforces a dynamic description of ethnic identity and language use.

Discussion of Data

The data demonstrate the ways in which individual speakers use language to construct meaning in negotiation with their interlocutors. When the speakers are bilingual, their discourse may also be described as bilingual. Bilingual discourse can be described as the use of two languages combined to perform a set of communicative functions. The bilingual children in this study exercise multiple options in terms of their choice of language for their everyday interactions with their peers and teachers. Monolinguals can draw upon styles, registers and other features of language variation to perform their communicative acts; bilingual speakers have a greater range of choice because they can draw upon any of the linguistic systems in their repertoire, or even combine them in a number of creative ways, to perform their communicative acts. Informants in this study can use Mirpuri-Panjabi only, English only, or combine Mirpuri-Panjabi with English to carry out a range of codeswitches at phonological, morphological, lexical, syntactical, semantic and organisational levels of language use. This perceived link between microsociolinguistic factors, language choice and the ethnic identity of speakers is a view confirmed by Bourhis (1979: 119) who identified features including 'the topic, setting, and purposes of conversation, as well as characteristics of the interlocutors' as factors that all influence language choice. These factors encompass Hymes' (1972b) taxonomy of situational determinants of speech as significant influences on individuals' language behaviour in given social contexts.

Situational Codeswitching

Situational codeswitching is identified in the literature as a common form of codeswitching behaviour. Situational switches are influenced by micro-sociolinguistic factors. They occur when the individual speaker's choice of language is guided by the prevailing rules and social norms of behaviour in a given situation. In these contexts switches can occur to mark in-group and out-group boundaries and can be observed when an in-group speaker intersperses their utterances with switches from the language of the out-group. In the case of the Box Hill Nursery, switches can be regarded as a device for maintaining and reinforcing ethnic group boundaries.

The data presented in this chapter demonstrate one facet of the children's linguistic repertoire. The range of language(s) that an individual can speak and/or understand can be likened to a personal life-history or autobiography. This linguistic autobiography is open to a number of influences and changes. It does not exist in isolation. It is part of a finely balanced ecosystem. These individual linguistic repertoires will be termed a *linguistic biography*. The concept of a linguistic biography will be presented in detail in Chapter 10. It has been demonstrated that even in the pre-school context there is evidence of language shift in the individual children's linguistic repertoires. This demonstrated shift in an individual's preferred language use away from Mirpuri-Panjabi towards English, the dominant language, demonstrates the impact that formal language planning policy at national level exerts on some individual speakers in public domains. Towards the end of the first term in formal education, none of the bilingual children is observed speaking only Mirpuri-Panjabi, even within the dense network of preferred interlocutors who are all bilingual English/Mirpuri-Panjabi speakers.

The Discourse of Schools

Recent studies in systemic linguistics have aimed to describe the generic patterns of discourse that define specific social contexts. The school as a specific social context has been described in linguistic terms. Wilkinson (1982) describes it as 'a unique communicative event'. Barton (1994: 177) suggests that schools are best understood as 'strange, not as normal'. He suggests that language plays a role in maintaining those 'strange' school practices which he describes as follows:

There are all sorts of practices which children are learning in schools: children are learning to conform, to be part of large groups, to sit still, to be regulated by time. Schools have their own ground rules of what you are allowed to do and what not, including rules about who may talk, when, to whom, and what about. These ground rules are different from those of home and community. There are many ways in which schools socialise children by the organisation of day-to-day rhythms of schooling; language use is a central part of this. (Barton, 1994: 179)

Fishman (1991: 395) identifies education as an important institution for addressing Reversing Language Shift (RLS). It is possible to speculate that the imposition of the English language, now decisively defined through the 1988 Education Reform Act as the only official language of educational institutions in England, is certain to have an impact on bilingual children's linguistic repertoire, both in the school setting and, eventually, beyond the school gates.

Factors Influencing Language Choice

In summary, there are a number of points to make:

(1) It can be said that codeswitching among the children in the nursery operates at a number of levels: the phonological, the lexical and at discourse turn. Codeswitches at the level of discourse turn influence the development of the discourse and set constraints on the subsequent speaker's discourse options or language choice.

(2) It is possible to identify from the data a pattern of characteristics that appear to influence the individual interlocutor's language use and language choice for specific utterances. These have been outlined in Figures 9.1, 9.2 and 9.3.

(3) The choice of Mirpuri-Panjabi within the dense friendship network, where all of the children are bilingual English and Mirpuri-Panjabi speakers, is interesting to note. Heller (1984) observed that a child's participation in social networks is a central feature in the formation of ethnic identity. From the data presented in Chapter 7 it can be seen that dense friendship networks emerge over the first term in school. The members of this friendship network share physical emblems of their ethnic identity. These indicate membership of a Pakistani background and of the Islamic community. They also share a common linguistic repertoire. The pattern of language choice or preferred language use within the networks demonstrates the tendency to use Mirpuri-Panjabi with those interlocutors who form the dense network. This

may be understood either as an explicit statement of perceived identity or as an act of linguistic solidarity.

(4) Codeswitching can be taken as evidence of the children becoming bilingual, because for codeswitching to be an option they need knowledge and understanding of both linguistic systems.

(5) Codeswitching can be taken as evidence of the children's developing sense of self and ethnic identity, of themselves as *different* from the monolingual children in the nursery who only speak English but *the same* as their Mirpuri-Panjabi speaking peers. In terms of Le Page and Tabouret-Keller's description of bilingualism, this preferred use of Mirpuri-Panjabi can be understood as a statements of an individual's values and their view of the world. It can be seen as an act that reinforces friendship boundaries, while the use of English reinforces separation and difference between the boundaries of both dense and loose networks, which are ethnically determined.

(6) Other factors that influence the children's codeswitching include:

- The individual child's linguistic repertoire (the language(s) which they speak and can understand).

- The presence of specific interlocutors: the potential participants (those individuals who are available for interaction); and the preferred participants (those selected for interaction).

- The presence of an adult; this confirms other research findings, such as those of Sylva *et al.* (1980), that speculate on the presence of an adult as an influence on child behaviour.

- The presence of preferred participants, or a coterie of significant others (Halliday, 1978) who form the dense friendship network.

The factors that influence language choice concur with the range of social factors identified by Romaine (1989: 115) as setting, topic and degree of competence. However, it should be noted that it is not suggested that it is possible to predict an individual's language use in any given situation. Rather, it is important to regard language choice as a discourse mode or communicative option which is available to bilinguals (cf. Gumperz, 1982) and which, in common with all discourse options, is open to external influences that make it impossible to predict outcomes even in specific interactions.

Summary

To summarise, Chapters 8 and 9 present data of the children's naturally occurring language use. Data from the audio-taped recordings of the children on their first and last day in the nursery have been analysed and the number of recorded utterances in English and Mirpuri-Panajbi have been compared. Analysis reveals:

(1) A small but significant increase in the number of utterances recorded in English over the term.

(2) The combined use of English and Mirpuri-Panjabi in some utterances.

(3) Four types of codeswitch, lexical, inter-sentential, intra-sentential and switches that correspond with discourse turns.

(4) Two generic patterns of language choice available to bilinguals.

(5) The use of codeswitching as a metaphorical device for establishing and consolidating group membership of the dense network of preferred participants.

(6) Patterns of preferred language use that vary according to interlocutors, settings and activities.

A number of influences on the individual informant's language choice or preferred language use have been identified. It has been suggested that the choice of a particular language for a given interaction is a matter of individual choice. In making these choices between one of the languages (English or Mirpuri-Panjabi) in their repertoire, or a combination of the two (codeswitching), bilingual children are demonstrating linguistic proficiency in a number of ways:

- a developing *communicative competence*, the ability to use language appropriately;

- an emerging *metalinguistic awareness* of the rules that govern both language systems; and

- a competence in managing and maintaining interactions with others, a *conversational competence*.

This chapter concludes the data analysis. Chapter 10 will build on the analyses presented in Chapters 5, 6, 7, 8 and 9 to argue the case for viewing language development as a way in which individuals expand and extend their linguistic repertoire and create a *linguistic biography* that reflects a number of elements from their life experiences. These include the social contexts in which they have participated and the people with whom they have interacted for a range of purposes.

Finally, to return to our starting-point and to the linguistic description of language as social semiotic which views language use and social behaviour as inseparable, in the words of Malinowski: 'a statement spoken in real time is never detached from the situation in which it was uttered … the utterance has no meaning except in the context of situation' (Malinowski, 1935/66: 310–311). Chapters 5 to 9 of data analysis have reinforced this view of the interdependence of the social and language behaviours of young bilingual children and have gone some way to supporting Malinowski's view of language as social action with reference to a particular group of young bilingual children who are learning a number of participant roles simultaneously. They are learning to be pupils, they are learning to be bilingual, and they are learning to be members of a minority ethnic community now permanently settled in Britain. Language plays a central role in all of these activities. These children differ from the monolingual pupils with whom they share the role of apprentice pupil, in that they require different languages for their social roles. They need to use both English, the dominant societal language, and their home and community language, Mirpuri-Panjabi. This is important for a number of social and personal reasons. Ventola (1987: 6) suggests that language is:

> a means of becoming a member of one's own culture, but it also enables one to participate in the social life of members from another culture. Learning … languages is learning how to behave linguistically in other cultures. Social encounters … organised linguistically help one in the process of becoming a member of another culture … permanently or temporarily.

Further, as Grosjean (1990: 107) writes, 'New situations, new environments, new interlocutors will involve new linguistic needs and will therefore change the language configuration of the person involved'.

Chapter 10
Linguistic Biographies

Everything about you ... ties you to something else: parents, the time in which you live. Who you are is where you come from. (Penelope Lively, *Perfect Happiness*, 1985: 162)

Introduction

Concluding the data analyses presented in earlier chapters, this chapter will present a framework for understanding individuals' social and language behaviour in the social setting of Box Hill Nursery School. It will be suggested that a developing communicative competence, including the linguistic repertoire, can be understood as an *linguistic biography* that is subject to a number of influences. These influences will be described. It will be suggested that the variety and range of influences account in part for the dynamic nature of an individual's linguistic repertoire.

The Concept of Ethnicity

Chapters 1 and 7 detailed the difficulties encountered in ascribing an individual's sense of identity to a sense of citizenship and nation identity. These are factors which are fluid and open to change and re-negotiation. There are historical and geographical features that combine to make this particularly problematic for British born people of ethnic Pakistani, Bangladeshi or Indian origin. The concept of ethnicity therefore, has been proposed as an alternative social categorisation appropriate to these groups. The concept of ethnicity is closely related to the value system and perceptions of the person attempting the definition. These definitions have varied. They include Fishman's (1989: 5) definition of ethnicity as 'an aspect of collectivity's self-recognition in the eyes of the outsider'; Gudykunst and Schmidt's (1988: 1) succinct definition 'social identity'; and Karl Marx, who predicted the extinction of ethnic groups, asking 'why should one continue to belong to archaic cultural groupings when one could become a worker?' (Roosens, 1989: 9). Other definitions include identifying characteristics. Edwards' (1985: 10) definition states:

Ethnic identity is allegiance to a group – large or small, socially dominant or subordinate – with which one has ancestral links. There is no
necessity for a continuation, over generations, of the same socialisation
or cultural patterns, but the same sense of group boundary must per-
sist. This can be sustained by shared objective characteristics
(language, religion, etc.) or by more subjective combinations to a sense
of 'groupness' or by some combination of both. Symbolic or subjective
attachments must relate, at however distant a remove, to an observably
real past.

This definition suggests internally perceived features, the subjective, together with externally acknowledged ones, the objective.

Thus it can be seen that the term 'ethnic identity' is used to represent a
wide range of phenomena, including what Gans (1979) terms 'symbolic
ethnicity'. For the purposes of the present discussion the multi-faceted
phenomenon ethnicity or ethnic identity will be defined as synonymous
with the term *unique identity*. Three characteristic features of unique identity (or ethnicity) are presumed:

- the collective term for group identity is self-ascribed;

- the membership is self-selecting and voluntary;

- the defining characteristics are dynamic and therefore may change
  over time.

In short, the group is dynamic and constantly changing because individuals opt in and out of the membership. The existence of a self-selected group
relies in part on the existence of other individuals and groups who are not
included in its membership. This marking of ethnic identity by boundary
phenomena was first clarified by Barth (1969), who argued that it was misleading to define ethnicity in terms of specific and unchanging
characteristics. He suggests an alternative, namely that the ethnic identity
of a particular group is created through the juxtaposition of that group
alongside other existing groups. Within this definition, 'a group' is the notion of group solidarity and collective identity which originates not from
internal features or shared characteristics but from comparison with other
groups and other individuals. Barth acknowledged that boundary markers
between groups do not remain static but vary from situation to situation
and over time. He suggests (1969: 11) a fundamental distinguishing feature
in determining ethnicity: that if a group (or an individual) 'identifies itself,
and is identified by others, as constituting a category distinguishable from

other categories of the same order', then that group (or person) can claim separate ethnicity. It will be regarded as distinctive.

In other words, group identity can be seen to originate in two ways. Unique identity can be regarded either as having its origins in shared internal characteristics, or inferred from the presence or absence of specific characteristics by comparison with other external agencies. That is to say, the definition of ethnicity can stem from either the presence or the absence of unique, defining features. In this sense Barth's (1969) definition can be held as different from that of Edwards' (1985), which suggests that both sets of characteristics are required to be apparent before unique identity or ethnicity can be claimed.

The approach favoured by Barth (1969) is an appropriate departure for the clarification of the related concepts of ethnic group, ethnic identity and own culture. Barth states that there should be a distinction between the ethnic organisation of a group and the ethnic identification of individuals within that group. He points out that an ethnic group is, first of all, a form of social organisation, in which the participants themselves make use of certain cultural traits from their past, a past which may or may not be verifiable historically.

The cultural traits by which an ethnic group defines itself never comprise the totality of the observable culture. The traits only combine some characteristics that the actors (or in-group members) ascribe to themselves and which they consider relevant. These traits can change and even be replaced by others in the course of time. For the indentification of the ethnic group, it is sufficient that a social border be drawn between the group and other similar groups, by means of even a small number of cultural emblems and values that make the group different in its own eyes and the eyes of others (Roosens, 1989: 12). Barth points out that the intensity with which a group profiles itself as an ethnic group, and with which individuals stress their ethnicity, generally increases when there is intense spatial-geographical and social contact between groups. More isolated 'traditional' groups probably feel the need to be less clearly ethnically defined. Ethnic groups are generally most clearly delineated in areas that have only one form of overarching political organisation. This view is however, debatable.

Nevertheless of all definitions and descriptions of ethnicity the most prevailing view is probably that of Barth. He describes (1969) the ethnic group as a 'social vessel' and suggests that ethnic self-affirmation is always related in one way or another to the defence of social or economic interests. Many people change their ethnic identity only if they can profit by doing so. This view is supported by Glazer and Moynihan (1975) who view ethnicity solely in material terms, as a struggle for material goods and status, in short for economic well-being and survival.

Barth attempts to define the concept of ethnic group from an anthropological perspective based on internal characteristics and traits. He states (1969: 14):

> It is important to recognise that although ethnic categories take cultural differences into account, we can assume no simple one-to-one relationship between ethnic units and cultural similarities and differences. The features taken into account are not the sum of 'objective' differences, but only those which the actors themselves regard as significant. Not only do ecological variations mark and exaggerate difference; some cultural features are used by the actors as signals and emblems of differences, others are ignored, and in some relationships radical differences are played down and denied.

This definition of ethnic groups makes certain assumptions about the nature of the group which Barth (1969: 10–11) outlines as:

- largely biologically self-perpetuating;

- sharing fundamental cultural values, realised in overt unity in cultural forms;

- making up a field of communication and interaction; and

- comprising a membership which defines itself, and is identified by others, as constituting a category distinguishable from other categories of the same order.

This ideal-type definition is not so far removed in content from the conventional proposition that a race equals a culture equals a language; and that a society equals a unit which rejects or discriminates against others. However, it does differ in significant respects. Barth (1969: 10–11) sets out his main objection to this ideal-type definition in the following way:

> Such a formulation prevents us from understanding the phenomenon of ethnic groups and their place in human society and culture. This is because it begs all the critical questions: while purporting to give an ideal type model of a recurring empirical form, it implies a preconceived view of what are the significant factors in the genesis, structure and function of such groups.

There are other objections to the traditional definition of a race equals a culture equals a language. Most critically, it allows us to assume that boundary maintenance remains unproblematic and could be taken to imply that racial differences, cultural differences, social separation and language barriers amount to organised enmity. It denies spontaneity. This traditional definition also limits the range of factors used to explain cultural diversity. It suggests that each group develops its cultural and social form(s) and traditions in relative isolation, perhaps chiefly in response to local ecological factors or through a history of adaptation by intervention and selective borrowing. However, groups in isolation could not borrow. Adaptation in the face of intervention, welcome or imposed, is familiar to historians. The idea of development in isolation is not borne out in reality. History has not produced a world of separate peoples, each with their own cultures and languages, separately organised into what are known as communities or societies. Indeed, it is frequently difficult to isolate these factors even for legitimate description. So for a number of reasons the traditional definition of a race equated to a culture with a language remains unsatisfactory.

In contrast with this definition with its emphasis on separate, discrete groups, Barth (1969) presents the concept of an ethnic group as a form of social organisation in which the participants themselves make use of cultural traits from their past (a past which may or may not be verifiable historically). These traits are postulated as external emblems (clothing, languages, etc.) and correspond closely to those emblems of ethnicity identified by Le Page and Tabouret-Keller (1985: 209). Other researchers such as Tajfel (1978) complement Barth's concept of the ethnic group with psychological factors, defined as 'that part of an individual's self-concept which derives from his (or her) knowledge of his (or her) membership in a social group (or groups) together with the values and emotional significance attached to that membership' (Tajfel, 1978: 63).

In addition to Tajfel, there are others who draw their definitions of ethnic identity from the non-economic, psycho-social dimensions of individuals (for example Roosens, 1989; De Vos, 1975; Epstein, 1978). They share the belief that in order to understand the dynamic force of individual and collective ethnic self-affirmation, individuals must be set within their own social dimension. Their concept of identity can be linked with the social psychology of the internal intrapsychic dimensions of 'self' that complement the social dimension of 'others'. Both internal and external dimensions are interwoven. Individuals experience the sense of belonging to a specific social category, network or group and for the duration of their membership or belonging they are partially determined by it. Individual members are simultaneously like, and different from, others who also belong to the same group. In turn, the group and its individual members are different from others who are members of comparable social units or groupings. This description allows each individual member to belong to several social units of collective identity simultaneously. At any one time, an individual may belong to a group known as a profession, a family, a religion or a political party, to name just a few of the many possibilities.

From this set of collective identities, it may be that a hierarchy of individual identities emerges. This hierarchy of self-ascribed identities would be different for individual members. It is also possible that it would also change over time and from context to context. So for example, in one context, say for example the office, one facet of identity would be paramount, the professional; while in a different context, say for example the supermarket, another would dominate. This change in the hierarchy of multiple identities would occur even when the participants in the contexts remained the same. For example, if a child and a parent were to attend the same school, the parent as a teacher and the child as a pupil, within the context of the school the professional pupil–teacher identities would dominate. However, in a different context, for example at home or even in the car travelling to and from school, different aspects of identity, the parent–child relationship, would take over. Definitions of ethnic identity that combine social and psychological aspects, and which allow for multiple identities to co-exist simultaneously, are compatible with the Hallidayan description of language as dynamic social behaviour.

Also, despite concerted national policies like the assimilationist education policy adopted in the UK throughout the 1960s, 1970s and 1980s, collective and individual identity based on ethnicity does not seem to be disappearing. Rather, the opposite seems to be the case. Roosens concludes (1989: 9): 'Ethnic groups are affirming themselves more and more. They promote their own, new cultural identity, even as the old identity is eroded.' This view is supported by others, including Glazer and Moynihan (1975) and Themstrom (1980), and can be witnessed in the recent dramatic events that are taking place in Europe (although these cannot be explained solely in terms of ethnicity).

The concept of ethnicity is particularly useful for descriptions of migrant groups now permanently settled within the UK. Their symbolic attachments to their past and homelands are evident in linguistic repertoires, the languages they speak and understand, rituals and celebrations that they uphold and continue, and the religious belief they observe, foster and teach to new generations. They are linked to their observable past, the homeland, through kinship and ancestry. The bonds are forged through a shared linguistic and cultural heritage. The concept of ethnicity is less ethnocentric than groupings based on national identity, which in any case would not be applicable to the new generation of migrants who are born in the UK. Neither is it applicable to those who migrated to the UK before the new nation states of Pakistan and Bangladesh were created, because their original homeland no longer exists with its original national and state boundaries and associated status. Language plays an important role in constructing and maintaining the ethnic identity of these groups and the new generation of children born into them.

Language and Ethnic Identity

Language and ethnic identity are related reciprocally, language use influences the formation of ethnic identity, but ethnic identity also influences language use and attitudes. This interrelationship between language and ethnic identity has been studied from a variety of perspectives. Haarman (1988) has written about the role of language in maintaining ethnic boundaries. He proposes a framework of ecological relations as a research tool for analysing the co-variance of language use and the dynamics of environmental factors. He suggests (1988: VIII) that formalising the concept of 'acculturation', a term used to mean the adoption to foreign cultural patterns, may provide broader insights into the phenomena of changing cultural patterns. He suggests that studies of language use will provide evidence of acculturation in contrast situations. He writes (1988: IX): 'It is precisely the most general macro-level and the most specific micro-level which are presently neglected in publications on ethnicity.'

Language and Ethnicity: A Network of Ecological Relations

A general and comprehensive framework of human relations can best be established in terms of ecology. In the introduction to this chapter it was suggested that it is possible to view an individual's linguistic repertoire as a *linguistic biography*. Following the basic assumption that the interaction between ethnic groups is the result of environmental factors that influence members, phenomena which are related to a collective ethnic body's identity can be analysed in terms of ecological relations (Haarman, 1988: 1). The interaction of individuals with elements of the environment reinforces the Malinowskian perspective of the centrality of context to linguistic behaviour and the interdependence of language and context.

The concept of linguistic ecology began when the concept of ecology was borrowed from the natural sciences. Hawley transferred the concept to sociology in the 1950s. It was Haugen in 1972 who first applied the concept to the field of sociolinguistics. He claimed (1972: 327):'Linguists have been concerned with [the ecology of language] in their work on language change and variability, on language contact and bilingualism, and on standardisation.' Grimshaw's view (1971: 93) is that 'the goal is to examine the interaction of language structure and social structure and of the interim implications of speech behaviour and social behaviour.' Language ecology should therefore cover the whole network of social relations which control the variability of languages and speakers' behaviours. The fundamental variables of language ecology are linked to speakers of a given language.

Natural language has no independent existence in social groups or society. It is always linked to individual speakers (or groups of speakers). It seems therefore appropriate to view an individual's linguistic repertoire as a linguistic biography. This term does not adequately conceptualise the external factors and changes that an individual linguistic biography experiences. The term linguistic biography is however sensitive to the independence of speakers, the social contexts they create through their interactions and their particular choice of language. It emphasises the consequences of changes, no matter how small, on language use, that other elements can exert. Within an eco-system, even small changes in one aspect can effect changes in co-existing quarters.

Haarman (1988: 258–260) makes six assertions that support the description of language use as an ecological system:

(1) The relativity of language in a network of ecological relations.

(2) The relativity of language in the processes of ethnic fusion and fission.

(3) The relativity of language in language-planning activities.

(4) The relativity of language in patterns of bilingual identity.

(5) The relativity of language in processes of adopting foreign cultural patterns.

(6) The relativity of language in a framework of prestige functions.

These are all of relevance, but numbers (4) and (5) are of central importance to this study, with number (3) relevant in the recommendations.

Bronfenbrenner's Ecological Systems Theory

A more detailed framework for understanding an individual's learning can be found in Bronfenbrenner's (1977, 1979) theoretical structure of the ecology of human development. The cornerstone, his Ecological Systems Theory (EST), was introduced in 1977 and reaffirmed in subsequent works. It is defined (1979: 188) as follows:

> The ecology of human development is the scientific study of the pro-gressive, mutual accommodation, throughout the life course, between an active, growing human being, and the changing properties of the immediate settings in which the developing person lives, as this pro-cess is affected by the relations between these settings, and by the larger contexts in which the settings are embedded.

Bronfenbrenner's ecological environment is conceived topologically as a nested arrangement of structures, each contained within the next. It views the child at the centre of four hierarchical levels of context: the microsystem, the mesosystem, the exosystem and the macrosystem. Although the detail of his definitions varies, (cf. Bronfenbrenner, 1977: 514–515; 1979: 226–230), the taxonomy of a hierarchy of systems at four levels, the micro-, meso-, exo- and macro-, remains unchanged. Bronfenbrenner's definitions of these, as presented here, combine the essential elements of both the 1977 and the 1979 versions, but in an attempt to provide a succinct description, they are selective, yet not intentionally distorted. His definitions of the four levels that constitute his ecological framework of human development are:

> The *microsystem* is the complex pattern of activities, roles and interper-sonal relations experienced by a developing person in a given face-to-face setting with particular physical and material features, in which the participants engage in particular activities in particular roles, for ex-ample, daughter, parent, teacher, employee etc., for particular periods of time, and containing other persons with distinctive characteristics of temperament, personality and systems of belief.

> The *mesosystem* comprises the linkages and processes, or interrelations, taking place between two or more major settings containing the devel-oping person at a particular point in his or her life (for example, the relations between home and school, school and the workplace). The mesosystem typically encompasses interactions among family, school, and peer group; for some children, it might also include church, sum-mer camp or workplace. Although the latter would be less common in

the United States than in some other societies ... A mesosystem is a system of microsystems.

The *exosystem* is an extension of the mesosystem embracing other specific social structures, both formal and informal, that do not themselves ordinarily contain the developing person but which influence processes within the immediate settings in which that person is found, and thereby influence, delimit, or even determine what goes on there. These structures include the major institutions of the society, both deliberately structured and spontaneously evolving. They encompass, among other things, the world of work, the neighbourhood, the mass media, agencies of government (local, state and national), the distribution of goods and services, communication and transportation facilities, and informal social networks.

A *macrosystem* refers to the overarching institutional patterns of the culture or sub-culture, such as the economic, social, educational, legal, and political systems, of which micro-, meso-, and exo-systems are the concrete manifestations. Macro-systems are conceived and examined not only in structural terms but as carriers of information and ideology that, both explicitly and implicitly, endow meaning and motivation to particular agencies social networks, roles, activities, and their interrelations. What place or priority children and those responsible for their care have within such macrosystems is of special importance in determining how a child and his or her caretakers are treated and interact with each other. Patterns of social interchange are embedded in each of these systems. (Bronfenbrenner, 1977: 514–515; 1979: 226–230)

All four levels in this ecological framework influence the child's experiences and subsequent development. There is other support for this view. Bronfenbrenner acknowledges that his conception of the environmental factors that influence an individual's learning (as foregrounded) draws heavily upon the 'topological territories' outlined by Lewin (1935). More recently Bruner (1986), Tizard and Hughes (1984) and other social psychologists have referred to what they term 'developmental environments', but without outlining the details to the same extent. There are a number of ways in which an ecological paradigm is appropriate for describing the language development of learning of individuals. It is important to emphasise that language learning as described, as a dynamic phenomenon, is not only applicable to child learners. It is remains pertinent throughout life as individuals continue to enhance individual linguistic repertoires with new forms of language which they learn in order to fulfil a wider range of personal and social functions.

At this point it seems appropriate to examine Bronfenbrenner's ecological paradigm more closely in order to explore more fully its relevance to the language development of bilingual children in nursery schools, beginning with the central tenet, the key definition of the ecology of human development which emphasises the nature of language learning as a dynamic phenomenon, influenced but not solely determined by the external influences of the immediate setting and wider society. This description of language development is supported by systemic linguists, beginning with Malinowski (1923/66) and continued by others including Firth (1957), Halliday (1978) and Harris (1952a; 1952b) who all share the view that 'a statement spoken in real life is never detached from the situation in which it was uttered ... the utterance has no meaning except in the context of situation' (Malinowski, 1923/66: 310–311).

Bronfenbrenner's microsystem is described as a complex pattern of activities, roles and interpersonal relations as experienced by the young child in a variety of settings, each of which can be characterised by specific physical and material features. This corresponds to what systemic linguists have termed the generic structure of social situations. A number of systemic semiotic frameworks have been described in detail. These describe the structure of social interactions in specific contexts such as doctor–patient interviews, bilingual courtroom discourse (Berk-Seligson, 1990), pupil–teacher interactions in classrooms (Sinclair & Coulthard, 1975) and sales service encounters (Ventola, 1987). Linguistic descriptions of the generic structures of written texts also exist. These include an account of the structure of nursery rhymes (Hasan, 1984) and stylistic analyses of both fiction (Hoey & Winter, 1982) and non-fiction texts (Hoey, 1983). All of these descriptions take account of the interdependence of the four elements in their analyses: the discourse, the participants, the social setting and the cultural context. Indeed, the terms used by Bronfenbrenner concur with those used by linguists working both before and after the publication of his Ecological Systems Theory. This observation is in no way intended to undermine or favour any particular contribution.

There are other ways in which EST concurs with sociolinguistic descriptions of language use. Bronfenbrenner's mesosystem stresses the interrelationship between the major settings which an individual experiences in life. Although the major setting for the young child will be the home, from a very early age children encounter new settings. These may include their own and other home settings and the nursery school setting. The settings are analogous with what linguists Fishman *et al.* refer to as 'domains' (1971). In their research into the language use of the Puerto Rican community in New York City they established, on the basis of interviews and observations, five domains in which either Spanish or English were used consistently. There is a definition for this term: 'a domain is an abstraction which refers to a sphere of activity representing a combination of specific times, settings and role relationships' (Romaine, 1989: 29). The five domains identified by Fishman *et al.* (1971) are family, friendship, the workplace, religion and education. These concur with the mesosystems contained within the EST and could be expanded in observations of different groups of speakers, to include place of work.

The value system operating within the exosystem is similar to the pressures of various kinds that have been described by linguists as influential factors operating on bilinguals' choice of language. The factors influencing language choice frequently originate outside the immediate setting or domain, but remain powerful and pervasive. These factors have been identified as economic, administrative, cultural, political and religious (Gal, 1988; Heller, 1988). They comprise both formal and informal social structures and include the major institutions of society, both the deliberately structured and the spontaneously evolving.

Finally, Bronfenbrenner's macrosystem, the economic, social, educational, legal, and political systems with their inherent value systems and the ways in which these are conveyed to society at large, also finds parallels in linguistic descriptions. A series of monographs edited by Bernstein and entitled *Primary Socialization, Language and Education* (1971; 1972/77; 1990) shows how in a coherent social theory a central place is occupied by language; that language is the primary means of cultural transmission. This is a view supported by linguists. For example, language as social behaviour (or 'socio-semiotic'; Halliday, 1978) describes language use within a cultural context, while Malinowski's (1923/66) description, which combines context with situation, reinforces the notion of language as potential social behaviour. The potential aspect means that from within a given framework of communicative competence or appropriate linguistic and social behaviour, there are a number of options available to individuals. Thus, for example, a mother or teacher attempting to regulate a child's behaviour will have a number of options available to them. They can choose from a range of strategies, including reasoning, pleading, threatening, and they also have the option of non-verbal responses.

Bernstein's (1971; 1972/77) theory of language and social learning suggests that *meaning* is only *realised* when the individual (mother or teacher) selects from the *semantic options* available. Meaning is realised in social contexts when individuals opt for a particular behaviour. The chain of realisations extends from the external society, to the specific social setting and can influence the choices which individuals select in their (social and linguistic) behaviour. Societal conventions determine the meaning potential by determining the acceptable range of behaviours available for selection, but it is the individual who realises acts of meaning. Societal and individual values operate to varying degrees. Macrosystems transmit information and ideology, both explicitly and implicitly. They act as potential determinants of the ways in which children and caretakers are treated and interact with each other. Patterns of social interchange are embedded in each of these systems. Appropriate behaviour is culturally determined and is context-specific. Learning to be a pupil in different cultures may require different patterns of behaviour (Willes, 1983). Learning a new language means learning how to behave in a new cultural context and the setting and domains (or sub-cultures) within the new community. This combines appropriate linguistic and social behaviour or *communicative competence* (Hymes, 1972).

Having established conceptual similarities and common concerns between Bronfenbrenner's description of the ecology of human development and linguistic descriptions of language use, these two will now be combined to present the notion of an individual's language development and use of language as an individual's *linguistic biography*.

Defining Linguistic Biographies

The concept of ecology arrived to linguistics from the natural sciences and sociology. Haugen (1972) was the first to link it to linguistics in his work on bilingualism and language contact. He defined the ecology of language (1972: 325) as:

> the study of the interactions between any given language and its environment ... the true environment of a language is the society that uses it as one of its codes. Language exists only in the minds of its users and it only functions in reality through these users to another.

More recently, Haarmann (1988: 4) proposed the general framework of individual; group; society; state. There are of course a number of problems in associating individuals' language use with hierarchical societal structures that embrace state and nationhood. This is particularly true of the informants in this study who are linked through heritage and language to the region known as the former state of the Panjab, which since 1947 has become three independent nation states. These are, from west to east,

Pakistan, India and Bangladesh, each with its own official state language, respectively Urdu in Pakistan, Hindi in India and Bengali in Bangladesh. This linguistic heritage has direct bearing on the linguistic group described here. However, leaving aside the ascription and linkage of individuals' language use to state, the concept of linguistics remains useful because of its sympathy with existing descriptions of language learning and use. For example, this concept is particularly appropriate as a framework for describing individual bilingual speakers and their language behaviour. It is a concept concomitant with the notion that natural language has no independent existence outside social groups. Language is always created by, and is therefore linked with, an individual speaker (or groups of speakers). The individual speaker is the *locus* of language use.

There are however a number of extraneous factors which influence individual use of language. From macro- to micro-level these include:

- the status of the official, state language;

- the influence of language planning policy;

- the domain of use, for example religious worship, family, friendship, education, official (Fishman *et al.*, 1972);

- the specific setting;

- the individuals present;

- the linguistic repertoires of those present and awareness of this;

- the discourse topic;

- other interlocutors.

The term 'ecolinguistic' is sensitive to these factors and to the interdependence of speakers and the social context which they create through their language use. Ecolinguistics acknowledges the consequences of even small changes in language use for other aspects within the contextual setting. It particularly accommodates the affective aspects of individual language use and the ways in which these can be seen to be influential on the linguistic and even physical behaviour of other interlocutors present in the contextual setting. The changes which individuals can precipitate across the linguistic chain reinforce the notion of the individual speaker as an active agent of linguistic change. Even the small changes and accommodations which take place between individuals in their interactions can have repercussions which resound across coexisting quarters. I should like to propose that the notion of ecolinguistics has three particular features: relativism, co-existence, and the interdependence of speakers.

The *relativism* of Preferred Language Use (PLU) or Language Choice (LC) refers to the ways in which speakers in this study change the language of their interactions and codeswitch between English and Panjabi. No category of switch can be described as conclusive or as a determining predictor of subsequent language choices. There is no way of absolutely predicting an individual's language choice in one particular setting with any individual or group of potential interlocutors. This remains consistent with Bernstein's view of *potential*.

The *co-existence* of speakers is evident from the ways in which individuals can be observed to influence each other during the course of their interaction(s). For example, the mere presence of an adult exerts an influence on the language used by the children. This can be seen in Ishtiaq's use of English to Mushtifaq when he says: 'You can do' (p.174).

The *interdependence* of speakers can be demonstrated by the ways in which individual speakers create social interactions through their language. It has been demonstrated in Chapters 9 and 10 that one speaker's utterance can impact on interlocutors and subsequent events in two ways. A speaker's utterance can have consequences for others, even those not participating in the discourse. A speaker's choice of language code can influence second speakers, discourse turns and subsequent discourse contributions. Discourse involves an ongoing negotiation between participants. Discourse turns are negotiated and are dependent in part on preceding speakers. Chapter 9 outlined generic patterns of adjacency pairs in the development of discourse. These patterns demonstrate the interdependency of speakers. The interdependence of speakers can be demonstrated by the ways in which discourse topics precipitate changes in preferred language use and the subsequent impact this has on individual interlocutors. For example, some monolingual pupils withdraw from play activity when the language shifts to Panjabi. The actual language choice is however one-dimensional. There are other non-linguistic features which are equally influential. These include the perceived status of individual speakers. For example, the presence of an adult authority figure can also be seen to influence PLU.

The three features suggested as components of ecolinguistics – relativism, co-existence and the interdependence of speakers concur with more established descriptions of language as a dynamic process, which does not merely facilitate but actually creates social situations (see for example

Halliday, 1978). To encapsulate this phenomenon of ecolinguistics as characterised by the three features outlined above, I use the term *linguistic biography*. The use of this term will not include a linkage of individual speakers or language use to the existence of state or nation. The absence of the link to higher social orders distinguishes this description from existing ones (Barth, 1969; Haarmann, 1988).

The notion of autobiography gains support from other quarters. Donaldson (1992: 274) reminds us that Bruner (1990) believes that individuals construct 'more or less coherent autobiographies centred around a Self acting more or less purposefully in a social world'. Bruner (1990) reinforces the notion that experiences from different spheres of personal experience combine when he suggests that families (and indeed whole cultures) invent traditions in essentially similar ways, based on what he terms 'the push for connectivity'.

Chapter 7 described the emergence of two types of social network among the bilingual children in Box Hill Nursery, pupil networks and friendship networks. The diagrammatic representation proposed to demonstrate these network ties can be combined with other environment influences described in Bronfenbrenner's (1977; 1979) micro-, meso- and exosystems. The influences exerted on individuals' linguistic biography can be presented diagrammatically. Figure 10.1 illustrates the Ecological Framework of social and linguistic development nested within a hierarchy of external influences which impact upon individuals' linguistic and social behaviour.

Linking Bronfenbrenner's EST to Other Theoretical Frameworks

In Figure 10.1 the *macrosystem* represents the highest and most official order of social organisation. It includes legislation, for example the 1976 Race Discrimination Act, the 1975 Sex Discrimination Act and the 1988 Education Reform Act. It also represents the institutional patterns, school organisation, social, political and economic strata that in the UK determine a stratified linguistic hierarchy with English as the official, dominant language.

The *exosystem* represents formal and informal social roles, such as being a pupil, being a friend. This level is deliberately structured and yet dynamic. The participants' orientation towards the relevant institutions (in this case towards the school or formal education) corresponds to what systemic linguists term the 'field'.

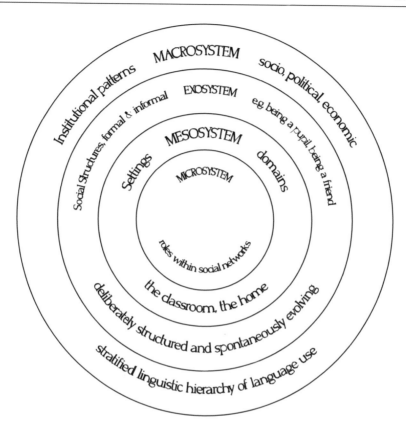

Figure 10.1 Ecological framework of social and linguistic development nested within a hierarchy of external influences

The *mesosystem* represents the settings or domains of interactions. These include the home, the classroom, the playground and other specific settings that demand particular codes of language use. Being able to behave appropriately in these contexts corresponds to being 'communicatively competent' in Hymes' (1972b) term.

The *microsystem* represents roles that participants play within the social networks they form. Children within their social networks assume the role of friend; within the pupil network, the role of pupil. Each role requires different types of language use and appropriate accompanying behaviour. Both language use and social behaviour are context-bound and culturally determined. Becoming a pupil in Britain requires children to learn to behave like a pupil and to speak English in the classroom. This requirement may be at odds with the natural behaviour of very young children. However, it has been domonstrated that they very quickly learn the rules of appropriate behaviour. They speak English and behave like pupils. Roles within the social networks and the relationships between individual participants correspond to what systemic linguists term the 'tenor'.

Finally, the choice of language between individual interlocutors is what systemic linguists term the 'mode'. It includes register choices, styles of talking that include the formal, the casual, the vernacular and, in the case of bilingual interlocutors, the choice of which language to use. This inevitably includes the possibility of codeswitching, using both language systems in juxtaposition.

Discussion

The data presented in Chapters 8 and 9 demonstrate one facet of the linguistic biographies of the children in the Box Hill Nursery Project, the school dimension. However, it has been shown that even in this context there is significant evidence of language shift in individual repertoires. This established shift in individuals' preferred language use away from Mirpuri-Panjabi towards English, the dominant language, demonstrates the impact that formal language planning policy at national level exerts on some individual speakers in public domains. This shift is noted in the trend evidenced by the preferred language use of the informants in the Box Hill Nursery Project. Towards the end of the first term in formal education, none of the bilingual children is observed speaking only Mirpuri-Panjabi even within the dense network of preferred interlocutors. The trend from the data is a shift in preferred language use or language choice and a decline in the number of utterances (or turns) recorded in the home and community language, Mirpuri-Panjabi, even when there is no increase in utterances in English.

The central tenet of a linguistic ecosystem is the effect experienced across a range of domains, interlocutors, and social contexts that even small changes precipitate. It is therefore possible to speculate that the shift in language use towards the dominant societal language, English, as experienced in the school context, will have repercussions across individuals' linguistic repertoire and will influence their use of language in other domains and other settings with other participants. If raised to a hypothesis, this speculation can only be verified by a longitudinal study to follow up the language use of these children as they progress through school. A follow-up study could include observations of these informants and their preferred language use in other social settings, for example within the family, the local community and other non-educational contexts.

The English language is central to learning and academic success in British schools and since 1988 it has been decisively defined as the only official language of primary school education. Evidence from other multilingual societies (Fishman *et al.*, 1971; Kroon & Vallen, 1994) suggests that legislation and formal language planning at national level can have dramatic impact on the languages that are *not* recognised within the national plans. The result is often a change in the domains and hence opportunities to use the non-recognised languages. While there is little disagreement over the occurrence of language shift (LS), opinion varies on whether it is a negative (Fishman, 1991) or merely an inevitable linguistic trend (Romaine, 1989).

Summary

This chapter concludes the report on the Box Hill Nursery Project with a proposal for a social and linguistic framework for describing an individual's linguistic repertoire as a linguistic biography. Three features of linguistic biography have been identified: the relativism, co-existence and interdependence of speakers. It is suggested that an individual's language use in one domain (for example, in the nursery school) will impact upon that individual's linguistic repertoire and has the potential to influence their preferred language use in other domains. In one sense it is clear that the informal social life of the individual is entirely outside the grasp of language planning efforts. However, to say that language planning has no impact on language use in informal situations belies the societal influences of language policy on languages perceived as low status within the stratified linguistic hierarchy of present-day British society. Social activity has linguistic consequences. To end with the words of Malinowski (1935/66: 311): 'linguistic material is ... dependent upon the course of activity'.

References

Agnihotri, R.K. (1979) Processes of assimilation: A sociolinguistic study of Sikh children in Leeds. DPhil thesis, University of York.

Alexander, R., Rose, J. and Woodhead, C. (1994) *Curriculum Organisation and Classroom Practice in Primary Schools.* London: HMSO.

Alladina, S. (1985) South Asian languages in Britain: Criteria for definition and description. *Journal of Multilingual and Multicultural Development* 6 (6), 449–466.

Alladina, S. and Edwards, V. (eds) (1991) *Multilingualism in the British Isles* (Vols 1 & 2). London: Longman.

Allen, W.S. (1956) Structure and system in the Abaza verbal complex. *Transactions of The Philosophical Society*, pp. 127–76.

Anderson, R.C. (1970) Control of student mediating processes during verbal learning and instruction. *Review of Educational Research* 40, 349–369.

Auer, P. (1991) Bilingualism in/as social action: A sequential approach to code-switching. In European Science Foundation (ed.) *Papers for the Symposium in Bilingual Studies: Theory, Significance & Perspectives* (Vol. 2: 319–352). Strasbourg: European Science Foundation.

Barnes, J.A. (1954) Class and committees in a Norwegian island parish. *Human Relations* 7 (1).

Barth, F. (ed.) (1969) *Ethnic Groups and Boundaries: The Social Organisation of Cultural Difference.* Boston: Little, Brown.

Bartlett, G. (1932) *Remembering.* Cambridge: Cambridge University Press.

Barton, D. (1994) *Literacy: An Introduction to the Ecology of Written Language.* Oxford: Basil Blackwell.

Beaugrande, R. de and Dressler, W. (1981) *Introduction to Textual Linguistics.* London: Longman.

Becker, F. (1963) *Outsiders.* New York: The Free Press.

Bennett, N. (1976) *Teaching Styles and Pupil Progress.* London: Open Books.

Berk-Seligson, S. (1990) *The Bilingual Courtroom.* Chicago: The University of Chicago Press.

Bernstein, B. (ed.) (1971) *Class, Codes and Control 1.* London: Routledge.

Bernstein, B. (ed.) (1972/77) *Class, Codes and Control 3.* London: Routledge.

Bernstein, B. (1990) *The Structuring of Pedagogic Discourse: Class, Codes and Control 4.* London: Routledge

Berry, M. (1975) *An Introduction to Systemic Linguistics 1: Structures and Systems.* London: Batsford.

Birdwhistell, R.L. (1971) *Kinesics and Context: Essays on Body Motion Communication.* Harmondsworth: Penguin.

Bloomfield, L. (1930/70) Linguistics as science. In C.F. Hockett (ed.) (1970: 227–30) *A Leonard Bloomfield Anthology.* Bloomington: Indiana University Press.

Bloomfield, L. (1933/43) *Language.* London: George Allen & Unwin.

Boissevain, J. (1974) *Friends of Friends: Networks, Manipulators and Coalitions.* Oxford: Basil Blackwell.

Bourhis, R.Y. (1979) Language in ethnic interaction. In H. Giles and R. Saint-Jacques (eds) *Language and Ethnic Relations.* Elmsford, NY: Pergamon.

Bourne, J. (1990) *Moving into the Mainstream*. Windsor: NFER-Nelson.

Bronfenbrenner, Urie (1977) Towards an experimental ecology of human development. *American Psychologist* 32, 513–31.

Bronfenbrenner, Urie (1979) *The Ecology of Human Development*. Cambridge, MA: Harvard University Press.

Bruck, M., Shultz, J. and Rodríguez-Brown, F.V. (1972) Assessing language use in bilingual classsrooms: An ethnographic analysis. In A. Cohen, M. Bruck and F. Rodríguez-Brown (eds) *Evaluating Evaluation* (pp. 40–56). Washington, DC: Center for Applied Linguistics.

Bruner, J. (1986) *Actual Minds, Possible Worlds*. Cambridge, MA: Harvard University Press.

Bruner, J. (1990) The narrative construction of 'reality'. Closing address to the Fourth European Conference on Developmental Psychology, Stirling, Scotland. August 1990.

Bruner, J. and Haste, H. (eds) (1987) *Making Sense: The Child's Construction of the World*. London: Methuen.

Byram, M. (1990) Return to the home country: The necessary dream in ethnic identity. In M. Byram and J. Leman (eds) *Bicultural and Trilingual Education*. Clevedon: Multilingual Matters.

Carroll, J.B. (1963) A model of school learning. *Teachers College Record* 64, 723–733.

Chomsky, N. (1968) *Language and Mind*. New York: Harcourt.

Churchill, S. (1986) *The Education of Linguistic and Cultural Minorities in OECD Countries*. Clevedon: Multilingual Matters.

Clark, M.M. (1988) *Children Under Five: Education Research and Evidence*. New York: Gordon & Breach.

Clarricoates, K. (1987) Child culture at school: A clash between gendered worlds. In A. Pollard (ed.) *Children and Their Primary Schools*. Lewes: Falmer Press.

Cleveland Research and Intelligence Unit (1989) *Cleveland's Ethnic Minority Population*. CR 668, September 1989. Cleveland County Council.

Cobb, J.A. (1972) Relationship of discrete classroom behaviours to fourth grade academic achievement. *Journal of Educational Psychology* 103 (63), 74–80.

Cohen, A., Bruck, M. and Rodríguez-Brown, F. (eds) (1977) *Evaluating Evaluation*. Washingston, DC: Center for Applied Linguistics.

Commission for Racial Equality (CRE) (1979) *Ethnic Minorities in Britain: Statistical Background*. London: CRE.

Commission for Racial Equality (CRE) (1982) *Ethnic Minority Community Languages: A Statement*. London: CRE.

Crystal, D. (1987) *The Cambridge Encyclopaedia of Language*. Cambridge: Cambridge University Press.

Crystal, D. and Davey, D. (1969) *Investigating English Style*. London: Longman.

Cummins, J. (1983) *Heritage Language Education: A Literature Review*. Ontario: Ministry of Education.

Cummins, J. (1984) Wanted: A theoretical framework for relating language proficiency to academic achievement. In C. Rivera (ed.) *Language Proficiency and Academic Achievement*. Clevedon: Multilingual Matters.

Denscombe, M., Szulc, H., Patrick, C. and Wood, A. (1993) Ethnicity and friendship: The contrast between sociometric research and fieldwork observation in primary school classrooms. In P. Woods and M. Hammersley (eds) *Gender and Ethnicity in Schools*. London and New York: Routledge.

Department of Education and Science (DES) (1975) *A Language for Life* (The Bullock Report). London: HMSO.

Department of Education and Science (DES) (1976) *Children and their Primary School* (The Plowden Report). Report of the Central Advisory Council for Education, London: HMSO.

Department of Education and Science (DES) (1981) *Circular 5/81 Directive of the Council of the European Community on the Education of the Children of Migrant Workers.* London/Cardiff: DES.

Department of Education and Science (DES) (1984) *Mother Tongue Teaching in School and Community.* London: HMSO.

Department of Education and Science (DES) (1985) *Education for All* (The Swann Report). London: HMSO.

Department of Education and Science (DES) (1988) *Report of the Committee of Inquiry into the Teaching of English* (The Kingman Report). London: HMSO.

Department of Education and Science (DES) (1989) *English for Ages 5 to 16* (The Cox Report). London: HMSO.

Donaldson, M. (1978) *Children's Minds*. London: Fontana.

Donaldson, M. (1992) *Human Minds*. London: Allen Lane.

Dunn, J. (1993) *Young Children's Close Relationships*. Newbury Park: Sage Publication.

Edwards, A.D. and Westgate, D.P.G. (1987) *Investigating Classroom Talk*. Lewes: Falmer Press.

Edwards, A.D. and Furlong, J. (1985) Reflections on the language of teaching. In R. Burgess (ed.) *Field Methods in the Study of Education*. Lewes: Falmer.

Edwards, J. (1985) *Language, Society and Identity*. Oxford: Basil Blackwell.

Epstein, A. (1978) *Ethos and Identity: Three Studies in Ethnicity*. London: Tavistock Publications.

European Community (EC) (1977) *The Education of the Children of Migrant Workers: EEC Directive 77/4861*. Brussels: European Community.

European Community (EC) (1984) *Report on the Implementation of Directive 77/486/EEC on the Education of Children of Migrant Workers*. COM (84) Final, Brussels, 10 February.

European Science Foundation (1991) Papers for the Symposium on *Codeswitching in Bilingual Studies: Theory, Significance and Perspectives* (Vol. 1). Strasbourg: European Science Foundation.

Field, S., Mair, G., Rees, T. and Stevens, P. (1981) *Ethnic Minorities in Britain: A Study of Trends in their Position since 1961*. Home Office Research Unit Report, London: HMSO.

Firth, J.R. (1957) *Papers in Linguistics 1934–1951*. London: Oxford University Press.

Firth, J.R. (1968) Ethnographic analysis and language with reference to Malinowski's views. In F.R. Palmer (ed.) (1968: 136–67) *Selected Papers of J.R. Firth 1952–59*. London and Harlow: Longman Green & Co.

Fishman, J.A. (1989) *Language and Ethnicity in Minority Sociolinguistic Perspective*. Clevedon: Multilingual Matters.

Fishman, J.A. (1991) *Reversing Language Shift*. Clevedon: Multilingual Matters.

Fishman, J., Cooper, R.L. and Ma, R. (1971) *Bilingualism in the Barrio*. Bloomington: Indiana University Press.

Gal, S. (1979) *Language Shift: Social Determinants of Linguistic Change in Bilingual Austria*. New York: Academic Press.

Gal, S. (1988) The political economy of code choice. In M. Heller (ed.) *Codeswitching* (pp. 245–63). Berlin: Mouton de Gruyter.

Gans, H. (1979) Symbolic ethnicity. *Ethnic and Racial Studies* 2 (1), 1–20.

Garfinkel, H. (1967) *Studies in Ethnomethodology.* Englewood Cliff, NJ: Prentice-Hall.

Geertz, C. (1975) *The Interpretation of Cultures.* London: Hutchinson.

Genesee, F. and Bourhis, R.Y. (1982) The social psychological significance of codeswitching in cross-cultural communication. *Journal of Language and Social Psychology* (1), 1–27.

Giles, H. (1979) Ethnicity markers in speech. In K.R. Scher and H. Giles (eds) *Social Markers in Speech.* Cambridge: Cambridge University Press.

Glaser, B. and Strauss, A.L. (1967) *The Discovery of Grounded Theory: Strategies for Qualitative Research.* Chicago: Aldive.

Glazer, N. and Moynihan, D. (eds) (1975) *Ethnicity: Theory & Experience.* Cambridge, MA: Harvard University Press.

Grierson, G.A. (1927) *Linguistic Survey of India.* Calcutta: Motilal Barnarasidas.

Grosjean, F. (1990) The psycholinguistics of language contact and code-switching: Concepts, methodology and data. In *Network on Code-switching and Language Contact* (pp. 105–16). Basel, Switzerland, 12–13 January. Strasbourg: European Science Foundation.

Gudykunst, W.B. (ed.) (1988) *Language and Ethnic Identity.* Clevedon: Multilingual Matters.

Gudykunst, W.B. and Schmidt, K.L. (1988) Language and ethnic identity: An overview and prologue. In W.B. Gudykunst (ed.) (1988) *Language and Ethnic Identity.* Clevedon: Multilingual Matters.

Gumperz, J.J. (1964) Linguistic interaction in two communities. *American Anthropologist* 66 (6), 137–54.

Gumperz, J.J. (1975) *Codeswitching in Conversation.* Unpublished manuscript, University of Berkeley, USA.

Gumperz, J.J. (1976) *Social Network and Language Shift, Working Paper 46.* Language Behaviour Research Laboratory, University of Berkeley, USA.

Gumperz, J.J. (1977) Sociocultural knowledge in conversational inference. In M. Saville-Troike (ed.) *Linguistics and Anthropology* (pp. 191–211). Washington, DC: Georgetown University Press.

Gumperz, J.J. (1982) *Discourse Strategies.* Cambridge: Cambridge University Press.

Gumperz, J.J. and Hymes, D. (eds) (1972) *Directions in Sociolinguistics: The Ethnography of Communication.* New York: Holt Rinehart & Winston.

Haarmann, H. (1988) *Language in Ethnicity.* Amsterdam: Mouton de Gruyter.

Hall, E. (1959) *The Silent Language.* New York: Doubleday.

Halliday, M.A.K. (1973) *Explorations in the Functions of Language.* London: Edward Arnold.

Halliday, M.A.K. (1975) *Learning How to Mean: Explorations in the Development of Language.* London: Edward Arnold.

Halliday, M.A.K. (1978) *Language as Social Semiotic.* London: Edward Arnold.

Hallowell, A. (1955/77) Cultural factors in spatial orientation. In J. Dolgin, D. Kemnitzer and D. Schneider (eds) *Symbolic Anthropology: A Reader in the Study of Symbols and Meanings.* New York: Columbia University Press.

Harris, Zellig S. (1952a) Discourse analysis. *Language* 28 (1), 1–30.

Harris, Zellig S. (1952b) Culture and style in extended discourse. In S. Tax (ed.) *Indian Tribes of Aboriginal America* (pp. 210–5). Proceedings of the 29th International Congress of Americanists, Chicago: Chicago Press.

Hasan, R. (1984) The nursery tale as a genre. *Nottingham Linguistic Circular* (13), 71–102.

Hasan, R. (1985) Meaning, context and text – fifty years after Malinowski. In J.D. Benson and W.S. Greaves (eds) *Systemic Perspectives on Discourse* (Vol. 2: 16–49). Norwood, New Jersey: Ablex.

Haugen, E. (1972) *The Ecology of Language (Essays)*. Stanford.

Heller, M. (1982) Negotiations of language choice in Montreal. In J.J. Gumperz (ed.) *Language and Social Identity* (pp. 108–18). Cambridge: Cambridge University Press.

Heller, M. (1984) Language and ethnic identity in a Toronto French-language school. *Canadian Ethnic Studies* 16 (2), 1–14.

Heller, M. (ed.) (1988) *Codeswitching*. Berlin: Mouton de Gruyter.

Hitchcock, G. (1982) The social organisation of space and place in an urban open-plan primary school. In G.C. Payne and E.C. Cuff (eds) *Doing Teaching: The Practical Management of Classrooms*. London: Batsford.

Hoey, M.P. (1983) *On the Surface of Discourse*. London: Allen & Unwin.

Hoey, M.P. and Winter, E.O. (1982) Believe me for mine honour: A stylistic analysis of the speeches of Brutus and Mark Anthony at Caesar's funeral in *Julius Caesar*, Act III, Scene 2, from the point of view of discourse construction. *Language & Style* 14 (4).

Hymes, D. (1967) Models of interaction of language and social setting. *Journal of Social Issues* 33 (2), 8–28.

Hymes, D. (1968) The ethnography of speaking. In J.A. Fishman (ed.) *Readings in the Sociology of Language*. The Hague: Mouton de Gruyter.

Hymes, D. (1972a) Competence and performance in linguistic theory. In R. Huxley and E. Ingrams (eds) *Language Acquisition: Models and Methods*. New York: Academic Press.

Hymes, D. (1972b) On communicative competence. In J.B. Pride and J. Holmes (eds) *Sociolinguistics*. Harmondsworth: Penguin.

Ingram, D. (1990) *The Teaching of Languages and Cultures in Queensland: Towards a Language in Education Policy for Queensland Schools*. Queensland Education Department, Centre for Applied Linguistics and Language, Griffiths University, Australia.

Kachru, B.B. (1978) Toward structuring code-mixing: An Indian perspective. *International Journal of the Sociology of Language* (16), 27–46.

Kachru, B.B. (1980) Socially realistic linguistics: The Firthian tradition. *Studies in Linguistic Sciences* 10 (1), 85–111.

Katzner, K. (1977) *The Languages of the World*. London: Routledge.

Khan, Farhat (1991) The Urdu speech community. In S. Alladina and V. Edwards (eds) *Multilingualism in the British Isles* (Vol. 2). London: Longman.

Kibrik, A.E. (1977) The methodology of field investigations in linguistics. *Janua Linguarum* Series Minor. The Hague: Mouton de Gruyter.

Kress, G. (ed.) (1976) *Halliday: System and Function in Language*. London: Oxford University Press.

Kroon, S. and Vallen, T. (1994) Multilingualism and education: An overview of the Dutch language and education policy towards ethnic minorities. *Current Issues in Language & Society* 1 (2), 103–29.

Labov, W. (1972) *Sociolinguistic Patterns*. Philadelphia: Pennsylvannia University Press.

Labov, W. (1981) Field methods used by the project on linguistic change and variation. *Sociolinguist Working Paper 80*. Austin, TX: South Western Educational Development Laboratory.

Lahaderne, H.M., (1968) Attitudinal and intellectual correlates of attention: A study of four sixth-grade classrooms. *Journal of Educational Psychology* 59, 320–4.

Lee, R. (1980) Codifications of reality: Lineal and non-lineal. In J. Spradley and D. McCurdy (eds) *Conformity and Conflict: Readings in Cultural Anthropology* (pp. 75–90). Boston: Little, Brown.

Le Page, R.B. (1968) Problems of description in multilingual communities. *Transactions of the Philological Society* (pp. 189–212). Oxford: Basil Blackwell.

Le Page, R.B. (1978/80) Projection, focusing, diffusion or steps towards a sociolinguistic theory of language, illustrated from the sociolinguistic survey of multilingual communities; Stage I: Cayo District, Belize; Stage II: St Lucia. School of Education, St Augustine, Trinidad: Society for Caribbean Linguistics Occasional Paper (9), reprinted (1980) in *York Papers in Linguistics* (9).

Le Page, R.B. and Tabouret-Keller, A. (1985) *Acts of Identity*. Cambridge: Cambridge University Press.

Lewin, K. (1935) *A Dynamic Theory of Personality*. New York: McGraw-Hill.

Linguistic Minorities Project (LMP) (1985) *The Other Languages of England*. London: Routledge & Kegan Paul.

Lubeck, Sally (1985) *Sandbox Society*. Lewes: Falmer Press.

Luria, A.R. (1978) The making of mind: A personal account of Soviet psychology. In M. Cole and S. Cole (eds). Cambridge, MA: Harvard University Press.

Malinowski, B. (1923/66) The problems of meaning in primitive languages. Supplement in C.K. Ogden and I.A. Richards (1923/66) *The Meaning of Meaning* (pp. 296–336). London: Routledge & Kegan Paul.

Malinowski, B. (1935/66) *The Language of Magic and Gardening (Coral Gardens and Their Magic*, Vol. 2). London: George Allen & Unwin.

McKinney, J.D., Mason, J., Perkerson, K. and Clifford, M. (1975) Relationship between behaviour and academic achievement. *Journal of Educational Psychology* 67, 198–203.

Mehan, H. (1978) Structuring school structure. *Harvard Educational Review* 48 (1), 32–64.

Mehdi, B. (1974) The final cry. In A. Jussawall (ed.) *New Writing in India* (pp. 207–8). London: Penguin.

Milner, D. (1984) *Children and Race 10 Years On*. London: Ward Lock.

Milroy, L. (1980) *Language and Social Networks*. Oxford: Basil Blackwell.

Milroy, L. (1987) *Observing and Analysing Natural Language*. Oxford: Basil Blackwell.

Milroy, L. and Wei, Li (1991) A social network perspective on code-switching and language choice: The example of the Tyneside Chinese community. In European Science Foundation (ed.) *Network on Code-switching and Language Contact* (Vol. 2: 233–52). Strasbourg: European Science Foundation.

Mitchell, J. Clyde (ed.) (1989) *Social Networks in Urban Situations*. Manchester: Manchester University Press.

Mitchell, T.F. (1975) *Principles of Firthian Linguistics*. London: Longman.

Mobbs, M. (1981) Two languages or one? The significance of the language names Hindi or Urdu. *Journal of Multilingual and Multicultural Development* 2 (3), 203–11.

Moffatt, S. (1990) Becoming bilingual: A sociolinguistic study of the communication of young mother-tongue Panjabi-speaking children. PhD thesis, University of Newcastle.

Moll, Luis C. and Dias, Stephen (1985) Ethnographic pedagogy: Promoting effective bilingual instruction. In E. Gacía and R. Padilla (eds) *Advances in Bilingual Education Research*. Tucson, AZ: University of Arizona Press.

Monaghan, J. (1979) *The Neo-Firthian Tradition and its Contribution to General Linguistics*. Tübingen: Max Neimeyer.

Mullard, C. (1984) *Anti-racist Education: The Three O's*. Coventry: National Association for Multi-Racial Education.

Muysken, P. (1990) Concepts, methodology and data in language contact research: Ten remarks from the perspective of grammatical theory. In *European Science Foundation Workshop on Concepts, Methodology and Data* (pp. 15–29), Basel, January 1990. Strasbourg: European Science Foundation.

Myers-Scotton, C. (1990) Constructing the frame in intrasentential codeswitching. Paper prepared for the Annual Meeting, *Societas Linguistica Europaea*, Berne, Switzerland, September 1990.

Nortier, J. (1989) *Moroccan Arabic and Dutch in Contact*. Doctoral thesis, University of Amsterdam.

Office for Population Census and Surveys (1977) New Commonwealth and Pakistani population estimates. *Population Trends* (9).

Pattanayak, D.P. (1981) *Multilingualism and Mother-tongue Education*. New Delhi: Oxford University Press.

Pfaff, C. (1979) Constraints on language mixing: Intrasentential code-switching and borrowing in Spanish/English. *Language* 55, 291–318.

Poplack, S. (1980) Sometimes I'll start a sentence in English y terminó en español: Towards a typology of code-switching. *Linguistics* 18, 581–616.

Pride, J.B. and Holmes, J. (1972) *Sociolinguistics*. Harmondsworth: Penguin.

Rist, R.C. (1972) Social distance, social inequality in a ghetto kindergarten classroom. *Urban Studies* 7 (3), 241–60.

Robins, R.H. (1971) Malinowski, Firth and the context of situation. In E. Ardener (ed.) *Social Anthropology and Language* (pp. 33–46). London: Tavistock Publications.

Roffey, S., Tarrant, T. and Majors, K. (1994) *Young Friends*. London: Cassell.

Romaine, S. (1984) *The Language of Children and Adolescents*. Oxford: Basil Blackwell.

Romaine, S. (1989) *Bilingualism*. Oxford: Basil Blackwell.

Roosens, Eugeen E. (1989) *Creating Ethnicity: The Process of Ethnogenesis*. London: Sage Publications.

Rose, E.J.B., Deakin, N., Abrams, M., Jackson, V., Preston, M., Vangas, A.H., Cohen, B., Gaitskell, J. and Ward, P. (1969) *Colour and Citizenship*. Oxford: Oxford University Press for the Institute of Race Relations.

Rothkopf, E.Z. (1970) The concept of mathemagenic activities. *Review of Educational Research* 40, 325–6.

Sacks, H., Schegloff, E.A. and Jefferson, G. (1974) A simplest systematics for the organisation of turn-taking in conversation. *Language* 50, 696–735.

Saifullah Khan, Verity (1977) The Pakistanis: Mirpuri villagers at home and in Bradford. In J. Watson (ed.) *Between Two Cultures*. Oxford: Basil Blackwell.

Saifullah Khan, Verity (1979a) Migration and social stress: Mirpuris in Bradford. In V. Saifullah Khan (ed.) *Minority Families in Britain*. London: The Macmillan Press in association with the Social Science Research Council.

Saifullah Khan, Verity (1979b) *Minority Families in Britain*. London: The Macmillan Press in association with the Social Science Research Council.

Sampson, G. (1980) *Schools of Linguistics*. London: Hutchinson.

Samuels, S.J. and Turnure, J.E. (1974) Attention and reading achievement in first-grade boys and girls. *Journal of Educational Psychology* 66, 29–32.

Sankoff, G. (1980) *The Social Life of Language*. Philadelphia: University of Pennsylvania Press.

Sankoff, D., Poplack, S. and Vanniarajan, S. (1991) The empirical study of code-switching. Papers for the *European Science Foundation Symposium on Code-switching in Bilingual Studies: Theory, Significance and Perspectives*. 1, 181–206. Strasbourg: European Science Foundation.

Saussure, F. de (1916/74) *Course in General Linguistics*. Suffolk: Fontana.

Saville-Troike, M. (1982) *The Ethnography of Communication*. Oxford: Basil Blackwell.

Schatz, H. (1989) Code-switching or borrowing? English elements in the Dutch of Dutch-American immigrants. *ITL Review of Applied Linguistics* 83/84, 125–62.

Schegloff, E. and Sacks, H. (1973) Opening up closings. *Semiotica* 7 (4), 289–327.

Scotton, C.M. (1976) Strategies of neutrality: Language choice in uncertain situations. *Language* 52 (4), 919–41.

Shultz, Jeffrey (1975) Language use in bilingual classrooms. Unpublished paper presented at TESOL in Los Angeles, CA,. Harvard University, Graduate School of Education, USA (mimeo).

Sinclair, J.M. and Coulthard R.M. (1975) *Towards an Analysis of Discourse*. London: Oxford University Press.

Sivanandan, A. (1982) *A Different Hunger: Writings on Black Resistance*. London: Pluto Press.

Smith, D. J. (1976) *The Fact of Racial Disadvantage*. London: PEP Broadsheet No. 560.

Smith, G. (1985) Language, ethnicity, employment, education and research: The struggle of the Sylheti-speaking people in London. *Centre for Language Education/Linguistic Minorities Project Working Paper 13*. London: University of London Institute of Education.

Sommer, R. (1967) Classroom ecology. *Journal of Applied Educational Science* 3, 489–503.

Spann, M.L. (1988) *Code-switching among Young Bilingual Panjabi-English Nursery School Children*. DPhil thesis, University of York.

Strong, M. (1983) Social styles and the second language acquisition of Spanish-speaking kindergarteners. *TESOL Quarterly* 17 (2), 241–258.

Stubbs, M. (1983) *Discourse Analysis*. Oxford: Basil Blackwell.

Stubbs, M. (1986) *Educational Linguistics*. Oxford: Basil Blackwell.

Sylva, K., Roy, C. and Painter, M. (1980) *Childwatching at Playgroup and Nursery*. London: Grant McIntyre.

Tajfel, H. (ed.) (1978) *Differentiation Between Social Groups*. Cambridge: Cambridge University Press.

Tajfel, H. (ed.) (1981) *Human Groups and Social Categories*. Cambridge: Cambridge University Press.

Tannen, D. (1979) What's in a frame? In R.O. Freedle (ed.) *New Directions in Discourse Processing* (Vol. 2: 137–83). Norwood, NJ: Ablex.

Taylor, M. and Hegarty, S. (1985) *The Best of Both Worlds?* Windsor: NFER-Nelson.

Thapar, K. (1982) *The Times*, 24 June 1982.

226   *Young Bilingual Learners in Nursery School*

Themstrom, S. (1980) *Harvard Encyclopaedia of American Ethnic Groups*. Cambridge MA: The Belknapp Press of Harvard University Press.

Tinker, H. (1974) *The New System of Slavery*. Oxford: Oxford University Press.

Tinker, H. (1977) *The Banyan Tree: Overseas Emigrants From India, Pakistan and Bangladesh*. Oxford: Oxford University Press.

Tizard, B. and Hughes, M. (1984) *Young Children Learning: Talking and Thinking at Home and School*. London: Fontana.

Tizard, B., Blatchford, P., Burke, J., Farquehar, C. and Plewis, I. (1988) *Young Children at School in the Inner City*. Hove: Lawrence Erlbaum Associates.

Tough, J. (1977) *Talking and Learning: A Guide to Fostering Communication Skills in Nursery and Infant Schools*. London: Ward Lock.

Treffers-Daller, J. (1991) French-Dutch language mixture in Brussels. PhD thesis, University of Amsterdam, Netherlands.

Troyna, B. (1991) Underachievers or underrated? The experience of pupils of South Asian origin in a secondary school. *British Educational Research Journal* 17, 361–76.

Tymms, P., Merrell, C. and Henderson, B. (1997) The first year at school. *Educational Research and Evaluation* 3 (2), 101–18.

Ventola, E. (1987) *The Structure of Social Interaction*. London: Frances Pinter.

Vos, G. de (1975) Ethnic pluralism, conflict and accommodation. In G. de Vos and L. Romamucci (eds) (1975: 5–41) *Ethnic Identity: Cultural Continuities and Change*. Palo Alto, CA: Mayfield.

Vygotsky, L.S. (1962) *Thought and Language*. Cambridge, MA: MIT Press.

Vygotsky, L.S. (1966) Development of higher mental functions. *Psychological Research in the USSR*. Moscow: Progress Press.

Vygotsky, L.S. (1978) *Mind in Society: The Development of Higher Psycholgical Processes*. Cambridge, MA: Harvard University Press.

Wei, Li (1994) *Three Generations, Two Languages, One Family*. Clevedon: Multilingual Matters.

Weinreich, U. (1953) *Languages in Contact*. The Hague: Mouton de Gruyter.

Wells, C.G. (1984) *Language Development in the Pre-School Years*. Cambridge: Cambridge University Press.

Wells, C.G. (1987) *The Meaning Makers: Children Learning Language and Using Language to Learn*. Sevenoaks: Hodder & Stoughton.

Wells, G. and Montgomery, M. (1981) Adult–child interaction at home and at school. In P. French and M. McLure (eds) *Adult–Child Conversation*. London: Croom Helm.

Westgate, D., Batey, J., Brownlee, J. and Butler, M. (1985) Some characteristics of interaction in foreign language classrooms. *British Educational Research Journal* 11 (3), 271–81.

Whiting, B. and Whiting, J. (1975) *Children of Six Cultures*. Cambridge, MA: Harvard University Press.

Wilkinson L. (ed.) (1982) *Communicating in the Classroom*. London: Academic Press.

Willes, M. (1983) *Children into Pupils*. London: Routledge & Kegan Paul.

Wong-Fillmore, L. (1976) *The Second Time Around: Cognitive and Social Strategies in Second Language Acquisition*. Unpublished PhD thesis, Stanford University.

Zentella, A.C. (1982) Code-switching and interactions among Puerto Rican children. In J. Amastae and L. Elias-Oliveres (eds) *Spanish in the United States: Sociolinguistic Aspects*. Cambridge: Cambridge University Press.

Index